PENGUIN

HIDDEN

Margaret Forster was born in Carlisle in 1938. Educated at the County High School, she won an open scholarship to Somerville College, Oxford, where she read history. Her many novels include *Georgy Girl*, *The Seduction of Mrs Pendlebury*, *Private Papers*, *Mother Can You Hear Me?*, *Have the Men Had Enough?*, *Lady's Maid*, *The Battle for Christabel*, *Mothers' Boys* and *Shadow Baby*. All of these titles are published by Penguin. Margaret Forster has also written numerous works of non-fiction, including a biography of Bonnie Prince Charlie, entitled *The Rash Adventurer*, a highly praised 'autobiography' of Thackeray, published in 1978; *Significant Sisters* (1986), which traces the lives and careers of eight pioneering women; a biography of Elizabeth Barrett Browning, which won the Royal Society of Literature's Award for 1988 under the Heinemann bequest; a selection of Elizabeth Barrett Browning's poetry; and her critically acclaimed biography, *Daphne du Maurier*, which was awarded the 1994 Fawcett Book Prize. *Hidden Lives* was nominated nine times in 1995 as Book of the Year.

Margaret Forster lives in London and the Lake District. She is married to writer and broadcaster Hunter Davies and they have three children.

MARGARET FORSTER

Hidden Lives

A FAMILY MEMOIR

PENGUIN BOOKS

PENGUIN BOOKS

Published by the Penguin Group
Penguin Books Ltd, 27 Wrights Lane, London W8 5TZ, England
Penguin Books USA Inc., 375 Hudson Street, New York, New York 10014, USA
Penguin Books Australia Ltd, Ringwood, Victoria, Australia
Penguin Books Canada Ltd, 10 Alcorn Avenue, Toronto, Ontario, Canada M4V 3B2
Penguin Books (NZ) Ltd, 182–190 Wairau Road, Auckland 10, New Zealand

Penguin Books Ltd, Registered Offices: Harmondsworth, Middlesex, England

First published by Viking 1995
Published in Penguin Books 1996
13 15 17 19 20 18 16 14

Printed in England by Clays Ltd, St Ives plc

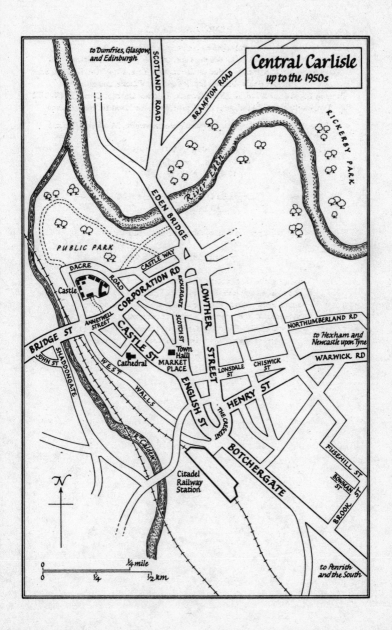

Central Carlisle
up to the 1950s

to Dumfries, Glasgow
and Edinburgh

SCOTLAND ROAD

BRAMPTON ROAD

RICKERBY PARK

River Eden

EDEN BRIDGE

PUBLIC PARK

CASTLE WAY

DACRE ROAD

Castle

CORPORATION RD

RICKERGATE

SCOTCH ST

LOWTHER STREET

NORTHUMBERLAND RD

to Hexham and
Newcastle upon Tyne

WARWICK RD

ANNETWELL STREET

CASTLE ST

Town
Hall

MARKET PLACE

LONSDALE ST

CHISWICK ST

BRIDGE ST

JOHN ST

SHADDONGATE

WEST WALLS

Cathedral

ENGLISH ST

THE CRESCENT

HENRY ST

R. Caldew

BOTCHERGATE

FISHERHILL ST

BOWMAN ST

BROOK ST

Citadel
Railway
Station

N

to Penrith
and the South

0   ¼ mile
0   ¼   ½ km

Prologue

Boxing Day, 1869. A Sunday. Snow lay thick on the ground, thick on the cathedral roof, thick on the stout castle ramparts. For days a bitter east wind had blown from the Pennines across the Eden plain, scudding across the heavily swollen waters of the river Caldew, splitting the opaque black surface into even darker ripples. There was a deathly silence in this snow-muffled night-time city of Carlisle except for the boom of the cathedral bells every four hours, a most sombre sound which carried far outside the city boundaries to the outlying Cumberland villages. The dawn that day was crude, the violent red of the suddenly lightening sky lurid against the startling white of the new snow, against the grim black of the many factories and mills in the district of Caldewgate. All of wide, wide Church Street was one mass of unbroken, crusty white and the side streets leading off it were silted up with snow. Where, in sheltered spots, cobbles showed through, these glistened with ice.

In a house in one of these turnings, John Street, a young woman, nineteen years old, was giving birth to her first child. The woman's name was Annie Jordan. She called her baby Margaret Ann. Three months later she had her daughter baptized in the church of St Mary. Not quite two years after that Annie Jordan died, aged twenty-one, leaving Margaret Ann an orphan.

*

The month of May, 1936. A Saturday morning in Raffles, the big new council estate on the west side of Carlisle where the poor of Caldewgate had been rehoused. Men were out in their gardens ferociously trimming hedges which were just beginning to mature, diligently mowing lawns now at last smooth and green, the weak growth of the first few years forgotten. Number 44 Orton Road was on a corner, facing the bus stop opposite, but the woman didn't come on a bus. She came by car. Cars were rare on the Raffles estate. When the black car pulled up outside number 44 it was assumed by those watching, and many were, if in an idle fashion, that a doctor would step out. But no doctor had been sent for. Instead, an elderly woman, short of stature and dressed in black, veil included, emerged and walked up the short path to the green door.

She knocked and waited. The door was opened by a graceful-looking young woman who looked startled to find anyone standing there. The visitor politely inquired if she was correct in believing Margaret Ann Hind lived here. The young woman said she was, that Mrs Hind was her own mother. The visitor asked if, in that case, she might have a few words with Mrs Hind? The young woman, Lilian, hesitated. It was rude to keep anyone on the doorstep but some instinct told her that it would be better if her mother was warned first. She didn't want to show this visitor straight into the living-room where Mrs Hind was sitting with her grandson Gordon, aged four, on her knee. So, with an apologetic smile, and wishing there was either a hall or a parlour where this woman could wait, she said she would go to get her mother.

Margaret Ann Hind, told there was someone at the door wanting her, lifted Gordon off her knee and stood up. She

2

had grown a little stout in her sixties but she carried herself so well, as straight backed as Queen Victoria, that it became her. She had a welcoming expression on her face but when she reached the tiny vestibule and saw her visitor it vanished. She seemed to freeze. She put out a hand to steady herself. Lilian saw that, for whatever reason, her mother was shocked and such shocks were to be avoided. Margaret Ann had suffered from angina for the past decade and the doctor had warned her to guard against agitation of any kind. But as Lilian, hovering in the background, asked if her mother was all right, Margaret Ann seemed to rally, to control whatever emotion she was feeling. She did not address this stranger by name but merely said to Lilian that she would take her visitor upstairs and began to lead the way. The stairs opened straight up from the vestibule. They led to two bedrooms, one occupied by Lilian and her husband Arthur and their son Gordon, and one by Margaret Ann herself. She was in the process of selling her house, though she had not yet emptied it of her furniture since she had not yet decided where she would live. Always in awe of her mother, Lilian did not protest, though it embarrassed her to realize there was no chair in her mother's bedroom upon which a visitor could sit. It was no place for a guest.

Lilian went back into the small living-room where Gordon was still looking at the picture-book his grandmother had been showing him. Arthur was in the garden, preparing the ground for his bedding plants. Soon he would take Gordon to visit his other grandmother and his grandfather. Lilian began to get Gordon ready. She had a sense of foreboding, but then she very often did. There was a fire burning in the black-leaded range even though it was May, and she warmed Gordon's jacket at it. Then she dressed him in it and sat him

3

on her knee, taking up the picture-book again and waiting for Arthur to come in and say he was ready. She could hear no sound from upstairs, not even the low hum of voices. She wondered if the two women were sitting side by side on the double bed. Were they whispering? It would be cold up there. It was a cold morning even if it was spring. A long time seemed to go by. Gordon became impatient. Finally, she went out to see how long Arthur was going to be. He was just finishing his digging. While he washed his hands in the kitchen sink she told him about her mother's visitor and how worried she was because her mother had seemed alarmed.

Arthur delayed his departure long enough to see Mrs Hind's guest leave. He stood back from the window, well back, and watched. The woman looked perfectly respectable, quite unthreatening, to him. What was the fuss? He admired the car. He was a mechanic and knew about cars. He couldn't see who was driving, just that the woman got into the back seat and was driven away without either a wave or look. Arthur set off, with Gordon, to visit his parents, not at all disturbed, and impatient with Lilian for being so. Worrying was a bad habit of hers.

When he had gone, Lilian went upstairs, wondering what had happened. She tapped on her mother's closed door and said, 'Mother? Are you all right?' There was silence. It frightened her, and this time, as she tapped again, she opened the door a little and peeped round it. Her mother was lying on the bed, her eyes closed, clutching a handkerchief. The constant kneading of this handkerchief was the only sign she was not asleep. 'Can I get you a cup of tea?' Lilian asked, and then, 'Shouldn't you take a pill now?' Her mother turned her face away, but not before Lilian had seen she was weeping, and said, 'Leave me. I'm resting. I'll come down presently.'

4

Presently turned out to be eight hours later. When Margaret Ann did come down she never once referred to her visitor or anything that had been said. Nothing. No explanation whatsoever. And Lilian, remarkably, never asked a single question. She was too afraid of her mother's evident distress to have the heart to pry. She saw how pale her mother was, how tired and sad, how defeated she seemed and it was too painful to probe. Margaret Ann drank some tea, ate some toast, then went back up to bed. Almost three months later she died, quite suddenly, and throughout that period there was an unhappiness about her which never seemed to lift.

The same year, 1936, 22 July. A hot day, most unsuitable for a funeral. It seemed so inappropriate to be standing at a graveside when the sky was a holiday blue and the sun shone so festively. It would have felt better to the mourners if it had been raining, if the weather had remained as unseasonably dreary as it had been three days earlier, the actual day Margaret Ann died.

Died quickly, dramatically, with Gordon sitting on her knee, shelling peas, slitting the pea pods open for him and letting him pop half the peas into his mouth. Arthur was at work, Lilian in the kitchen washing dishes. Gordon suddenly cried out. He didn't know what had happened, only felt the rim of the metal colander, into which the peas were supposed to go, dig painfully into his fat little tummy, pushed forward by the weight of his grandmother's slumping on top of him as she collapsed without a sound. Gordon struggled and cried and the budgerigar flapped wildly in its cage in a panic. It was the bird Lilian heard, and she came through from the kitchen, hands still wet. She saw Gordon red-faced and wriggling and her mother's body curved over him. The

5

hands she released from around her son were warm and soft but she knew at once that her mother was dead. She didn't know what to do. Gordon was sobbing, the bird screeching. There was no telephone, no way of getting help without leaving the house.

She ran to the end of the road, still clutching the wailing Gordon, to the public telephone outside the Horse and Farrier pub. She rang the doctor but he was out on his calls and she could only leave a message. Re-entering her house was dreadful – seeing the dead body lying so unnaturally, so awkwardly, in the chair. She wished her sisters, Jean and Nan, were with her or that Arthur had come home for his dinner, but it was only half past eleven, another hour to go before he cycled back from the Metal Box factory. But the doctor came quicker than expected, before Arthur arrived. Margaret Ann had died of a heart attack. Dr Honeyman was surprised there had been no definite warning signs, no complaints of breathlessness or acute pains. But this was in character everyone later agreed. Margaret Ann Hind, née Jordan, was brave, she was stoical, she had had a hard life and was used to suffering of every sort.

This was what they all said to each other on that sunny day, the day of the funeral. They sat, the three daughters – Lilian, Jean and Nan – and the two sons-in-law – Arthur and Dave – and Nan's boyfriend, Jack, and said what a wonderful woman Margaret Ann had been and what a hard life she had had. None of them knew exactly how hard, though they were convinced of its hardness, because Margaret Ann never talked about her background. No one knew where she had been born or brought up. In the Newcastle area, it was believed. She had not liked to be asked and such was the strength of her character and of her dislike of any questioning that nobody's curiosity ever got the better of them. She was allowed to have had no past until the age of twenty-three when she was quite happy to acknowledge that she had begun work as a domestic servant to the Stephenson family.

A life suspected to have been hard, then, but over now. Her three daughters had wept copiously, even Nan, the youngest, the wild one, the defiant one, the one who had caused her mother most anxiety. Guilt as well as grief hung in the air, the usual guilt feelings of adult children who fear they never expressed their love and gratitude sufficiently to the dead parent. And extra guilt in this instance, the guilt that came from knowing none of them had properly taken their mother into their own homes. Jean had tried. Her mother, while her house was being sold, had come to Motherwell, intending to stay, but she'd been unhappy and returned to Carlisle. Jean worried that she had not tried hard enough to make her mother part of her family, but it had been difficult in a room and kitchen only, with a husband and two children, to give her mother the peace and privacy as well as the warmth she needed. Nan had not even had a home to offer her mother (who didn't know she was living in sin with Jack in Glasgow). And Lilian, to whom their mother had come after the abortive Scottish trip, worried that she had not urged her mother to make her stay with her permanent and not the temporary thing she spoke of.

So it was a miserable gathering as befitted the occasion. Three daughters, aged thirty-four, thirty-one and twenty-eight, and their three men, all crowded into the front parlour of their mother's house in Bowman Street from which everything was to be cleared the following day. There had been others present, cousins and friends, but they had all left. They had been Hind relatives, not Jordans, no one from their mother's side at all, not a single Jordan. Their mother had had friends but no family, a fact well known to them.

It was warm in the parlour, close, being such a hot day. No one had lived in their mother's house for the last four months. The first sale had fallen through, and the second dragged on and on, and meanwhile their mother had vacated the place and it had not been regularly aired. The blind was down and the thick velour curtains drawn and the house baked in the afternoon heat. There were sighs as they sat in the stifling heat and the gradual removal of hats and gloves, the opening of jackets and blouses – only a discreet button or two but a relief. The men were restless. Jack stood in front of the empty fireplace, legs apart, hands behind his back, immaculate in his elegant suit, lifting himself every now and again on the balls of his feet, eyes only for Nan, the lovely spirited Nan, longing to get her away, hating these rituals and only with difficulty respecting them. Dave was splayed out in an armchair, all six foot of him, neat enough in his best suit but hair rumpled, eyes closed with fatigue (and whisky), thinking only of the few hours left before his next shift. And Arthur, whistling soundlessly, head bowed, was sitting on a stiff-backed chair, dreading Lilian's sustained grief and wondering why she always had to be twice as upset as anyone else.

Jack looked at his gold watch and said to Nan it was time to leave. Leave in their car. Nobody else in the family had a car, only Jack, flash Jack with his public school education, his southern ways. Nan got up and straightened her beautifully cut skirt and picked up her crocodile-skin handbag and at that moment there was a knock at the door. Quite a timid knock, three gentle-enough taps with the brass knocker in the shape of a lion's head. More flowers, arriving too late? Nan said she would go, she was going anyway. They heard Nan go to the door and open it and then, indistinctly, another voice speaking words too muffled to be heard in the parlour. Nan came back, looking astonished. 'It's a woman,' she said. 'She says she's come to see if there is anything for her.' The others stared at her. 'Anything *for* her?' echoed Jean. 'What does she mean, who is she, do you know her?' But it was Lilian who next went to the door, the ever-polite, grave, eldest daughter.

There was indeed a woman standing at the door. A woman, and behind her a man. Lilian took in the man's face before the woman's. She felt she'd seen him, or someone like him, before. A burly fellow with a big moustache. Maybe she'd seen him in the market, maybe he was a butcher. But the woman she had never seen. She was perhaps forty, quite tall, good posture, a square not unattractive face with large brown eyes which seemed both fierce and frightened. 'Can I help you?' said Lilian, at her most gracious. 'I've come to see if she left me anything,' the woman said, and then, seeing Lilian's bewilderment, 'in her will.' 'You mean,' said Lilian, 'my mother's will?' 'Yes,' said the woman firmly. 'I've come to see if she's left me anything. I want to know, has her will been read yet?' 'My mother's will?' repeated Lilian, still dumbfounded by the question, aware of Nan and Jean now behind her in the narrow passage. 'Why should my mother leave you anything? Who are you?' 'I'm her daughter too,' the woman said.

Lilian, Jean and Nan stood utterly still and stared at this mad creature. Patiently, the woman on the doorstep repeated yet again that she had come to find out if she had been left anything. 'We've just buried our mother,' said Jean angrily. 'We don't know anything about any will.' 'I think you should show some respect,' Nan chimed in. 'And take yourself

9

off, coming at a time like this, you've no manners. Close the door, Lily.' But Lilian had no chance to do so before the woman burst into tears and turned and ran down the street. The man hesitated, then, before following her, said, 'It's right enough. She is her daughter, and if she has been left anything you'd better see she gets it or I'll set the law on you.'

Shock could not adequately describe the sense of outrage in the parlour. It was a trick. What else could it be but a disgusting attempt to extort money? Jean's and Nan's faces were flushed with fury, Lilian's pale with distress. The men wished they had gone to the door and dealt with this intruder. Dave said it was a damned cheek, Jack said such vermin should be reported to the police, and Arthur said nobody should have talked to the woman in the first place. Then, as Jack and Nan prepared once more to drive off, Jack said, casually, very off-hand, 'Is there a will, by the way?' Everyone stared at him. The idea had still not entered their heads. Once he and Nan had gone the others discussed this possibility. 'When Father died there was no will,' Lilian said, troubled, 'and Mother said what a mess there was, with there being no will. I wouldn't be surprised if she has made one. There was the money from this house to leave and a bit more.' 'If there is a will,' said Dave, 'it will be with a lawyer.' 'Or among her things somewhere,' Arthur said. 'Maybe still in the house.'

It was in the house, in the bedroom, in the right-hand small drawer of the chest of drawers. The last will and testament of Margaret Ann Hind, widow, of 14 Peter Street, made on 7 December 1915, three months after her husband died. Lilian found it and at the words on the envelope – My Will – could not at first open it. She handed it to Jean and they both sat down on the bed. 'Oh God,' Jean said, 'suppose . . .' 'No,' said Lilian, suddenly resolute, 'not Mother, never. Give it back to me.' And taking the envelope she opened it and extracted the document inside and quickly scanned it. 'I knew it was a lie,' she said triumphantly and passed the will over to her sister. It was unequivocal. It gave and bequeathed all money and possessions to be shared equally between 'my three daughters, Lilian, Jane and Annie'. No mention whatso-ever of any fourth daughter. No need for panic. No need to revise the revered character and conduct of the good, the wise, the kind, the gentle, the generous, the honest, the almost saintly Margaret Ann, their beloved mother.

The autumn of 1946. A dusty church hall in Raffles where twenty-four Brownies are gathered round Brown Owl. Badges have been competed for, beanbags thrown and caught, and now the whole pack is sitting cross-legged on the floor, attentive and a little breathless from all the Wednesday evening excitement. Brown Owl has something special to say. She is talking about history. First she talks about the history of the Girl Guide Movement and how the Brownies came into being, then about how each Brownie has her own little history, special to her. She wants them all to go home and come next week with their own personal family histories. They are to ask their mothers and fathers and grandpas and grandmas and aunts and uncles and anyone at all related to them, ask them to write down when they were born and married and how many children they had, and with all this information they are to make their own family trees. It will be fun, it will be instructive.

One of the Brownies, Margaret, can hardly wait to get home. She is such a keen child, keen at school, keen at Brownies. She goes straight into her home and begins asking for names and dates, pencil poised, sheet of paper ready. Her mother, Lilian, likes to see her children keen to learn and is only too pleased, at first, to cooperate. She gives Margaret her own birth date and her sisters', their marriage details, and she shows her daughter how to set all this out. She gives her husband Arthur's dates and those of his parents and his brother's and his brother's wife's, and now the tree is filling up, it is as complete as Lilian can help to make it. But not enough for the keen-eyed Margaret. 'Your mother's dates,' says the child. 'I've got those, but not *her* mother's. Who was she?' 'We've done enough,' Lilian said, 'time for bed.'

The following week, Margaret takes her family tree to Brownies. She has more names and dates on her sheet of paper than anyone else, far more, and all so neatly set out. Brown Owl's brother is with her that evening and is most impressed. He is at university and is studying History and Brown Owl has brought him along to tell the Brownies why history is important and how they are all part of it. Only Margaret pays much attention and Brown Owl's brother is most gratified. He looks closely at this keen child's family tree. She points out the gap, where she has been unable to put the names of any maternal great-grandparents. She says her mother doesn't know who they were. Brown Owl's brother says if she likes he'll come home with her and help her mother find out, tell her how she might trace these ancestors. Margaret is thrilled. She dances into the house with Brown Owl's gawky brother rather sheepishly following her. Lilian is, as usual, polite. She listens to what Brown Owl's brother has to say about parish registers and so forth, but then becomes distant, rather aloof and cold. She thanks the young man but says that really she would prefer not to carry out any investigation into her mother's background. A howl of protest from Margaret, but Brown Owl's brother blushes and leaves.

That is the end of that. For the time being.

Four fragments, full of facts but full of hearsay too, the very stuff of family history. Over and over again we get told stories by our parents and grandparents, and sometimes, if these stories are treated seriously and checked, that is all they turn out to be – stories, unsubstantiated and often downright contradicted by the actual evidence in records. But sometimes beneath the stories lurks the history of more than an ordinary person. Sometimes their story is the story of thousands.

My grandmother's story seems to me representative in that kind of way. When my mother died, in 1981, I felt freed from the taboo she'd placed on any attempt to unravel the background of Margaret Ann. I could hardly believe that she had never insisted on knowing the identity of her mother's visitor. Surely, once her immediate distress was over, she could have been asked? But no. My mother was too afraid of the truth. My grandmother's birth certificate, easy enough to obtain, told a familiar, sad little tale: she was the illegitimate daughter of a servant girl. How pathetic, I thought, that all the mystery was just to hide this banal fact. How ordinary, how disappointing.

But then I began to think about the various stories handed down. Who was the woman in the car, the woman in black, who came to visit my grandmother not long before she died? What news did she bring? And who was that other woman, the one who turned up on the day of my grandmother's funeral claiming to be her other daughter? Why did my grandmother give the impression she was from the Newcastle area when she was born in Carlisle? No wonder Brown

Owl's brother was shown the door ... What puzzles to solve, what secrets to reveal. How little I really knew of my maternal grandmother and how much I suddenly wanted to know, becoming convinced that her history was somehow essential to understand better not simply my own but that of a whole generation of working-class women (and perhaps of a great many middle-class women too, those who may have had the means and education to be independent but who believed their marital duty was to put their family first).

MARGARET ANN

1869–1936

I

I hadn't known the name of my maternal great-grandmother, but once I did I thought that might be all I ever would manage to find out. Annie Jordan, the nineteen-year-old who gave birth to her illegitimate daughter on Boxing Day 1869, was and remains almost totally obscure. There is her daughter's birth certificate, some census information and her death certificate and that is that. My grandmother was lucky to be born at all. The local paper in Carlisle was full, at that time, of pitiful stories describing how unmarried servant girls tried first to conceal their pregnancies and then, when their babies were born, delivered without assistance, to kill them.

The same month Annie Jordan gave birth there was an inquest in Carlisle on the body of a baby found 'in the river Eden, among the branches between the bank of the river and some old weiring. A sod was laid upon it . . . a woman was seen near the place where the child was found, leaning against some railings, apparently in distress and crying.' The woman was arrested and when it was discovered she was the mother of the dead baby she was sent to prison for six months. Annie Jordan could so easily have been driven to that solution or else to giving birth in her place of employment, as Sarah Potts did a few weeks later. Her employer 'had occasion to go into Sarah's bedroom on Saturday morning and observed marks which induced her to believe a child had been delivered. On searching the room she found the child in the

17

chamber-pot.' Meanwhile, Sarah was scrubbing the kitchen flagstones, busy pretending nothing had happened.

But young Annie had her child and kept her and had her christened and managed to continue working until in 1871 she became ill and died in five days of 'epilepsia convulsions, delirium tremens'. She died on 18 December, eight days before her daughter Margaret Ann's second birthday. On her death certificate she is described as the widow of Joseph Jordan, a butcher, whereas on her daughter's birth certificate no husband or father of her child is cited. There is no trace of any marriage between Annie and Joseph even though she used his surname (her own was Roscow). Joseph Jordan, whose widow she claimed to be, had died, aged twenty-three, the year before, soon after Margaret Ann's birth. But though there is no evidence of any marriage, Annie was buried in the same grave as Joseph so their union was recognized by their families.

Pointless to hope to find out any more about poor insignificant Annie, about what she looked like, what kind of personality she had, but not pointless or hopeless trying to piece together the sort of life she led. Carlisle, in 1869, the year Annie gave birth to her only child, was still a small, compact city, easy to imagine and reconstruct. It had always been from Roman times a frontier settlement which, from the reign of Henry I, gradually became a city of importance in the North. A castle was built, a mint established, a priory and cathedral endowed and a town charter granted. But Carlisle's most important function remained a military one – it was a city constantly filled with soldiers to keep the Scots at bay. The needs of this permanent garrison stimulated trade and by the end of the thirteenth century Carlisle was the centre of the textile trade in Cumberland, so that later, much later, when the industrial revolution began, Carlisle was perfectly placed to become the fourth most important textile-producing city in the whole of England. The medieval city within its walls remained much the same but without them the change was dramatic. Annie Jordan's short life spanned the middle period of that change.

At the very beginning of the nineteenth century all that caught the eye of anyone standing on the city walls and looking west was a general emptiness, the lack of any significant landmark or building. Coming out of the walled city in this direction a bridge crossed the river Caldew, and then beyond there were meadows and an open stream, Dow Beck, running down the wide, cobbled road, Church Street, which led eventually to the sea. Edward I was carried along it to his lonely death out on Burgh marsh, and Robert the Bruce had made his camp here while he contemplated attacking the castle. The city stopped at Caldew Bridge and what lay beyond was of no importance compared with the lives lived in the elegant houses near the cathedral. This outer district was called Caldewgate, a poor district. Into it the Irish and the Scots flocked, looking for work and, as the century progressed, finding it in the mills which had suddenly mushroomed. The water of the Caldew was found to be excellent for use in the textile trade and by 1850, when Annie Jordan was born, Caldewgate had become an industrial suburb. Now, anyone standing on the city walls and looking west saw huge chimneys and factories and scores of houses crammed together.

There were four printed-cotton works in Caldewgate, a soap boilery, tanneries and breweries, and factories where hats and whips and fish hooks were made. The Dixon family had built a huge factory on the banks of the Caldew (with a chimney said to be the highest in England) and the Carr family, who made biscuits, another on the other side of Caldewgate. But what had changed the area most from being open meadows and marshland to having every square yard filled with houses or factories was the coming of the railway lines running through it. The Carlisle to Newcastle line opened in 1838, the track running under the city walls alongside the river Caldew, and every year after that it seemed another railway company entered Carlisle, and Caldewgate was scarred even more by their lines. The noise and filth of the trains added to the noise and filth of the factories made the district ugly and unhealthy.

Annie Jordan lived in the middle of it. Her mother Mary ran one of the many public houses in Caldewgate. The Carlisle Relief Committee, founded in 1862, worried about the all too visible poverty in the district. Conditions required soup-kitchens to be set up with monotonous regularity to cope with the larger than usual influx of migrant workers. Annie's mother, as a publican, benefited from these workers – they drank themselves silly. Beer was cheap and so was gin. Every street in Caldewgate had at least one pub – Mary's was the Royal Oak in Church Street – and all the city's breweries were in this one district. Annie's 'husband's' family, the Jordans, were publicans too. Thomas Jordan, Joseph's father, ran the Queen's Head, also in Church Street, but he had another trade, he was a butcher. Caldewgate was almost as full of butchers as publicans, with half the animals butchered coming from across the border with Scotland, captured in dawn raids. There was a flat area of land, a sort of island off the banks of the river Eden, called the Sands where cattle and sheep were auctioned. Before the animals were slaughtered the butchers who had bought them would graze them on what was left of Caldewgate's meadows. Meat was big business. Carlisle was full of meat markets, whole streets given over to different animals. There were other markets – Carlisle was after all a market town even before it became anything else – but nothing compared with the sale of meat. The butchers had rows of lock-up stalls, called shambles, in the area known as Rickergate, where the slaughterhouses and pigsties were mixed in with the houses, making the district even poorer and less salubrious than Caldewgate.

Annie had her baby not in her mother's pub, nor in the pub where she worked as a domestic servant, but in the house of one of her husband's family. Straight afterwards she went to live in West Walls – described by one observer as 'broken down in places and crumbling away and almost disgusting with filth'. She lived at number 19 three months after her daughter's birth, when she was christened, but by 1871, when there was a census, she was back outside the city walls in Caldewgate, living with her mother and two sisters. When she died at the end of that year she hadn't moved more than a few hundred yards from where she had been born. The same can still be said for many of the population of Carlisle.

All Annie left behind her was her baby Margaret Ann, aged two. From 1871 to 1893 this baby, my grandmother, disappears from all records. But she, unlike her mother, can be clearly identified and described even if there are gaps, gaps she went to great lengths to keep empty. During her lifetime she managed to conceal everything she wished to conceal. After her death not all her secrets have remained secret.

There is only so much that can be done when trying to find out what happened to an obscure two-year-old child in the late nineteenth century. The records are meagre. School registers rarely survive, if they were kept at all, and school logbooks, though they do contain names of individual pupils, seldom list entire classes. The best bet for this kind of search are census returns, especially if an exact locality is known. But Margaret Ann Jordan, though born in Caldewgate and baptized at St Mary's, does not exist in the census for 1871, when she would have been sixteen months old (the census was in April). There are four under-two-year-old Margarets in that census for Caldewgate and one Margaret Ann. She is registered as the daughter of Walter and Elizabeth Graham, who lived at 16 Bridge Street, next door to number 18, where Annie, my Margaret Ann's mother, died. Was her child already living next door with the Grahams and so became part of their family when, a few months later, Annie died? Perfectly possible, even likely, but no proof at all.

In the 1881 census the position is the same: no eleven-year-old Margaret Ann Jordan in Caldewgate or anywhere in Carlisle. In the 1891 census still no Jordan but Margaret Ann Graham turns up as resident servant to the Stephenson family at 4 Paternoster Row, a smart street directly beside the cathedral. This is the family my grandmother said she began working for in 1893 and the house from which she was married in 1899. This, in fact, is where she allowed her own history to begin. How curious that she must therefore have taken over from a young woman her exact age and with her Christian names. Curious, but also acceptable as coincidental. And there is still my grandmother's only bit of information given to her daughters that she was from the Newcastle area.

One sister, Nan, was still very much alive and alert when my mother died and I began this search. I showed her Margaret Ann's birth certificate and she was shocked. It wasn't the proof of Margaret Ann's illegitimacy which shocked her – though it did – so much as the evidence that she was born in Caldewgate. Nan and her sisters really had believed their mother was from the Newcastle area. But maybe she was. Maybe the infant Margaret Ann was taken to relatives in the Newcastle area and brought up by them, returning to Carlisle only at the age of twenty-two.

Newcastle even then was bigger than Carlisle, but not so large that its census returns are too enormous to search. Plenty of Jordans in the Newcastle area and many of them involved in the pub trade, the same as in Carlisle. But no Margaret Ann Jordan in the whole of the census returns for 1871, 1881, or 1891. Was she concealed at every census? Or simply forgotten about? Possible with a child under two, virtually impossible for a girl of eleven or a woman of twenty-one to be omitted. Was she always travelling during each census? Highly unlikely. Whatever the case, my grandmother, whether living under a different name, or miraculously escaping detection, or being in neither Carlisle nor Newcastle (though when she travelled to Scotland at the age of sixty she said Newcastle was the furthest she'd ever been before), simply disappears for twenty years.

Mothers spend half their time referring to their own childhoods as a point of comparison when bringing up their children, but apparently not a wisp of a memory ever escaped my grandmother's lips. Nothing. A blank. She was a mother who had had no childhood, or a childhood so unhappy that she wiped it out, leaving only an impression that whatever she had suffered was too awful to remember. Her daughters were afraid of what she suppressed without knowing what it was. They were nervous, agitated, even after she was dead, at the thought of what might be uncovered if their mother's past was exhumed.

But I am not. I want to know. I have even come to believe I need to know.

The story has to start, for the time being, in 1893 when Margaret Ann acknowledged she was living with the Stephenson family in Paternoster Row. She was only, living there, yards from where her own mother had lived in West Walls when she was baptized, only five minutes' walk from where she herself was born over the bridge in Caldewgate, but she could have been in a different city so great was the contrast.

She talked freely to her daughters, in later years, about that period and they, my mother's sisters, especially Nan, were equally free passing the stories on to me. Life in Paternoster Row was literally dominated by the cathedral. Margaret Ann said she loved it, loved coming out of number 4 and looking straight at the splendour of it. Walking down the Row to Abbey Street, she passed the Abbey gateway, leading into the cathedral precinct. The doors were huge and solid, massively thick and iron-studded, with one short ladder hanging either side of them, used by the porter to light the gas lights. There was a right of way through the precinct which she often took for the pleasure of passing so close to the cathedral. It ran alongside the Fratery, with its ivy-covered ancient walls, and she would linger there, listening to the choirboys rehearse, as they did every morning. She would linger again, as she neared the doors of the cathedral, if there was a service on, so that she could hear the chanting and singing and the organ playing, a splendid organ recently renovated and fitted with air pumps driven by a gas engine. It made her happy living so close to the cathedral; feeling its holiness and beauty somehow touched her.

The Stephensons' house gave her almost the same satisfaction. She liked living there. Number 4 seemed to her exactly what a house should be – not too large, not too forbidding, a family house of the best kind with an elegant but modest appearance. It was only two storeys, built of red brick with pale sandstone dressings round the doorway and with a good slate roof. What she admired most was the doorway with its panelled door and pretty fanlight and its stone columns either side. She thought the one bay window (in Mr and Mrs Stephenson's bedroom) gave the house a more interesting aspect than the other flat-fronted ones in the Row. Mr Stephenson had told her that when the house was built, only forty years ago in 1855, the workmen had discovered a Roman road running underneath where the cellar was to go. Margaret Ann liked to think about that. She had some sense of the importance of history (even if she denied her own). She often said how exciting she had found living above a Roman road, connected like that to ancient times.

Number 4 Paternoster Row was a smart address lived in by a prosperous family. Mr Henry Stephenson was a glass merchant, head of a firm of glass makers, painters and decorators. His work premises joined on to his house with an arched opening between the two parts. Behind was the warehouse, partially blocking out Tullie House, an elegant seventeenth-century house recently converted into the Carlisle Museum and Library. His wife, Hannah, was ten years younger than him and they had four sons, William, Ernest, Alfred and George, and one daughter, Annie. Looking after them all was Margaret Ann, their resident domestic servant.

It was fortunate Margaret Ann loved the house and its situation, because the work inside it was hard. Four sons, aged eighteen, twelve, nine and seven, when she started work in 1893 (if that was indeed when she did start) and one daughter of fifteen made for heavy work. There were many sheets to be washed and ironed, many plates and knives and forks to clean, many meals to shop for and prepare. But Margaret Ann was supremely capable. She had heard Mrs Stephenson boast she was a gem, a treasure. But she had help. She was not expected to do quite everything herself. The Stephensons also employed a cook who came in every day except Sunday, and two young girls who did menial tasks under Margaret Ann's supervision (though she sometimes expressed the opinion that they were more trouble than they were worth).

Her wage, her annual wage, was eighteen pounds and her keep. She thought this keep good. She had her own room at the back of the house, above the scullery, overlooking the yard between house and warehouse. It was small but it had a carpet on top of the linoleum, quite a luxury for a servant, a comfortable bed, a wardrobe and a wash-stand, all fitted in somehow. There was a tiny wrought-iron fireplace in which a few coals could be burned during very cold weather (and there was plenty of that). Mrs Stephenson complimented Margaret Ann on how she had managed to make her room pleasant – 'You have quite a flair,' she told her and wondered aloud where it had come from. There was little enough scope for 'flair', but within the strict limits imposed by the size of the room, and by the amount of furniture, Margaret Ann had demonstrated it. The wallpaper was a heavily embossed cream, and Mrs Stephenson had offered Margaret Ann a pink and blue patterned quilt for her bed and pink and white flowered curtains to cheer things up. The cheering up had been declined. Margaret Ann said she had a crocheted bed-cover of her own. It was plain white. And she chose from Mrs Stephenson's linen cupboard a pair of off-white cotton curtains which had been makeshift ones for Annie's room until the red velvet pair were ready. The carpet was dark brown so it was a white and cream and brown uncheered-up room except for some artificial flowers, pale lilac, in the white jug on the narrow mantelpiece. The room was simple, quiet, like the servant herself.

Mrs Stephenson's only criticism of Margaret Ann, or the only one she ever admitted, was that she was not very forthcoming. She realized, she said, that most people would consider this quality an asset in a live-in servant, but she thought Margaret Ann carried quietness too far. She was not sullen, she must not think she was being thought sullen, far from it, she had a lovely smile, often in evidence, but she rarely initiated conversation nor did she seek to prolong those conversations begun by others . . . To Mrs Stephenson, Margaret Ann's words were usually considered and few and, quite frankly, it rather hurt her employer, or so she said. She would have wanted her devoted servant to *respond* more, that was all. Mr Stephenson, hearing this once, had laughed and said that Margaret Ann was too intelligent to go in for gossip (Margaret Ann left the room instantly on hearing this, mortified). Ever afterwards she felt Mrs Stephenson was studying her for visible signs of this intelligence and failing to find it and becoming annoyed with her husband for alleging it was there.

But Annie Stephenson agreed with her father. She adored Margaret Ann, who was not so very much older than herself. She thought her not just intelligent but beautiful, much to Margaret Ann's embarrassment − she did wish Annie would not say such foolish things and especially not in front of her brothers, who guffawed rudely even though they too liked Margaret Ann and showed it. She knew she was not beautiful.

Her hair was an ordinary brown and she wore it in an old-fashioned style. Her face was too square and her jaw too strong for beauty and her figure – well, she would rather not think about it. She was thick-waisted, not tall and slender like Annie. Annie, she knew, was only being kind to make her care less about not being married or having a suitor.

Annie herself, greatly preoccupied with her own chances of matrimony, could never understand why Margaret Ann was not married. Sometimes she asked, as tactfully as possible, if she had turned down offers? Margaret Ann said she had not. She said she had always been too busy to think of suitors and, mercifully, Annie left it at that. And it was true, she worked so hard that all she wanted to do in her spare time was rest in her room or go to church. She rose at six in the morning and was never in bed before midnight. The hardest work was in the morning. She wore a dark blue dress with a grey overall on top, because so much of the morning's work was, if not dirty, messy. The dress came down to her ankles and underneath she wore thick black stockings and clogs, though not heavy clogs with clinkers. She found clogs more comfortable than shoes. They were better for her feet which often were swollen with all the standing she did. The first thing she did every morning was get the fire going in the kitchen range, thankful one of the girls black-leaded it once a week, a truly filthy job she hated. Then she boiled the kettle, the big iron kettle hanging from a hook above the fire, and began mixing the dough to bake bread for breakfast. Her breath would be coming out mistily all this time and the cold sweeping up her skirt from the stone flags until the fire took a hold. Even then the fire, however fierce, hardly spread its warmth beyond a radius of two feet. It was movement,

28

constant movement, which kept Margaret Ann warm. She was on the go all morning, making porridge, making tea, rushing backwards and forwards to the dining-room laying and clearing the table and carrying heavy trays. Breakfast for a household of seven took two hours from that first descent into the cold kitchen to the last dish emptied and washed. Mrs Stephenson was the only one who did not appear for breakfast. She had it in bed. Margaret Ann was always grateful if Annie took in her mother's tray and if William, who was very kind, volunteered to carry up the cans of hot water needed for baths. Really, she counted herself fortunate to be servant to such a considerate family.

She felt less fortunate as the morning progressed. There was so much to do, time was her enemy. 'How's the enemy?' she would ask the girls as dinner-time loomed. Dinner was eaten in the middle of the day, at half past twelve. Everyone came home for it. The daily cook shopped for and cooked it, but she needed the two young girls to run around for her, so Margaret Ann managed everything else. She made everyone's bed, a laborious business with so many blankets and quilts and eiderdowns to shake and spread, and dusted all the furniture, dusted scores of cluttered surfaces and endless mirrors, and then she sorted the washing to be sent out. On Mondays she lifted the carpets and took them into the yard and beat them to expel the dust; on Tuesdays she cleaned the silver; on Wednesdays she ironed, her wrist aching from the weight of the heavy stone iron; on Thursdays she polished every piece of furniture in the over-furnished house; on Fridays she scrubbed the kitchen out before Cook arrived – she hated Fridays; on Saturdays she cleaned the windows, though one of the girls helped. Every morning was always a long morning, what with the essential regular jobs and each day's particular extra one, and it ended with a gallop, with the serving of dinner.

It always seemed that half this housework was done in semi-darkness, though 4 Paternoster Row was not an especially dark house. There was not much natural light coming through the windows, heavily shrouded in net, and the gas lamps were not lit until late afternoon. Those lamps were the very devil in any case, always needing attention. Hours it took getting them to burn properly, nearly as difficult to manage as oil lamps. There was talk of electricity being installed soon, but there was no Electric Lighting Station in Carlisle yet (it wasn't constructed until 1899). Margaret Ann was more interested in the thought of Mrs Stephenson purchasing a gas oven. It would be such a blessing, doing away with so much mess. It seemed to her that the two biggest headaches in her working day were dealing with the dirt caused by coal and battling against bugs. Dust from coal spread everywhere and then there was the menace of soot from the chimneys and the filthy ash which had to be cleaned out from the fireplaces. As for bugs, constant vigilance was necessary. The mattresses, the pillows, the carpets, the curtains – they all had to be inspected and treated to keep the bugs at bay. Margaret Ann was exhausted at the end of every morning with the fight against all forms of dirt.

Afternoons were more restful. Cook baked in the afternoons and sometimes she helped her, especially with scones and pastry. Cook had a heavy hand with both, and Margaret Ann a light touch. They baked for tea, high tea as well as afternoon tea, tarts and rock-cakes and several kinds of bread and scones, and the kitchen would suddenly seem a pleasant, warm place. Or Cook would bake on her own while Margaret Ann mended. There was always heaps of mending, stacks of socks to darn and buttons to sew on and even collars to turn (because Mrs Stephenson didn't believe in throwing a good shirt away just because the collar was worn on the inside). She would have enjoyed the mending more – at least she was sitting down – if Cook hadn't talked so much. She rambled on in a disjointed way and sometimes she was foul-mouthed which Margaret Ann hated. She was always tempted to leave the kitchen and retreat to her bedroom with the mending, but this would have caused such offence she endured Cook's bouts of swearing and tried to show her disapproval by her absolute silence. Other afternoons she sorted the larder, tidied drawers and made clothes for Mrs Stephenson. Early on Mrs Stephenson had discovered that her servant could not only darn so that these darns were virtually invisible, but that she could sew beautifully. She even knew how to make paper patterns and cut out material. If Mrs Stephenson could have spared Margaret Ann from her other work she would have had her dressmaking every day, all day.

Tea was at four, just for Mrs Stephenson and Annie together with anyone invited to join them. High tea was for the men, at six, after work and school. The men ate mountains of food, great heaps of Cumberland sausage and eggs and pies and cold meats, followed by scones and cakes, and all of it washed down with gallons of tea. It took a long time to prepare this feast and a long time to clear the debris away and put the kitchen to rights. Cook and the girls would have gone by then and Margaret Ann was responsible. It was well after eight before she was done and free to retire to her room with the eternal mending. That was the best time of day. Sometimes she didn't go to her room; sometimes she stayed in the kitchen. There was an old but very comfortable armchair there and she'd sit with her feet up and savour the peace. Sometimes Annie would come and talk to her, mostly to complain about trivial things, about being made to go on learning to play the pianoforte, at her age, and about her boredom with Carlisle, with her dull life. Margaret Ann listened but passed no comment, offered no advice. She went to bed around midnight and said her prayers and mostly slept deeply. Mostly, but not all the time. She dreaded having nightmares and crying out in her sleep. Only Annie ever heard her, but by the time she had come to Margaret Ann's door to inquire what the matter was Margaret Ann was awake and in control of herself.

Nothing, she always said, nothing was the matter. It must have been something she ate. Never, all those years later, when she related this to her daughters, did she give them any clue as to what her nightmares had been about or why she had cried out. And they were stopped from asking her for the usual reason they always gave – 'she was upset, even remembering'.

II

My grandmother's life was, then, a narrow life, a predictable one, shared by scores of domestic servants in Carlisle in that last decade of the nineteenth century, by thousands in the whole country. Hardship was only relative to Margaret Ann Jordan. Her life was no harder than any other woman's in her position, the point precisely. The physical hardship, the sheer energy and strength needed to get through each day, was commonplace. She *expected* to be down on her knees scrubbing, up to her elbows in boiling or freezing water washing and rinsing dishes, rocking on her feet with weariness after hours of running up and down stairs. It was what she was paid for. When she reminisced later in life – as she often did, her daughters remembered – it was always without any trace of resentment. Her expectations were low. She expected to carry on as she was until she dropped. Or married.

Marriage was always an option. Marriage was possibly, but not definitely or even probably, an escape from servitude. If she married, she knew she'd still have to cook and clean and wash and mend, and without the help of the kind of servant she was to the Stephensons unless she married a rich man. The chances of this happening were nil. Who, in Carlisle, among the servant class, married rich men? Rich, eligible men were few and far between, and girls like Annie Stephenson from good families ever on the lookout for them. But there was rich and rich, after all. Plenty of tradesmen around who did quite well for themselves by Carlisle standards, tradesmen who could afford to rent or even buy decent houses and to lead comfortable enough lives. The market was full of them. Plenty of money there, especially among the butchers, with Carlisle being such a big meat-eating place.

On Saturday afternoons Margaret Ann would go to the market to buy the joint for Sunday. She'd walk to the end of Paternoster Row, cross Castle Street, where the potato stalls were lined up in front of the cathedral railings, and cut through to Fisher Street into the splendid new covered market. She went through the glass doors and down the little cobbled hill where the shambles now were. Some butchers had more than one shambles. They had three or four together, positive empires. The meat hung from the ceiling on hooks, whole carcasses of pig and lamb and beef, and on the tiled counters below lay the cut-up portions: the bright red stewing steak, the dark slabs of liver, the great coils of pale, putty-coloured Cumberland sausage, the crimson mounds of mince, the stiff rows of chops. Meat was so important, it was every housewife's mainstay, it could not be done without. Every meal that professed to be a real meal had to have some kind of meat content. The Sunday joint was naturally the most important meat purchase of the week. It was a serious business. The joint had to do the family for Sunday dinner and then provide cold meat for Monday with enough left over to make rissoles or shepherd's pie on Tuesday, and preferably leave a well-covered bone to use for stock. The responsibility of this purchase lay heavily on Margaret Ann every week. She actually hated the sight of meat. It made her feel sick, all that bleeding red, that reminder of killing . . . She had to control herself carefully. She found beef the worst to buy, but it was the Stephensons' favourite. Best sirloin, that's what they liked, or rib of beef. The meat had to have yellowy fat round it, not white lardy-looking stuff, and it had not to be a suspicious bright red but rather a dull brown in colour. She knew that meat, to be properly inspected, should be touched as well as looked at – she saw other shoppers removing their gloves and prodding the meat, but she couldn't do that, she was too squeamish, too fastidious. She had to rely on the honesty of the butcher, of Thomas Hind.

Thomas Hind was proprietor of numbers 4 and 12 shambles, but whether he himself served at either of them she didn't know when first she began patronizing his stall soon after she came to work for the Stephensons. The reason she bought meat at number 4, usually, was because this shambles was so clean. The carcasses didn't drip blood, the meat on the counter did not lie in puddles of it, the bin for fat – cut off before purchase – wasn't nauseatingly visible. The floor of Thomas Hind's shambles always seemed freshly sawdusted, the aprons of the assistants were spotless and their heads always covered. But his prices were not the cheapest. Margaret Ann had reported this to Mrs Stephenson who sanctioned paying higher prices willingly, quite proudly, asserting that she was in agreement with her servant that cheapest was not always best, indeed not. There was always a queue at Thomas Hind's, but Margaret Ann was a patient queuer. She never attempted to push herself forward but waited her turn calmly. She engaged in none of the banter other customers seemed to like. She stated her requirement and that was that beyond a please and a thank you.

These were exactly the qualities which aroused Thomas Hind's interest. He noticed her precisely because of her curious quality of stillness. He didn't go in for banter either, though he was capable of it. He met dignity with dignity and hoped

35

it would get him somewhere. In 1893, when Margaret Ann first began buying meat from him, he was thirty-five years old and unmarried. His father had been a butcher and so had his grandfather, and as the only son he was always expected to take over the family business. His father had died when Thomas was a child and his mother, Jane, had become a butcher herself in order to keep the business going for Thomas to inherit. His debt to her was strong and he acknowledged it by now supporting not just her but two of his three sisters (the third had married). He was prosperous enough by then to marry but as yet had given little thought to it. He was notoriously hard to satisfy and was teased about his high standards by his sisters who despaired of him ever approving of any girl. For four years he observed Margaret Ann quite contentedly, and then, when his mother died in 1897, decided the time had come for him to court her seriously. Nothing impetuous about Tom.

He knew Margaret Ann was a servant to the Stephensons of Paternoster Row and that she was a regular attender at St Mary's church to which his sisters also belonged, but beyond that he was surprised to find he could discover very little. No one seemed to know this quiet woman. There were Jordans in Caldewgate but he asked around and none of them knew her. She wasn't claimed by any family, not even as a distant relative, which puzzled him, Carlisle being the place where everyone knew everyone else, or at least someone who did. So it was a slow affair, this courtship, three years of best boned-and-rolled sirloin, shoulder of lamb, leg of pork, three years of pounds of Cumberland sausage, best back bacon, ham on the bone. A lot of meat, a lot of pleasantries, a lot of cap-doffing on Tom's part and head-inclining on Margaret Ann's. He never went to Paternoster Row, he was never a gentleman caller. One Saturday, towards the end of the afternoon, when he himself was serving and there were no assistants to hear and smirk, no customer other than Margaret Ann to hear and speculate, he asked her if she would care to ride with him and his sisters out to Burgh marsh for a breath of sea air. He was very much afraid she would refuse, even be offended, but no, she smiled and said she knew his sisters from church and she would be glad to accompany them if she could get time off (knowing, of course, that she could, that Mrs Stephenson would gladly give permission).

The four of them went in a pony and trap, quite a squeeze, with both Maggie Hind and Sarah Jane Hind being large women, and Tom himself over six foot and big with it. It was lucky Margaret Ann was so small and light. She had so rarely been driven anywhere that it was quite a thrill to bowl along through Caldewgate and out on to the Moorhouse Road into the country towards the coast. The Hind sisters were jolly and great pointers-out – sheep, trees, cottages, all called forth excited exclamations and their guest found it quite hard to sustain the level of enthusiasm they seemed to desire. They were also great eaters. Each had a bag of sweets in her lap into which she frequently dipped. It took a long time to get to Burgh marsh, some seven miles away, a place Margaret Ann had never been, but with which the Hinds were familiar since their grandmother came from Burgh. She was surprised to find the sea so hard to glimpse, with such great expanses of marsh between it and the road, and felt a slight sense of disappointment, quickly suppressed. They went on to Port Carlisle – just a few houses, a shop, two pubs, strung out along the marsh road – and here they got down.

The Misses Hind were tactful. They claimed not to have the energy to walk about and encouraged Margaret Ann to take a walk, if she felt so inclined, with their brother. The two of them strolled off, not far but far enough to be out of earshot. They stood admiring the vague outline of the Scottish coast and made polite conversation. Tom asked Margaret Ann if she was happy with the Stephensons and she said she was. Then he asked her if she saw much of her family and immediately there was a stiffness on her part as she said she had no known family which warned him off. She seemed to find it a painful topic so he tried to joke about his own family, saying how overwhelming they were, how he wouldn't mind a bit of a separation from them without wishing them ill. There was no response. Hurriedly he turned to talking about bowls. He played bowls for the Turf Club and was quite a champion, without wanting to boast. Would she care to come to watch some evening? She said she would.

It was certainly preferable to meeting over meat. All summer of 1898 Margaret Ann went regularly to watch Tom Hind bowl. She wasn't at all interested in the game, couldn't see the point, but she loved the lush smoothness of the bowling green and the white coats of the players and even the bowls themselves, so satisfyingly heavy and solid, making such a dramatic click as they knocked against each other. She enjoyed being in the fresh air, sitting on a comfortable chair Tom had fetched out of the clubhouse for her. He brought her tea and was in every way attentive. She told Annie Stephenson about his attentiveness only because Annie saw her being escorted home and was half mad with curiosity. 'Will he propose, do you think?' Annie asked breathlessly. 'And will you accept if he does?' Margaret Ann was silent. She gave nothing away. 'Promise,' Annie pleaded, 'that if you do marry I can be your bridesmaid?' She dreaded Margaret Ann leaving and told her so, even though she wanted her to marry happily. Mr Stephenson had just died and Annie dreaded being left to cope with her mother's distress and depression – Margaret Ann could do this so much better. So a double promise was given: Annie could be at any wedding of Margaret Ann's (though not as bridesmaid, she didn't see herself having bridesmaids) and Margaret Ann would not leave the grieving widow until she was more reconciled and settled.

Finally, on Thursday, 14 September 1899, Margaret Ann Jordan married Thomas Hind, according to the rites and ceremonies of the Established Church, in St Mary's. Thomas gave his age as forty, though he wasn't forty until December, and Margaret Ann gave hers as twenty-eight, though she was twenty-nine. Under Father's Name, Surname and Profession Margaret Ann drew a line. The marriage was announced in the appropriate column of the *Carlisle Journal*, a perfectly conventional notice except for one curious thing: Margaret Ann styled herself 'granddaughter of the late Thomas Jordan'. Most unusual to refer to oneself as granddaughter rather than daughter, and in her case rather a nonsense, for if her father was unknown – hence the blank first on her birth certificate and now on her marriage certificate – how did she know Thomas Jordan had been her grandfather? And why did she wish to draw attention to this? This grandfather died when she was fifteen. Had she lived with him those fifteen years? Not according to any census return nor according to her own later assertion that she was from the Newcastle area. It was a strange and perhaps significant little proclamation, a desperate-looking desire to claim some family, at least at the time of her marriage.

September 1899 to September 1915, almost sixteen years to

the day. The best years of Margaret Ann's life. She was mistress of her own house, though it was rented not bought: 29 Corporation Road. Not an elegant house like Paternoster Row but her first real home. It was very small, a living-room and kitchen and scullery downstairs, two bedrooms (though no fixed bath, no indoor lavatory) upstairs, but a neat, compact, well-built workman's house with a yard at the back and opening straight on to the cobbled street in front. It was one in a terrace, near to the Sands where the cattle auctions were held and very near to the market, highly convenient for Tom's work. The river Eden was only yards away and so was the park where, later, God willing, children could play. Looking after this house was easy compared with looking after 4 Paternoster Row. There were only a few stairs, no passages, no fine furniture to polish and only Tom and herself to cook and wash for.

But to balance this less gruelling life as a housewife there was the butchery business to help with. Margaret Ann never wanted Tom to know how much she hated this helping. It would have been ungrateful to let him realize her loathing of meat and everything to do with the butchering of it when their prosperity depended on the trade. She forced herself to seem eager to aid him and he was pleased. At the end of every day she helped to scrub down the shambles in the market, remembering how the very reason she'd bought Tom's meat in the first place was because of the cleanliness of his stalls. Now she learned the cost of such pristine conditions. Buckets and buckets of water it took to swab the place down, carried in heavy metal buckets from the communal tap to the stalls and flung over ground and shelf and walls and counters, and then scrubbing, while the water was still running, running red, running fainter pink, scrubbing with big, hard bristle

40

brushes that took strength and ingenuity to lift and man-
oeuvre. The water ran into a gully at the front and the gully
had to be cleaned of the bits of bone and gristle which could
block it, a hateful job, scooping it out, making sure the water
ran freely. It took an hour, all of them working together, the
assistants inspired, or at least encouraged, by Mrs Hind's
example.

A small price to pay, though, for her own home and
husband. Tom was doing well. He took on a third shambles
in partnership with another butcher and between them they
were the most important in the meat market. Tom was
saving to buy their own house, but there was enough to spare
for his wife to have new clothes which she made herself on
the sewing-machine the Stephensons gave her as a wedding
present. She still made clothes for Annie and Mrs Stephenson
but now they paid her and she put the money into Tom's
bank, proud to be able to do so. Tom joked that at this rate
their sons would inherit a fortune as well as a butchery
business.

But there were no sons. On 14 September 1901, their
second wedding anniversary, Margaret Ann gave birth to a
daughter, named Lilian. Tom said he didn't mind a lass
coming first, she could help look after the lads that came
after. He loved his Lily – Margaret Ann always called her
Lilian, but Tom and everyone else called her Lily – who was
a pretty, quiet baby with her mother's blue-grey eyes and her
father's fair hair and complexion (though the hair quickly
turned dark, like Margaret Ann's). He was old to be a father
for the first time but he relished the role and just hoped he
wouldn't have long to wait before his son arrived and he
could train him as the butcher he was destined to be. On 28
June 1904 another girl was born and christened Jane. This

time Tom was not so delighted and Margaret Ann felt a failure. Jane was not as docile as Lily. From the start she was fractious, as if she was protesting against the disappointment she knew herself to be. Not as big a disappointment as Annie, though, the third and last child, the last hope, with Margaret Ann almost forty. Annie was born on 23 May 1908 and that, said a resigned Tom, would be that.

Three daughters, admirably spaced (Tom was always known as a considerate man). They were all bright, though Lily was the brightest, all sound in wind and limb, all pretty, though Jane, when young, not as obviously pretty as the other two. Annie was the prettiest, with enormous blue eyes (which, however, turned out to be short-sighted) and beautiful blonde silky hair, but she was the most trouble, more trouble than the already troublesome Jane. Lily was the good, the dependable one and her mother thanked heaven for her every day. Give Lily a task to do and it would be perfectly executed without complaint. She liked to please. For a child she had a highly developed sense of duty; too highly developed her father often thought and said so. 'Go and play, Lily,' he'd urge her, but Lily didn't seem to understand the concept of play. She had no playmates. Tom worried about this and said he'd have to have a playmate specially made for her. Jane and Annie played out in the street the whole day long, played like urchins with hoops and balls and skipping ropes, always running around shrieking and laughing with other children, while Lily watched from the window. She was always usefully employed helping her mother. Once she began school she became the teacher's darling, good at every lesson, top in every test. 'We've got a professor here,' said Tom, and 'I don't know what we're going to do with our Lily. She's too smart for a lass.'

Lowther Street Infants, where Lily started school in 1905, was not a good school. It was one of the Board Schools opened after the Education Act of 1870, when local authorities were instructed to take on the task of educating the children of the city and pay for it out of the rates. The Board School style of architecture in Carlisle tended towards the Gothic – classrooms were enormous, with high ceilings, and interconnected, separated by sliding partitions. The floors rose in tiers and pupils sat at long desks with sloping lids. His Majesty's Inspectors were extremely critical of this Lowther Street School (Infants and Mixed) during the period Lily was there, though they acknowledged 'the children come from very poor and neglected homes' and therefore admitted teaching was difficult. Lily's own home wasn't neglected or particularly poor but it was true that Corporation Road, while respectable in itself, was on the edge of Rickergate, Carlisle's worst slum area.

The HMI report in 1909 was damning. The whole school was said not to reach a very high level of proficiency and the teaching was criticized as far too restrictive and ill-prepared. A Mr Bolt had broken a cane, as well as regulations, in caning two girls with unnecessary vigour, for which he expressed regret (though whether for breaking the cane or beating the girls was not made clear). Violence was the only kind of discipline and the Inspectors sound most enlightened in their condemnation of this régime of terror. They pointed out in their detailed report that violence did not work because even with it there was 'in no class the order that could be desired'. In general they were in despair about Lowther Street where 'there is an absence of that bright and sympathetic treatment under which young children best develop their natural activities of mind and body'. Quite.

43

After this verdict a few heads rolled – Mr Bolt's for one – and by 1912 things were a bit better for eleven-year-old Lily and her contemporaries. But HMI came down in favour of the boys and against the girls, suggesting to the teachers that the sexes should be separate 'so that the girls do not hold back the boys who, as a whole, show more interest and power'. Their advice was not acted upon and the following year this decision was vindicated: of fourteen pupils put in for the Merit (an examination held to determine which sixteen pupils in the whole of Carlisle should have free places at the new Higher Grade School) only two were selected and both were girls. One was Lily. Tom was bursting with pride – 'Our Lily beat all the lads' – and very much in favour of the Higher Grade. It was a school specially designed to provide an extended and better education for clever working-class children leaving the Board Schools at thirteen and not having the means to go on to the boys' Grammar School or girls' High School, both of which had their own entrance exams and were fee-paying (fifteen pounds a year at the High School as opposed to a pound a year for paying pupils at the Higher Grade). The new school had opened in 1899 and was an instant success. By the time Lily won her free place there its premises had moved from a church hall to the top part of Lowther Street Board School, after a plan to build a completely new school had failed. Conditions were far from ideal – ventilation and acoustics were both poor – but they didn't seem to matter. HMI were in raptures over 'the spirit of industry which pervades the school . . . the pupils benefit to an extraordinary degree'.

Lily loved the Higher Grade. There was no need for caning or any kind of brutality there. Discipline was no problem in spite of the hopelessly inadequate classroom

44

arrangements (with three classes often sharing one room). The peace and quiet after the hurly-burly of the Board School were bliss and she made rapid progress. Her reports show that she was good at everything, consistently top in History, English and Geography with marks in the high eighties and scoring 100 per cent for Arithmetic term after term. At the end of her first year she was the only girl in Form 1 to win a prize. She was much too clever and industrious for the Higher Grade, yet no one ever appears to have suggested she should try for a scholarship to the far superior High School which, since 1909, had been under the jurisdiction of the Cumberland Education Authority and, since 1914, jointly under the Carlisle City Education Department. The High School was indisputably the best school for girls in the whole area and a certain number of places were set aside for scholarship girls. Lily never applied, perhaps for the very reason that the High School was superior – it was no place for a working-class girl, however clever. Better to go to the Higher Grade and learn shorthand than go to the High School and learn Latin. Then, one had a future, one's aspirations were quite high enough.

The education Lily received at the Higher Grade was adequate in most respects and excellent in some, but if she had been a boy in that school she would have been better off. The headmaster obviously thought it nonsense that, as the nineteenth-century feminists argued, there was no sex in intellect. Boys in his school had a different and harder curriculum to follow. Boys were taught fractions and equations while girls had to be content with multiplication and division; boys learned Physics, girls Physiology; boys had Chemistry lessons while the girls had Botany. But at least both boys and girls took commercial classes. These were very popular

45

because, as was well known, knowledge of everything to do with commerce led to office jobs and everyone wanted those, even the brilliant Lily who certainly didn't think an office job too lowly for her academic talents. Ask her what she was going to do when she left school and she'd say, get a job in an office *if she could*. She had no other ambition. Nobody mentioned university or college, an outlandish notion for a working-class girl, and she never thought of it herself. She hoped to get a good job, then eventually marry and have children. It was what girls did.

Yet in spite of her happiness at school, and her success there, Lily had an anxiety about her which her father could not understand. She was always worrying. It seemed to Tom abnormal for a young girl to fret so much when there was nothing to fret about. Really, nothing at all. She had a loving mother and father and two sisters and times were good, and yet there was this ever-present apprehension in Lily's eyes. Even on Sundays, when Tom took his girls in the pony and trap to Wetheral, a village on the river Eden, five miles away, and then out in a boat – even then Lily seemed anxious. If he told her to cheer up, it might never happen, she took this as a criticism and tears filled her eyes. So Tom just had to let his favourite daughter be. She liked to sit up at the front of the trap with him, holding his thumb, and then she'd smile and he'd think he'd been exaggerating her solemnity. She just wasn't noisy and giggly like Jane and Annie, that was all.

Margaret Ann never went on these Sunday outings to Wetheral. She said the river gave her a headache, which was strange because it was a very peaceful river, broad and pretty with lovely trees coming right down to the edge of it, and absolute silence the length of it except for the plop of salmon.

But she went with Tom and the girls on their rarer outings to Silloth and loved it. Silloth is a small town on the Solway Firth, twenty miles from Carlisle, much loved then as a holiday resort, imbued with a special quality for all working people – going to Silloth was exciting. It was a comparatively new town then and had all the virtues of a planned town, laid out like a square with straight streets at right angles to each other. These were wide and well paved and planted with trees. Between the streets and the sea was the Green, thirty-six acres of fine turf bordered with pine shrubberies. There was a sea wall, perfect for promenading along, and *all* manner of amusements to hand – donkeys to ride, an eighteen-hole putting green, a pavilion where regular shows were put on, and the Silloth Town Band.

Tom took a house every July and the whole family went for a holiday, as did half Carlisle. The normal population of Silloth was under two thousand but in July it was swollen to over six thousand. Margaret Ann and the girls adored being there – it was the best of times. All of them were happy in their different ways and wished they could stay for ever. Tom fished for codling and flounders, and Margaret Ann sat crocheting on one of the seats on the front, and Jane and Annie and even Lily rode on the donkeys and paddled and watched the Pierrots, enraptured. Why, there was never a dull moment even if it rained, and in all their memories it never once did.

It was a good life, and then it ended.

III

All those sixteen years, the best of her life, the good years, my grandmother was hiding a secret. Not only the greater secret of her first twenty-three years, shrouded in general mystery, but a more specific one. At some point before the good life ended with her husband's death she was obliged to confide in him. Maybe she did it when he proposed, or maybe he had always known of it because he was part of it and it was his secret too. It is impossible to know.

Thinking about the woman who claimed to be my grandmother's fourth unacknowledged daughter, I decided to check through the whole of the birth, marriage and death registers for all the five parishes then in existence in Carlisle. My grandmother's surname of Jordan made the task not too difficult – it was unusual enough not to crop up with the monotonous frequency of Graham, or Armstrong. I knew she was born in 1869 and so began searching for any birth to a Margaret Ann Jordan from 1893, the year she said she started work for the Stephensons, the year from which she dated her adult history. Immediately, it was there: to Margaret Ann Jordan, general domestic servant, aged twenty-three, on 12 April 1893 a girl, named Alice, born in Wetheral, the village Tom took his girls to, but where Margaret Ann would never go. No father was named. Several weeks later she had the baby baptized, though not in her own church of St Mary's but in Holy Trinity, Caldewgate. She gave as her address a house in St Cuthbert's Lane in which, two years earlier, at the time of the census, had lived one Elizabeth Jordan, an elderly woman, on her own.

Equipped with Alice's birth certificate, I hoped to locate her in the Carlisle of the turn of the century by tracing her address through school records. But those school logbooks for all the local schools between 1898, when Alice reached five, and 1906, when she was thirteen, and likely to have left school, reveal no Alice Jordan. (These logbooks are not registers in any case but sometimes they do list the names of the reception class each term.) I turned to the marriage registers. If Alice was born in 1893 it was likely that if she ever married it would be between 1909 and, say, 1929. Again, it was easy. On 1 January 1915 Alice Jordan, father unknown, married William Muir, a pork butcher of 48 Brook Street. There were three witnesses to her marriage. One of them was Thomas Hind. What was my grandfather doing as witness to the marriage of his wife's unacknow- ledged, illegitimate daughter? Then I noted Alice's address: 14 Peter Street, the house to which my grandparents and their girls had recently moved. Was Alice merely using that address for some reason but never resided there? How could she have lived in a small house with half-sisters of thirteen, ten and six without them knowing? Impossible. Curiouser and curiouser.

It occurs to me, as it surely would to anyone, that Thomas Hind was a witness to Alice's marriage because he was her father. The story of the slow courtship, which his daughters loved to hear, and which in turn was relayed to me, may not have been entirely untrue but it could have had a quite different and earlier beginning. Suppose Tom knew Margaret Ann before 1893 and when she became pregnant could not for some reason marry her? His mother Jane, the butcher, depended on him and he may have been afraid to leave her and marry. Or, though a bachelor, he may have been involved with someone else . . .

But no, I don't think Thomas Hind was Alice's father, but perhaps this is because I don't want to. Tom was always described to me as a kind and gentle man who loved all children. To find that he had been party to the abandonment of Alice would make the whole thing worse. There must be some other reason why he, and not Alice's mother, attended her marriage. Nor do I believe Alice really was residing at the address she gave, my grandparents' new home in Peter Street. Yet where had Alice been from 1893 to 1915? Surely Margaret Ann, who had suffered all her life from the stigma of illegitimacy, had not abandoned Alice? Even if there had been reasons why she could not keep her baby in 1893, solid economic reasons, why did she not claim her and take the child into her own family in 1899 when she married? Alice was only six then, young enough to be moved from wherever she was. Had Alice been given to some family who would not part with her? Had a deal been made in 1893 that Alice should never know who her real mother was if some other woman took her in? Did Alice herself break the agreement and discover Margaret Ann?

Where, oh where, had Alice been?

It was a good life, and then it ended, in 1915, but not because of the war. Tom was too old for the war. It was Margaret Ann's immediate thought when war was declared and so many men rushed to serve King and Country. Tom was fifty-four and, as yet, not needed. He was safe and for the first time Margaret Ann was glad she had borne him no sons.

Carlisle was not particularly affected by the war. A few

wooden huts were erected near the castle, though no one quite knew what for, but there was no blackout, and rationing, when it came, was not severe. The only way Carlisle noticed there was a war on was through observing the lack of men on the streets. And in the market. By 1915 the meat market was showing signs of losing its porters and it was the older men, like Tom, who were having to do the heavy work they thought they'd left behind them. Tom was big and strong but not as fit as he had once been. Carrying carcasses, something he'd once done with such ease, now tired him, but there were no young men left who could swing a whole pig over their shoulders and think nothing of it, so he had to do it. Margaret Ann always felt that the strain of returning to this kind of physical effort had weakened him so that when he caught a chill he did not have the resistance to throw it off.

He came home on the evening of 3 September 1915, looking awful – grey-faced, his breathing one long wheeze, his skin clammy. His wife knew immediately that this was no ordinary chill. It was a beautiful late summer's evening but Tom complained of feeling cold, so she lit the fire and sent Lily to boil the kettle and mix hot water and lemon while she found a shawl, a big heavy woollen shawl, and wrapped it round his burly shoulders. He groaned and croaked that whisky was the best medicine but she persuaded him to take the lemon and water together with two aspirins. He sat there for an hour, the wheezing getting worse, his eyes shut, though he wasn't asleep. He wouldn't eat, not even soup. About nine o'clock he said he'd be better off in his bed but he had trouble standing, said he felt dizzy and couldn't seem to see properly, and even more trouble getting up the narrow stairs. It took Lily behind him, doing her best to push, and his wife in front, pulling, to get him up. He collapsed fully clothed on to the bed and didn't want to be bothered undressing, so they loosened his collar and removed his shoes and left it at that till later.

Margaret Ann never knew whether he slept that night or not. She certainly didn't and neither did Lily. They both heard the dreadful breathing, quite shatteringly loud and laboured, and both longed for morning so that a doctor could be sent for. By morning Tom seemed delirious. Lily went first thing to Dr Edwards with a note and he came back with her. He examined Tom and said straight away it was a case of pneumonia. The very word terrified Margaret Ann, but Dr Edwards assured her that her husband was as strong as an ox and his constitution would see him through together with the careful nursing he knew she would give him. After he'd gone Lily asked her mother what was the matter with her father and, seeing the child's scared face, Margaret Ann didn't mention pneumonia, only said Tom had a chill but he was strong as an ox and so would soon be on the mend. Lily, as ever, was so good. Jane and Annie were packed off to school but Lily stayed at home and sat all day with her father, wiping his brow, trying to get him to drink those quantities of fluid Dr Edwards had advised. At ten o'clock her mother sent her to bed. Her friend Annie Broadhead had arrived to sit through the night with her. 'You've been a little angel, Lily,' her mother said.

Lily slept deeply that night and had a lovely dream about Silloth, about all of them sitting by the sea at Silloth, and her father in his shirtsleeves laughing at them from the boat where he was fishing. She woke up feeling happy, but then felt the deep silence around her. No sound of her father's wheezing. Did it mean he was better? But then her mother appeared in the doorway and her face was enough. She had her finger to her lips and gestured to where Jane and Annie were sleeping. Lily crept out of the room and followed her mother. Her father lay with a sheet up to his chin. His eyes were closed but they had pennies on them. She stared at the pennies, the dull copper circles where his blue eyes should be, and heard her mother say, 'He's gone to Jesus, Lily. Don't cry.' Lily didn't cry. She was too terrified to cry. She backed out of the room without a word and ran down the stairs and shut herself in the cupboard underneath them. There she crouched among the dustpans and brushes. She buried her face in the apron hanging on the back of the door and only then began to sob. It was dark in the cupboard, not even a sliver of light coming through the tightly fitting door. She had her back wedged against the wall and her knees drawn up and only just fitted in. Still in her white cotton nightgown, she pulled it over her knees until it stretched tightly and enclosed her cramped legs. Her heart was pounding and there was a pounding somewhere in her head too. She heard her mother's plaintive call – 'Lily!' – but she couldn't answer it, she couldn't leave her hiding-place. She heard the door-knocker. It was already muffled, tied up with a rag, but she heard the soft thud, thud, thud, and her mother's feet going slowly down the stairs above her head, and the door being opened and then shut, and the rise and fall of whispering voices. People went backwards and forwards, past the cup-board without guessing she was there. Her eyes grew used to what had been the intense dark. She made out the suitcase jammed in the corner, the one used for Silloth. The thought of Silloth and her happy dream made her cry harder and now she was hiccuping. They wouldn't be able to go to Silloth ever again. How would they manage without their father, what would they do? Terror joined grief and she rocked and rocked in the small space.

Jane and Annie knew where she would be. How she hated hearing them cry. 'Lily will be in the cupboard under the stairs, she will, she will!' Then there were taps on the cupboard door, and entreaties to come out, but she wedged her feet firmly against it and it could not be budged. She could hear her sisters, all excited, squealing as though she was a trapped animal. Her head ached, she felt sick and her throat burned, but she wanted to stay in this hole for ever, to die in it and be buried like her father soon would be. But thinking of his burial made her want to vomit and she had to swallow the bile which rose up and try to control her desire to scream and scream at the vision of his dead body and the worms eating it. She drummed her heels on the wooden floorboards and shivered, but she was hot, not cold, feverish, her nightgown drenched in perspiration. All the activity outside her sanctuary seemed to have stopped. It was quiet again. Jane and Annie had disappeared. She heard her mother say softly, 'Lily? Come out, I need you. There's only me now.' Guilt stopped her sobs. Common sense told her she couldn't stay in this cupboard for ever – she was Lily, the sensible one. She put her head on her knees and cried some more and then she was sensible. She opened the door and crawled out like a dog, her hair matted and damp, her face blotchy and disfigured. 'Oh Lily!' her mother said. 'Oh Lily, Lily, look at you!'

But even out of the cupboard and trying to be sensible she didn't yet speak to anyone. She did what she was told, but with her eyes lowered, and silently. Jane and Annie disgusted her. They cried every now and again but she could tell they were not really sad. They brightened up so quickly when they were measured for their mourning clothes. Their mother had their photographs taken when they were dressed in these, but Lily refused to pose. She couldn't. Let Jane and Annie preen themselves. But she was glad to have her own black dress, though she wished it even uglier and less becoming than it already was. It made her feel better to be clothed so drably and she had no desire for the lace collar Jane pleaded for, and got, nor for the sash conceded to Annie – plain, harsh, unadorned black suited her feelings. So did the funeral, every awful minute of the ride to the cemetery and the long walk down the main path to the plot near the huge copper beech tree where her father was to be buried. Jane and Annie cried for real then, whimpered pitifully and hid their faces in their mother's skirt, but she stood straight and unyielding, watching the coffin descend every inch of the way, hearing the thud of the soil on the varnished wood, tiny stones hitting the brass fittings with an almost musical noise.

That was not the hard bit. The funeral was satisfying, what she felt to be appropriate if dreadful. It was the period after the funeral which was much more terrible, those first weeks without her father when her mother's worries about money became her own. There was no will. Mother explained to her what a will was and why it was important to have one. And Tom had left no will, no will and no immediate access to the money Margaret Ann knew to be in the bank, the money he had said only recently was now more than enough to buy them a house, outright, at last. There was only five pounds in cash in the house. A man came to see Margaret Ann and he said there would be no problem since she was Thomas Hind's legally married wife and would be granted something called probate with no difficulty. But it would take time and since there was a war on maybe as much as three times the normal minimum time of six weeks. He said a loan could be easily arranged, but Margaret Ann said at once that she would not take a loan, she would manage somehow. She acted immediately. First she moved her family out of Peter Street, where the rent was nine shillings a week, to a house in Kendal Street, Caldewgate, where it was only four shillings. Then she took in two women lodgers and put them in one bedroom while she and her girls all slept in the other. Lastly, she got a job.

She had hoped to get a job as a seamstress, at Bullough's, but when she applied she was told she was too old (at forty-four) to join the twenty-five girls (average age twenty) who worked in the shop's alterations department. The only job she could get, apart from scrubbing houses or offices, was as a waitress, at Robinson's, Carlisle's first emporium, a huge department store, everything from clothes to ironmongery, which had taken over a whole block of buildings in English Street. Robinson's had a Jacobean café on its second floor and here she worked, carrying laden trays backwards and forwards, on her feet for eight hours at a stretch and her legs aching more than they had ever done while she was working for the Stephensons. At home, she relied on Lily, who gave Jane and Annie their meals and did all the housework after school. Lily wanted to leave school and earn money so that her mother wouldn't need to work, but Margaret Ann was adamant. She reminded Lily of her father's pride in her and how he had planned for her to stay on at the Higher Grade until she was sixteen and had learned all there was to learn. Then she could leave and get a good job, far better than any she could get now at fourteen. 'See sense, Lily,' her mother said, and sensible Lily did.

After all, mother had told them many times about her years in service, of the hopelessness of obtaining any other kind of employment for a girl of no means with no training except as a maid-of-all-work. Mother had said over and over that she didn't want her girls spending their youth down on their knees scrubbing other people's floors, nor did she want them later in life only to be fit for what she was doing now, being a waitress. They were all to stay at school and do well and make something of their lives. So Lily did. She worked harder than ever. But life was more different than even she had feared it would be and that difference was not only to do with the lack of money. It was the sudden fall in both status and expectations which took her by surprise and was hard to bear. The death of her father, the breadwinner, the one whose efforts had made them all relatively prosperous (for the times, for Carlisle, for their station), threw them into a wobbly world where nothing was certain and visions of abject poverty rose in front of them. Margaret Ann was not a widow who went to pieces – she could, and did, cope splendidly, managing by the practice of a brutal economy (which turned out to be unnecessary) to keep up appearances. But there was no joy in their home any more. Never had Lily realized how much her father had been the one to bring that joy into their family life. He was the jolly one, the lively, boisterous parent, full of confidence, a natural optimist and not prone to worry. Their mother was quiet, not a gregarious woman, forever counting her blessings in a fearful way and not imagining they would last. Once Tom was dead, this gravity of their mother's settled over the girls like a pall.

Jane and Annie resented it and struggled against it. They tried to lift the gloom by bringing their noisy friends home, hating their mother's, and Lily's, preference for peace. When this didn't work they played outside more and more, anywhere to avoid the dreariness of the house. Only Lily was ever at home when her mother got in, exhausted from waitressing. 'I don't know what I'd do without you, Lily,' she said, every day. She depended on her utterly, often voicing the reflection that when Lily married she would be lost. Lily said she would never marry, she would stay and look after her mother. It made Jane and Annie laugh to hear her say it, so solemnly, so virtuously. They certainly had no intention of staying at home with mother. Annie was, at seven, already planning to tour the world and have beautiful clothes and jewels. How? By marrying a rich, a very rich, man. How else? Jane just wanted to have a good time. What kind of good time? She couldn't be specific, though, aged eleven as she was, she already loved dancing. She wanted to dance all the time, to have fun, to have a life of variety. Neither of these two sisters had the slightest desire to go to the Higher Grade School like Lily. They intended to leave the moment they were thirteen and get jobs and have money to spend on themselves, and never mind if Lily said Mother needed it.

After the first six months, Margaret Ann didn't find herself in such terror of dire poverty. She had overreacted. Tom had died intestate but, just as she had been promised, there was no difficulty about his money passing to her. He had left £771 2s. 11d., which was a quite princely sum to her – no wonder he had said they could now buy a house and still be comfortable. But she didn't buy a house, that would be folly, when any fool could see that spread over the coming years, the years until all three girls were working, Tom's savings would soon evaporate. When he died he was bringing in two hundred pounds a year. His savings would only last four years if they continued to live at the same rate (not that they

58

were going to). Her own wage as a waitress was meagre – £1 18s. 0d. a week. Her plan was to make Tom's money spread over six years, until Lily was twenty, Jane seventeen and Annie thirteen, and all of them working. So there would be no house buying. The only concession she made was to move back into Peter Street, their old home, as soon as it was vacant, though she took one of her lodgers with her.

She wondered, in spite of being relieved to have got Tom's money safely, what had happened to his share of the shambles in the market? Surely his partner should buy her out? But he didn't offer to and she thought perhaps she should consult a solicitor but was afraid of incurring ruinous expense. Instead she went to see this partner, in her widow's weeds, but suffered the humiliation of being told, on numerous occasions, that he was not at home. She got Lily to write to him, at her dictation (claiming Lily's handwriting was better than hers, which from the evidence of her signatures on various certificates was true enough to plant doubts as to how well she could write at all). There was no reply. She thought about confronting this man, Mr Pattinson, in the market but couldn't bear the idea of any scene. Instead she tried to earn more money by dressmaking every evening after she'd recovered from the tiredness of waitressing, but this didn't bring in a fraction of the butchering business. She'd made clothes for the Stephensons and friends and Tom's family all her married life and thought the money she earned prodigious until suddenly she had to rely on it and found it not to be substantial at all.

The war had already, in 1916, made widows of so many women that Margaret Ann was fully aware that compared with some she was still well off. The good years might be over but her situation was far from bad. She had a roof over her head, money in the bank, a job, no debts and three healthy daughters. It didn't matter to her that she had no life of her own – her pleasure was her family and everything she did was towards supporting them and giving them the best life she could. Her family came not only first but second, third, all the way down to last. A family was what she had always craved and now she had it, even if the head of it was dead. She impressed people by saying she was more grateful for what she had than resentful because of what had been taken away from her.

But how did poor Alice fit into this?

By 1921 Margaret Ann's circumstances had changed quite dramatically, and very much for the better. All three girls were working, Mr Pattinson had grudgingly given her if not half the share of the shambles at least a lump sum of four hundred pounds (shamed into it by public opinion among the butchers in the market), which satisfied her and she was able to leave her job as a waitress. She stopped working in 1919, once Lily was established in her job and giving all her money to her mother.

Lily loved her job. She became a clerk in the Public Health Department in 1917, as soon as she left the Higher Grade (with a clutch of impressive certificates and prizes). The competition to get this job had been tough. First there was a two-hour written examination in the Town Hall, with forty other applicants, men and women, then an interview, together with the other five who had done best in the written part, with Dr Beard, the Medical Officer of Health. The interview clinched it. Dr Beard was immediately taken with the attractive, calm Miss Lilian Hind – she of the top marks in Arithmetic, the faultless typing, the almost perfect shorthand taken at impressive speed. He had an eye for a pretty girl, did Dr Beard, for all he was married, but that wasn't enough to make him appoint a clerk on looks. He was a demanding employer with a demanding job and he needed a clerk – there were no secretaries as such then in Carlisle's Health Department – who could cope. He reckoned this young woman could. She seemed temperamentally suited as well as highly qualified.

He was right in his judgement. Lily became one of the four clerks in the Department, two men who were senior to her and another woman, Mary Purdham, who started at the same time. Mary was the exact opposite of Lily in looks and personality, though almost her equal in ability (except for shorthand). She was squat, whereas Lily was willowy, and had a permanent scowl on her square, heavily fringed face, whereas Lily's habitual expression was pleasantly tranquil. Mary was grumpy and people were frightened of her. No one was frightened of Lily who was immediately popular even with Mr Barrow, the chief clerk. What impressed Mr Barrow was Lily's shorthand – he was a shorthand fanatic and could hardly credit the standard (120 words a minute) this slip of a girl had reached. He could understand why Dr Beard made Lily into his right hand almost from the start, junior though she was.

Going to work gave Lily such joy and Margaret Ann the deepest possible satisfaction. Quite apart from the prestige of the job – and it was prestigious, people were in awe when told where Lily worked and for whom – the place of work in Fisher Street in the centre of Carlisle was so pleasant. The room where Lily and the other three clerks and the three Health Visitors spent their working day was large and airy, on the ground floor with windows facing on to the street.

There was a long desk running the length of these windows, the old-fashioned sort with a sloping lid, and the clerks sat together in front of it on comfortable seats, not stools. Mr Barrow sat behind them by himself and behind him was a table upon which rested two important-looking typewriters, one for Lily and one for Mary. The atmosphere was relaxed, in spite of Mr Barrow's air of vigilance, and friendly – not even Mary's grumpiness spoiled the pleasant feeling of camaraderie. It was a busy room most of the day but never noisy even though a stream of people passed through the edge of it, presenting various kinds of chits entitling them to payment of some kind. Sometimes these chits were for free milk tokens, sometimes for actual cash. The greatest number were for having killed rats. As part of Carlisle's Pest Control programme a rat's tail was worth tuppence. The tails had to be shown to the Destructor Attendant at the Municipal Dump, as evidence that a rat had been killed, and he would sign a chit which then had to be surrendered to a clerk in the Public Health Department. But Lily didn't have much to do with such lowly traffic. She was almost always in Dr Beard's office taking dictation and then busy at her typewriter preparing his letters for signature.

There were always a great many letters. Dr Beard worked her hard but she didn't mind. She started at nine o'clock prompt, signing her name in the attendance book. A line was drawn across the page at precisely nine by the chief clerk and it was a disgrace to have to sign one's name under it. Officially she left at six o'clock, except on Saturdays when the office closed at one, but she and the others often worked until later and there was virtually no objection except from Mary who was constitutionally made for objecting to all manner of things. There was a generous lunch break of one hour and twenty minutes, ample time for them to get home and eat. Everything Lily did in her job interested her but then she'd joined the Public Health Department at quite a significant period in its existence. It was expanding rapidly at the beginning of the 1920s because of all the additional services local authorities were now obliged to provide under the recent Acts of Parliament, passed in a flush of post-First-World-War enthusiasm to improve the health of the nation. A new maternity hospital was opened and an infant consultation clinic and ante-natal clinic too. Fresh measures were taken to combat scarlet fever (still an average of 150 cases a year in the city), diphtheria (about the same) and tuberculosis (even more, a veritable epidemic). These involved Dr Beard in complicated administrative procedures and a great deal of practical organization. He was engaged in permanent battles with the town council's committee on health, with architects, with builders and with other doctors who did not always support him. No wonder Lily had so many letters to write.

Dr Beard had once practised as a barrister and had a barrister's eloquence even on paper. Lily marvelled at how fiercely and cogently he argued with anyone who opposed him, and thought the letters he dictated had a magnificent ring to them, unlike those he received in reply – poor squibs of things, in her opinion, written in stilted official language and very often, as Dr Beard would contemptuously point out, positively ungrammatical. But if Lily admired Dr Beard's way with words, he admired what he told her was her 'natural feel for language'. If he was searching for the right word (which was admittedly rare), he was surprised to find young Lily could often supply it. He asked her if she read a lot and she was embarrassed to confess that no, she did not, only novels by Annie S. Swan and suchlike. He couldn't work out either how Lily came to be such a good speller if she didn't read widely – it was most unusual and intrigued him, this proof of an innate linguistic sense. But then he was intrigued by her in general, as well as attracted, though any attempt on his part to demonstrate either the esteem he held her in or the attraction he felt for her seemed to embarrass her. A hand put over hers and kept there, an arm round her shoulders, an invitation to move her chair closer – all were met with a flush of discomfort and an uneasiness which warned him off. He was, she knew, old enough to be her father.

There were others in the department who were also smitten with Lily's charms, but she kept her distance from them. Everyone assumed Lily must have a suitor but when asked if she was spoken for she said no with such firmness she was completely believed. She loved her job and it was perhaps relevant, the other clerks thought, that they knew matrimony meant the instant loss of it. The rule was inflexible: married women must resign. If they didn't, they would be sacked. A woman could be engaged, though even that was frowned upon, but not married. Married women belonged at home. They were the clear responsibility of their husbands. Married women took the jobs men needed more, that was the thinking. It was not only greedy of these women to cling on to jobs but it showed a lack of both responsibility and pride in their husbands – husbands were shamed by their wives working, or at least those in Carlisle.

By 1920 Lily was earning £2 4s. od. a week. But, though she had by far the best job of the three sisters and earned the most money, with her salary rising all the time, Lily's was not the only source of income in the Hind family. Jane was working too and contributing some of her wage, though she wasn't called Jane any more; she was called Jean, which she much preferred. She hated the name Jane with its connotations of 'plain', and the moment she left school at thirteen changed it to Jean, refusing to answer to Jane. Margaret Ann was exasperated and told her daughter her father would have been most upset because Jane was called after his own mother, but the newly styled Jean said he was dead, so it didn't matter what he thought, frankly.

Jean started work at Carr's, the biscuit factory in Caldewgate, built in 1831 by Jonathan Dodgson Carr, the Quaker. He was a good employer who gave his workers a reading-room and a library in his factory and provided a bathroom where those without baths at home (virtually the entire workforce) could have a hot bath. By the 1920s, when Jean worked there, Carr's employed three thousand people, most of them women. It was a fine sight to see them streaming along Church Street towards the factory, clad in their white overalls and turbans, but Jean didn't wear either because she worked in the offices, hardly a factory girl at all. She'd had to get a special certificate, proving she was over thirteen, before she could start work there or anywhere else – the Factory and Workshop Act of 1901 required it. Her job was that of a very junior trainee clerk which for the first three years meant being at the beck and call of everyone, and doing nothing more interesting than carry things from one place to another, sharpen pencils, fill inkwells and clean floors and desks. It was a long, long time before she did any clerking but she earned ten shillings a week all the same and benefited from being able to use the factory's facilities for its workers.

The best of these was the canteen. Carr's had a breakfast- and dining-room for employees which provided food at prices well below the cost of the ingredients. A cup of tea – a large cup, and the tea was very good quality – was only a ha'penny. Every day of the week had a set menu, all good nourishing stuff. Monday there was a choice of browned beef at tuppence a plate, or peas and potatoes for a penny, but the favourite day was Thursday when there was hotpot for tuppence. If you couldn't afford that – though Jean could – you brought your own food and as long as it was handed in to the kitchen by a certain time it would be cooked for you free of charge. Breakages had to be paid for, naturally – thruppence for a broken cup, fourpence if it was a glass – but Jean was careful and never broke anything. She was also good at sums, which had got her into Carr's offices in the first place, and progress for a bright girl with a head for figures was rapid once this was recognized. There were set rates of pay up to the age of twenty-one, but after that it was quite likely she could earn as much as Lily in spite of her slow start.

It was at this stage – with two daughters earning and a third about to begin – that Margaret Ann took a deep breath and bought a house. Tom's money had lasted the six years she had counted on (and was still not done) and now she had the money from his business partner, as well as two wages coming in, it seemed the right thing to do. And the girls were urging her on, desperate to get out of Peter Street and say goodbye to lodgers (though their mother wanted to keep them on as a kind of insurance policy). They moved to Bowman Street, on the southern side of Carlisle, near the City General Hospital. Amazingly, it was near Brook Street, where Alice lived with her husband William Muir and his brother and family. Why did this not inhibit Margaret Ann from buying this particular house? Bowman Street lies at a right angle to Brook Street – the two streets could not be closer. If my grandmother had had no contact whatsoever with Alice since her wedding day in 1915, then she may have assumed the Muirs had moved, but people did not move house easily then and she could not have counted on it. How could she bear to run the risk of being confronted by Alice every time she went out? But she went ahead and moved into Bowman Street. It was only half a mile from Peter Street, and the house, although technically a much better one, was not, to any but a discerning Carlisle eye, all that superior. True, it had three bedrooms and a parlour – oh, the joys of a parlour at last! – and the rooms were bigger, but nevertheless it still opened straight into the street and had a yard, not a garden. It was bought outright in 1922 for just under four hundred pounds, the exact amount exacted from the shambles share. Perhaps Margaret Ann would have been wiser, better advised, to put only half the money down but, psychologically, knowing the house was hers gave her a tremendous confidence. Whatever happened, she now had a house to sell and was full of awe at the thought – to be a house owner was a fine thing, something she had never thought she'd rise to.

Her daughters still didn't get a bedroom each. Margaret Ann insisted on keeping their one lodger, to pay the gas bill, but since this was a cousin, Florrie Stubbs, daughter of one of Tom's sisters, the girls didn't mind so much. Jean and Annie shared one room, Lily and Florrie another, and Margaret Ann had the small boxroom on her own. She was back to being a housekeeper again but of a house she owned, which made all the difference, and with the help of four young women. Well, of two of them: Lily and Florrie. Jean and Annie were hardly there – except it was now Jean and Nan, if you please. Nan copied Jean. She'd always hated Annie as much as Jean hated Jane, because it reminded her of 'little orphan Annie', certainly not in keeping with the image she wished to project. Her mother thought the name Nan ridiculous, not a proper name at all, and did not give in as readily to her youngest daughter's whim as she had done to her middle daughter's. Eventually, though, so many people called Annie Nan that she found herself following suit, to her annoyance.

Nan was a puzzle to her mother. She grew up to be far prettier than her sisters, her hair still blonde, her skin flawless, her complexion the envy of all, and with these attractions went a liveliness, a pertness, which made the most of them. Nan was selfish and fierce, constantly on the lookout for ways of grabbing attention and profiting from it. She had a terrible temper and what provoked it most was not having enough money for the many things she craved – she couldn't *bear* not to have new dresses, money for this and money for that. It drove her to a frenzy. But she could sew. It amazed her mother that it was Nan who had inherited her own natural skill as a dressmaker. She'd expected Lily to, but Lily was hopeless, all thumbs in spite of her general gracefulness. And Jean, though an expert knitter – Lily could only knit laboriously, another odd failing – was too careless to make a good seamstress. No, it was Nan who had the talent, who picked up the tricks of her mother's trade quite effortlessly. She could cut out material deftly, follow a pattern without help and on the treadle she had a natural rhythm. It was obvious that she should try for a job at Buck's, the shirt manufacturing factory in Denton Holme, where indeed she started work at the age of thirteen.

Buck's was not as good a place to work as Carr's. This was not a Quaker-owned factory and there wasn't the same care shown for the welfare of the workers, but in some ways girls preferred Buck's. Here they could learn a valuable trade, one they could carry on when they married and practise at home. The factory itself was a little intimidating, a tall brick-built edifice like so many others in this little industrial suburb, but there was a tremendous spirit among the three hundred women who worked the looms there. But Nan didn't work on the looms. She started in the machine-room on the second floor, sewing on buttons, then progressed to sewing shirt parts together, some by hand, some by machine. She was good at machine work. She had a steady hand and quickly mastered the quite tricky business of feeding often very fine material under the flying needles. And at work she was a different girl, her temper firmly under control, wanting very much to learn so that one day she could have her own business and be rich (not like mother who never charged enough and half the time made things for nothing). It was lucky she had this attitude because her job was the hardest of the three sisters' and she was the most delicate – her mother worried about the strain on such a young girl of all that noise in the factory and the exhaustion of the long walk there and back when she was so tired. But ambition kept Nan going, her sights fixed on starting up as a seamstress on her own as soon as possible.

She was never too tired to go out enjoying herself anyway. By the time she was sixteen there wasn't a dancehall in Carlisle where Nan Hind and her friend Peggy Farish had not put on exhibitions which drew admiring gasps – what a sight they were, these two pretty girls, demonstrating the Charleston, the Black Bottom, the Tango, laughing wildly, tossing their heads and whirling around, like mad things, in the lovely dresses they'd made themselves, then collapsing, half hysterical with the pace and fun of it all. Margaret Ann had never been in a dancehall in her life. She was suspicious of them, didn't like young Nan – *so* young – frequenting them, especially the one that had opened near George Street, where she was told there were flashing lights round the walls and where sometimes *all* the lights were put out. But Jean went dancing too. It was what girls did, the way they socialized, the way they met boys. Jean had, if anything, more boys after her than Nan, even if she wasn't as obviously pretty. They came to the front door in Bowman Street when others were coming to the back door and it was too much for Margaret Ann. She was bewildered by these two fun-loving daughters who seemed to think of nothing but having a good time.

But there was always Lily. Lily thought of other things and didn't rush out every night as her sisters did. When she did go out, it was to more sedate gatherings, to the Girls' Club in Union Lane, a most refined affair run by a church organization, and always chaperoned. The Girls' Club discussed the Bible and had talks from visiting missionaries and, when they did have a social, boys came by invitation only and their names were carefully scrutinized. Jean and Nan thought it was a hoot, Lily's club, and gave up going before they were sixteen, whereas Lily went on attending at the great age of twenty. No young men called for Lily, and that became another worry for her mother. On the one hand, she fretted over Jean and Nan flirting and having too many boyfriends, and on the other over Lily, seeming to have none. But it was Nan she worried about most. She was forever talking about money and especially in relation to boys. She liked boys who could afford to take her to dances at the Crown and Mitre and preferably drive her home (though there were precious few with cars) or pay for a cab.

She liked well-dressed young men who could buy her presents and who had some style and she never had made any secret of being on the lookout for a wealthy husband. Her mother couldn't imagine where Nan had got these standards from. Not from her, not from Tom. Nan had such contempt for how her mother had spent her life, how she had always accepted her lot without complaint and counted whatever blessings she had. Even a little thing like watching her mother wash dishes aroused Nan's contempt – 'I'm *never* going to wash dishes,' she vowed. 'I'll have paper plates in my house and throw them away when they're dirty.' Good for a laugh in the Bowman Street kitchen, but she meant it. It made Margaret Ann feel spineless, cowardly somehow, to see how Nan regarded her labours. It depreciated the currency of what had been her entire life and she wondered what women were coming to, thinking, like Nan, that their lives could be different.

What on earth was going to happen to Jean and Nan? And what, for that matter, had already happened to Alice? If Alice ever had a job, there is no record of it, but maybe her husband kept her in comfort – and before he did, who? – and she had no need to work. Maybe she was still expecting to have children. Would it have changed Margaret Ann's apparent attitude to her if she had? Or would Alice's children also have had visited upon them whatever it was kept Margaret Ann away from her?

At any rate by 1920 Alice was respectably married, she was secure. Her half-sisters were not, not yet, not in the way their mother wished them to be.

IV

It was almost as though another phase of the good life had begun but Margaret Ann, though grateful throughout the 1920s, was always apprehensive. True, all three of her girls had jobs, all three of them were climbing their respective ladders and earning more money than she had ever earned in her life. True, she had her own house and with the money she made from dressmaking together with the contributions of her daughters – substantial, in Lily's case – she was better off than she had been since Tom died. True also that her home was full of the most pleasant kind of activity – the girls rushing in and out with their many friends, full of chat – and she was never lonely, but all the same she had her fears. They could be summed up in one word: men.

Men had to enter her daughters' lives. She knew that, and she wanted them to, if they were the right sort of men with the right sort of intentions. She wanted to see her girls properly courted, properly married and, eventually, properly brought to bed of children. But where, among Jean's and Nan's endless stream of giddy youths, were these proper husbands? She could see no sign of them. By the time Jean was twenty-five she had gone through any number of so-called 'beaux' and none of them impressed her mother. These young men, she was sure (and said so, in guarded but easily interpreted language) were only after one thing and it was the one thing Margaret Ann could not bear the thought of.

Suppose Jean got into trouble, trouble that began with an 'e' for 'expecting'? All the girls noted how hard their mother was on women who had illegitimate babies, how horrified and censorious this normally gentle and tolerant woman became. She took to recounting clearly symbolic anecdotes about girls who had fallen, girls who had been taken advantage of, girls who had thought they could get away with 'it' but were 'caught'. 'Oh, for heaven's sake, Mother!' Jean would say, exasperated, 'I wasn't born yesterday.'

Lying awake at night, hearing Jean being brought home by one of her many swains, Margaret Ann had no faith in Jean's confidence. She heard the scuffles, the suppressed laughter, the groans and prayed and prayed that the worst would not happen (without ever admitting to any of her daughters that it had happened to her and that in her case the worst, poor spurned Alice, was living one street away). She didn't want Jean or Nan to give up all the fun they were having – the dancing, the outings in charabancs to Blackpool, the holidays in the Isle of Man – when they worked so hard, but she wanted them settled as soon as possible before the worst befell them. Jean had her offers but turned them all down. Her mother warned her that good offers, and at least two had been from respectable, sober citizens, did not grow on trees but she was ignored. When Dave Wallace came on the scene everything changed and marking this change Margaret Ann was full of a quickly expressed foreboding. From the first, she was wary of this Dave. He wasn't a Carlisle man. He was a Scot whom Jean had met at Blackpool, on a Carr's works outing. So far as could be ascertained, he had picked Jean up on the promenade, just like that, and taken her to a dance. He lived in Motherwell, near Glasgow, and that should have put a stop to any blossoming of romance but it didn't. No

73

sooner was Jean home than Dave appeared, coming down from Motherwell on the back of a friend's motor bike and staying at a bed-and-breakfast for truck drivers in Warwick Road. Every weekend he came and every weekend Margaret Ann grew more and more alarmed: Dave Wallace was dangerous, she was afraid of him.

She supposed what she feared was Jean's obvious attraction to him. He was attractive, Margaret Ann could see that – he was tall, fair, lively and he had been to America which gave him a kind of glamour. But he was only a fitter and he was a Scot who, if he wooed Jean successfully, would take her away. He liked a good time as much as Jean, did Dave Wallace, liked to dance and sing, also – very bad news – to drink. Many times Margaret Ann heard Dave and Jean come singing home late on Saturday night and she was sure the singing was more than happy, it was *slurred*. They'd been drinking, both of them. She tackled Jean about this but only got more of 'for heaven's sake, Mother!' She became upset, pleaded with Jean to give Dave up, but no, Jean wouldn't. The whole point of her week now was to get through it until the bold, singing Dave arrived. Yet no proposal of marriage was made. Dave was not well off and he had a widowed mother he supported. If Jean had been officially engaged Margaret Ann would not have been so apprehensive, but she was not. Dave might disappear at any moment leaving Jean – well, leaving her – leaving her 'caught' if what her mother suspected was going on was indeed going on.

Hardly less of a worry was Nan. She'd done so well by 1928, actually got herself set up in a couple of rooms above a shop in Lowther Street in a dressmaking business with Peggy Farish. It was remarkable how Nan's ambition had fuelled her to achieve such a thing – only twenty and with her own business. Margaret Ann had visited the rooms and been impressed. Nan and Peggy were so organized. They had made the rooms look efficient and attractive, what with their respective sewing-machines – saved for and bought out of their own wages over many years – set up on tables covered with bright pink sateen and a basket chair (from a second-hand shop) for customers to sit on, and a pretty floral curtain in front of an alcove where they could change in privacy. In the other room was a long trestle table (a throw-out from the market) which had been scrubbed and scrubbed – Nan wasn't too proud to scrub when it was for her own ends – and upon which they did their cutting out, and a swing mirror (loaned by the shop below) and a chest of drawers. They had plenty of business. Two pretty, lively, flirtations girls who were themselves walking advertisements for their own dressmaking – no problem. Margaret Ann was scandalized at the prices Nan and Peggy charged, but they were not a bit embarrassed. Their work was *quality*, they explained haughtily, and for quality people were prepared to pay, especially for quality wedding-dresses which was what eventually they chose to specialize in.

All this success of Nan's and yet what was she now doing? Risking the loss of everything by associating with a most alarming man, far more alarming than Jean's Dave Wallace. He'd picked up Nan, though in a different way from how Dave had picked up Jean. Nan thought it a wonderfully romantic story but her mother didn't. One wet, windy day Nan had been crossing Lowther Street, leaving her work to go home, when her umbrella was blown out of her hand and down the street. There was a car waiting at the crossing for Nan to cross the road and the moment her umbrella blew away a man got out and dashed to retrieve it. He bowed to

Nan as he presented her with her now damaged brolly and asked if he might drive her home since she would no longer be sheltered under its broken and bent spokes. He was an immaculately dressed, incredibly handsome *rich*-looking stranger with a posh accent and Nan never hesitated, she was in his car like a flash. The drive to Bowman Street took less than five minutes but it was long enough to learn that this gorgeous man's name was Jack Marshallsay and that he was only passing through Carlisle.

He passed through the next week and the next and the next, and each time he took Nan out in his car. He took her for dinner to the Crown and Mitre and presented her with flowers. When he left, he always gave her 'a memento' – perfume (*Je Reviens* – he kindly translated the meaning for uneducated Nan), chocolates, lipstick (Passion Pink, which needed no translating). After three months of this it was Nan's birthday and he gave her a necklace. The moment Margaret Ann saw it she felt apprehensive. The necklace was a pearl necklace and she knew at once that these were not artificial pearls. Mrs Stephenson had had a real pearl necklace. Real pearls were creamy-coloured, just like these. 'Give it back to Jack at once,' she said to Nan, snapping shut the blue velvet-lined case. Nan said she certainly would not, she loved pearls, she had always wanted pearls, and she defiantly put the necklace on there and then, with her jumper and skirt, not even bothering to wear a good dress. When Jack next came to pick her up, Margaret Ann could not bring herself to greet him. Who was he, anyway? Nan said he was a gentleman, quite out of the run of Carlisle men. Certainly he looked and sounded like a gentleman, and he had the clothes and car for the part, but what was his background? Why was he always just passing through Carlisle? He was a completely unknown quantity and the more he apparently doted on Nan without ever proposing marriage the more suspicious Margaret Ann became.

Thank God for Lily. Lily did, at last, go out with young men, but always in groups. Her mother was glad about this. She approved of Lily going for a holiday to the Isle of Man with two other young women and three young men, the women staying in a boarding-house and the men in a camp. She had new clothes to go in, a cream shantung dress and a fawn coat and a white beret, and when she came back she was so beautifully tanned that in the dark of the back kitchen all that could be seen when she came through the door on her return were her bright blue eyes. One of the young men on this holiday trip was very keen on Lily and had been for several years by 1928. Arthur Forster had got himself invited to a Girls' Club social and then he had pursued Lily ever after. She didn't seem so keen on him and Margaret Ann could understand why. Arthur was not Lily's type (even if Lily in fact had no type). He was perfectly presentable, quite good-looking really, and smart, but his personality was at odds with Lily's. Anyone could see that. Lily was quiet, elegant, fastidious, altogether what her mother labelled 'naturally refined'. Arthur was . . . Well, he was not refined in any way. He was gruff and awkward; his manners left a great deal to be desired. He was a mechanic, working at Pratchitt's, and he lived in Denton Holme. At least that was something to be said for him. He was a Carlisle man who, should he win Lily over, would not take her away. And he adored Lily, his expression said it all. But what did Lily, aged twenty-seven now, think of him? She seemed embarrassed by his devotion, if anything, and she was sensitive to careless remarks made about him, remarks especially from Nan – 'Ugh! A mechanic. You shouldn't waste yourself on him, Lily.' Instead of laughing at her sister for being a silly little snob, Lily blushed.

The first of Margaret Ann's daughters to marry was Jean. She married Dave Wallace on New Year's Day 1930. A quick wedding, speedily arranged, with suspicions inevitably running high in spite of the bride having known the groom for over two years. Jean offered no explanation for the sudden decision to marry. She just said to her mother that her mind was made up at last and there was no point in waiting. Dave had some time off over the New Year holiday and it would be a good start to marry on New Year's Day, the first day of a new decade. She hoped it snowed. It would be so romantic to be a snow bride, it would bring luck.

It didn't snow nor was the wedding very romantic. Dave had been up all night celebrating Hogmanay and looked terrible. Jean looked even worse, absolutely ashen, but it seemed she had a chill on her stomach and had been sick that morning (and the one before and the one before that . . .). Margaret Ann was less than happy as she attended Jean's wedding in St John's church, London Road – not even her own church, but then Jean never went to it, only Lily was a church-goer. Arthur Forster was best man and Lily and Nan maids of honour, but there was no sense of occasion. After-wards, Margaret Ann gave a wedding breakfast at Bowman Street but the celebrating was half-hearted, what with Dave's head feeling as if it was going to split into two and Jean's 'chill' bothering her. There was no honeymoon. The newly married pair left that evening for Motherwell to stay with Dave's mother, whom Jean had never met, until they found somewhere of their own. The farewells were emotional and painful, with all the women weeping, even Nan. Jean looked so pathetic, surrounded by her cases and boxes, so small and thin beside the tall Dave. Margaret Ann could hardly bear it, though her tears were the most restrained. Jean swore she would write regularly but what use were letters? Facts had to be faced: this daughter was leaving the family and that was that. The ninety or so miles to Motherwell might as well be nine thousand for all they would now see of her. And what sort of life was she going to lead, so far from her own family, surrounded by strangers and with a 'chill' already? Margaret Ann had never had to part with a mother, she had never known what it was to leave one family for another. It was the first time, she said to Lily and Nan when Jean had gone, that she was glad of it.

But Jean kept her word and did write, long letters too, quite surprising for one who had never shown any taste for the written word. She and Dave had found a room and kitchen in the Buildings on Belshill Road. There was a bed-in-the-wall in each room, so her mother and sisters could come to stay. The rent was a scandalous ten shillings a week, which on Dave's wage of thirty-five shillings a week was far too much but there was nothing else available. Lily and Nan encouraged their mother to go to visit Jean, to have a holiday in Motherwell. When had she last had a holiday, after all? Fifteen years ago, in Silloth. So she went, in March, when the weather was a bit better. Lily and Nan put her on the train and Jean met her at the other end. She saw straight away Jean was expecting – she was too thin for her pregnant state not to be extremely obvious. September, the baby was due in September, Jean said. It was March. Margaret Ann looked at Jean but said nothing except that she was delighted. Jean was safely married, after all. This child would be born within wedlock, *well* within wedlock, and it would probably be possible to claim it was premature. There was no point in expressing, at this stage, any disapproval or sorrow as to the date and circumstances of its conception. But Jean was relieved her mother did not inquire. Dave said it was ridiculous but she'd been so nervous about telling her mother she was expecting – her mother was so moral, so hard on anyone who gave in to temptation.

That first visit to her married daughter's home depressed Margaret Ann. She shook her head sadly and sighed when she told Lily and Nan about Jean's situation. God knew her own life had been hard enough but when she started married life she had been going up in the world in every sense. It seemed to her obvious that Jean was going down. The room and kitchen in which she lived were dingy and inconvenient, with steep steps at the back down to the row of wash-houses and lavatories, each with its own big iron key which had to be carried back and forth. It was far worse than popping out into one's own back yard and made Margaret Ann feel she had been privileged in every house she'd lived in. Then there was the constant noise above and around Jean's rooms. The Buildings swarmed with families and there was rarely any peace. Outside at the back was a giant slag heap, the bing, and in front a busy road to Glasgow. Jean knew no one but then she had just arrived. She was alone, trying to make something of her rooms, and cooking in a tiny corner near the door to the steps, until Dave came home. They went out only on a Saturday night and not any more to dances. Jean wasn't having the fun she loved and she missed her job desperately. Her mother saw she was trapped, that all her daughter's fine ideas of quite another sort of existence were finished and she tried to describe Jean's new life in such a way that Nan and Lily would take heed and think hard before they followed suit.

Nan, it seemed to her, was doing no thinking at all. She had just announced that she had been offered 'a good opportunity' in Glasgow by a friend of Jack Marshallsay's and that she was going to take it up. Margaret Ann knew immediately what that meant, she wasn't stupid, and questioned Nan closely. What was this 'good opportunity'? How could it be better than the already thriving business she had with Peggy? What about letting Peggy down? Where would she live in Glasgow, a big city, a city she didn't know and no place for a young woman of twenty-two. She was angry with Nan for being so deceitful and, for once, though direct confrontation was never her way, challenged Nan to admit she was going to Glasgow not because of any 'good opportunity' but because it was where Jack Marshallsay now lived and worked since he had stopped his mysterious passing through Carlisle. Nan glared, turned red, but admitted nothing. Her mother asked outright. 'Has he proposed? Any decent man would have proposed by now. He's leading you on and you're letting him. You should be ashamed of yourself, Nan Hind.'

But Nan was not ashamed. She knew by then that the reason Jack had not proposed was that he was already married, but she didn't dare tell her mother that. Jack had applied for a divorce and the moment he was free they would marry, and then her mother would be told the truth. Jack was so honest. He hadn't tried to hide anything. His marriage had been a mistake, a case of youthful folly. His family – a good family who lived in Surrey – hadn't approved and they'd been right. His father was a surgeon and lived in a big house which would be Jack's one day (and Nan's, too, naturally). Jack had been to a public school and had trained at Guy's Hospital to be a doctor but gave it up. He was too sensitive to be a doctor which was why he had now decided, after a few career fluctuations, to be an optician. All this Nan believed implicitly. Some of it was true but the most important thing was not: Jack had not applied for a divorce. He had set no divorce in motion by the time he tempted Nan to come to Glasgow and live with him. He had married one Lily Howard in 1927 when he was twenty-two, only one year before he passed through Carlisle and raced after Nan's umbrella on the Lowther Street crossing. On his marriage certificate he gave as his profession 'commercial traveller in costumes' not medical student. There is no record of his ever having studied medicine and his father was a dental surgeon not a surgeon.

Yet Nan was not really wickedly deceived because Jack did truly love her and had no intention of seducing her and then deserting her. He was just in a mess, afraid to ask his wife for a divorce and wondering how and when he could persuade her to give him one when she didn't even yet realize that he had left her for good. In any case, none of this could be told to Nan's mother, and the pretence had to be kept up that Nan was going to make her fortune in Glasgow working for a well-known firm of tailors and living in a most respectable boarding-house. Nan was excited by this adventure and took very little persuading. The only thing that made her hesitate, and not for long, was her mother's anger and distress. There was a terrible day when Margaret Ann went to see Peggy Farish privately to beg her to use her influence to stop Nan going off to Glasgow. Peggy, relating what had taken place, described to Nan the state her mother had been in, how horrified at the prospect of her youngest daughter running off with Jack Marshallsay about whom so little was known. Peggy could only say that Nan was determined to go and nothing she could do would stop her.

So Nan, too, left Carlisle and Margaret Ann had only Lily

now. At least it was the right daughter to have near her. (Though the unacknowledged Alice was also near her, just round the corner in fact.) Lily would never get herself into trouble, or run off to Glasgow without being married. It affected her, though, the fortunes of her sisters. When Jean's baby was born, a boy, on 15 July 1930, Lily was rather subdued, even though she said all the right things, and when she went through with her mother to see the new baby, Stuart, she seemed quite wistful. Lily was almost twenty-nine, time to be thinking about babies before it was too late, and she was the one, not Jean or Nan, who had always loved children. Then she was affected in a different way by Nan's passion for Jack Marshallsay, her utter delight in his company. Her mother never talked to her about it but tried to make it clear that this kind of feeling of Nan's for a man wasn't necessarily crucial for happiness. Nan was Nan, Lily was Lily – they wouldn't be likely to feel the same, to respond in the same way. But Jean's lovely baby son and Nan's impetuous flight to Glasgow seemed to influence Lily. She decided, in the autumn of 1930, to marry Arthur Forster in the April of the following year.

On the whole, Margaret Ann was pleased. No rush here. Lily had known Arthur now for very nearly nine years and he had shown himself to be steady and reliable and devoted throughout that time. He wasn't the kind of man everyone had imagined Lily would marry – someone from the office or some doctor, they'd thought, when speculating – but she had never had any other serious suitor, rather to their surprise (and her own). Plenty of admirers but no offers, it seemed, except from Arthur. Everything was proper enough to satisfy Margaret Ann's desire for respectability and this time she enjoyed the wedding preparations. Lily and Arthur even had a house to move into when they were married. It was a council house, one of those newly built on the estate of Raffles, to the west of the city. This was a vast estate, with nearly two thousand houses planned. Carlisle City Council were proud of being the first in the country to snap up the subsidy offered by central government towards the cost of new housing. They claimed, with some justification, that their building plan was the best in Britain, that they had responded the most whole-heartedly and eagerly to the King's Speech of April 1919 in which he had said 'the only adequate solution to the housing question is to build houses specifically for the poor'. This, His Majesty had added, was 'the foundation of all social progress'. The men coming back at that time from the trenches to homes in slums must be given somewhere to live worthy of their wartime endeavours and suffering. Carlisle didn't have great numbers falling into this category but the political parties represented on its council were for once united in agreeing that housing for the poor would be their priority in the decade after the end of the First World War.

The first council estate in Carlisle was ready for occupation by 1922 and how proud the City Council were, inviting other cities to send their representatives to inspect it. It was on the west of the city, at Longsowerby, beyond the small industrial Denton Holme area, and it consisted of only six hundred houses. But each house was well built of good materials, no skimping just because these were houses for the poor. Many of them had parlours with bay windows, and some even had proper bathrooms and indoor lavatories. They were so attractive that, to the great indignation of the council, white-collar workers, who could well afford to buy their own houses, or at least rent privately, were taking tenancies. The slums of

Rickergate and Caldewgate were certainly not being cleared by any happy exodus to Longsowerby – it was a cheat, and an expensive one. There were furious protests made by Labour councillors that too much money had been spent on too few houses when it should have been spent on building many more basic, cheaper homes for the thousands who needed them. So when Raffles, where Lily and Arthur went to live, was planned it was in quite a different way. The main thrust in the 1930s was to be genuine slum clearance with provision for unskilled and semi-skilled workers only.

The Raffles site was purchased in 1926 – ninety-eight acres for ten thousand pounds – and the city architect was told to get as many houses of the non-parlour variety out of it as possible, but nevertheless to make this estate into a community with provision for a park, shops, a church and other kinds of social amenities. The specification that there were to be few parlour-type houses had one Labour councillor thundering that 'the working classes are as entitled as everyone else to a parlour', but in general the thinking behind the directive was approved. Percy Dalton, the city architect, was also enthusiastic about the community brief – he envisaged Raffles as a miniature garden city with the required housing but plenty of green spaces, even apart from a park. The houses were to have front and back gardens and there would be land set aside for allotments and trees lining some streets. But he was handicapped by what had happened at Longsowerby – the materials used in the Raffles houses would have to be poorer to satisfy those outraged by the cost of the top-quality materials used there. As for the proper bathrooms, very few houses would have those. To save money, the two-bedroomed houses were built with lavatories incorporated into the fabric of each house but in order to reach them the tenant had to go out of the back door and in at the separate lavatory door. Better than having to go to the bottom of a yard, or share a privy with ten other families, as many were still doing in the city, but a ludicrous economy all the same. Wash-houses were built in the same way, part of the house but not reachable from it without going outside.

By 1930, when Lily and Arthur were planning to marry, the Raffles estate was near completion and already reckoned a great success. The houses were plain, meant to be neo-Georgian in style with flat frontages (though the few parlour-type had the same bay windows as in Longsowerby) and built in a pleasantly varied combination of terraces and semi-detached blocks. People came out to Raffles to walk round the estate and admire that very garden feeling the architect had envisaged. Those who were allocated these new houses were greatly envied and in awe themselves of the splendour of their new homes. The council kept its word and it was the industrial workers mainly from Caldewgate – Raffles lay beyond Caldewgate, to the far west of the city – who were rehoused. By 1931 91 per cent of the heads of households in Raffles were manual workers. The average rent was six shillings a week, paid out of an average wage of £2 3s. 2d. The clamour to be put on to the Raffles estate was great, not just because of how attractive the place seemed but because it was near to all the main factories – Carr's, Buck's, Dixon's, Pratchitt's – unlike some of the other council estates being built at the same time to the south and south-east of the city where the distance travelled to work, for the majority of tenants, was three times as great.

Lily and Arthur were lucky to get a house in Raffles. There was a waiting list of 1,521 families by 1931 and they were newly married with no family and no real claim to be housed. Arthur was a manual worker but he lived in his father's privately owned house which had three bedrooms, and Lily was a most superior white-collar worker who lived with a widowed mother, also in a house with three bedrooms and privately owned. Young couples who could perfectly well live with their families were not entitled to any council housing but there was a faction on the council, on the Housing Committee, which thought the composition of Raffles should from the beginning be balanced. They were enlightened enough to see that the future of the estate would be better served by including some childless-as-yet couples who would grow with it and have a stake in its prosperity. A member of the Housing Committee who knew someone in the Housing Department mentioned this desire on the part of some members to have young couples as well as slum-clearance large families, and he in turn mentioned it to Lily in the Public Health Department. In this roundabout way Lily was told that if she and Arthur put in a written application they could have one of the two-bedroomed, non-parlour, semi-detached houses on the boundary road, Orton Road.

Margaret Ann went with them to view the house as soon as the builders had finished. She was quite impressed. There was only one living-room but it was a decent size and the range along one wall had a good oven even if it was of the old-fashioned kind (strange for a modern house). One of the bedrooms was fairly large, larger than her own in Bowman Street, and the other big enough for a double bed. There was also a bathroom which was literally that, a room with a bath but no sink, and no lavatory, which was outside. There was a garden round three sides of the house which was at that moment all mud but Arthur would soon transform it. Lily was anxious about what she would think, so she said what she thought – 'Compared with Jean's rooms in those Buildings this is a little palace.' Nan, naturally, was not so complimentary. 'It wouldn't suit me, Lily,' she said. 'I'd want a proper bathroom and a lounge.' (Nan didn't say 'parlour' any more – Jack was educating her, a veritable Professor Higgins.) It was such a stupid, thoughtless, Nanlike thing to say because Lily would have liked those too. She was settling for 44 Orton Road because it was the best she could get.

The bigger question was whether she was settling also for Arthur Gordon Forster? Nan went on about this endlessly to her mother, who didn't really want to hear what she had to say. Nan in her own way loved Lily. She admired her, she worried that Lily was too good and, even though she was seven years older, too innocent and trusting. She didn't see ahead the way Nan did, and what Nan saw was a sister who loved her job giving it up to marry a man for whom she felt no passion and who was wrong for her, and doing all this because she so much longed to have children and her own home. To Margaret Ann there was nothing wrong in this. To her that was more or less what most women had to do. But to Nan, high on her own passion for Jack, and proud of her ability to earn her living, set up as an independent dressmaker, Lily was making all the wrong choices. 'No woman should marry without being passionately in love,' said Nan, and 'No woman should sacrifice her career for marriage.' 'Don't be so dramatic,' her mother said. 'Don't be so silly, Nan.'

But Nan, though certainly dramatic (always) wasn't silly. She saw that marriage to Arthur would drag Lily down just as marriage to Dave had already dragged Jean, and Jean was far tougher than Lily. Those rooms which even Margaret

Ann had found miserable had appalled Nan – she couldn't bear to see Jean confined to them with one baby already and another on the way and very little money to manage with. 'What a life!' Nan had exclaimed, and noticed Jean did not rush to claim that her life was actually what she wanted, if not wonderful. Lily's fate, in Nan's gloomy estimation, would be worse because at least Jean had loved Dave with the requisite amount of passion, and they were a pair. They liked the same things, they had a similar outlook. Nan was damned if Lily and Arthur had. Jack, who admired Lily too (he thought nothing of Jean), said Arthur had not the class for Lily. She could do better for herself than marry a manual worker in a factory. The worst of it, both Nan and Jack agreed, was that Lily had thought about this marriage so carefully and for so long and could not be accused of not weighing up the pros and cons. She'd weighed them and made her bargain, trading a job she loved and good money, and a comfortable home with her mother, whose company she found more than congenial, for marriage to a man she cared for, but for whom she did not feel overwhelming attraction, in order to fulfil her destiny as a woman and have those children for whom she yearned.

Nan made Lily's wedding-dress, not white, though there was no one more virginal than Lily, but a pale blue silk gown, long, with a soft draped collar, a graceful dress to suit graceful, modest Lily. The hat was, Nan felt, a little unfortunate, too close-fitting and too low on the brow for Lily. Her own was much more flattering, but then it had come from Newcastle where she got all her hats – in Nan's opinion Carlisle did not *know* about hats – and Lily wouldn't run to the expense of it. Nan thought her own dress, as brides-maid, nicer too, a shimmering deeper blue taffeta with a deep

V-neckline. Arthur was smart in a new three-piece suit and a startlingly white shirt with a collar stiff enough to cut his neck and a blue tie which, rather sweetly, matched Lily's dress. Margaret Ann had a new dress, not made by Nan but bought for her by Lily at Bullough's. Privately, Nan thought it a disaster – her mother was now too stout for spots, for mercy's sake, and the double chiffon it was made of clung unattractively. It was not formal enough for a bride's mother either. Arthur's mother, Agnes, though not at all elegant or good-looking, looked better in a simple light-weight grey woollen suit and cream blouse, with a dark cream hat. It was with a struggle that Nan kept these thoughts to herself (only to trot them out, whenever Lily's wedding was mentioned, for years and years to come).

Margaret Ann gave a wedding breakfast, a much happier affair than Jean's had been. No one on Dave's side had been at his wedding, but Arthur's were well represented at his. His parents were not the easiest of guests. George, his father, was so taciturn and abrupt he made his son seem positively sophisticated, and Agnes, his mother, was excitable and nervous. Margaret Ann had been to have tea with them in their house in Richardson Street on the far side of Denton Holme. George Forster was only a fitter at Pratchitt's but he'd bought his own house through judicious gambling on horses. His brother was a bookie and rather to Margaret Ann's alarm – gambling was almost as bad as fornication and drunkenness – young Arthur was proud of having obliged his uncle by doing a bit of 'running' (laying bets) for him. Agnes was clearly under George's thumb and was always on the lookout for his approval. She only spoke freely when he was not around, but then at least she was extravagant with the compliments about Lily. She had no daughters, only Arthur and his young brother Bob, to her everlasting regret. She described most piteously to Margaret Ann how she used to sit in her parlour on Sunday afternoons crying with envy as she watched other women walking past with their daughters and craving her own. Lily was everything she had wished for and she would treat her as hers.

Once Lily had married, Margaret Ann was living by herself. Jean was in Motherwell, Nan in Glasgow (best not to mention exactly where or with whom) and even the lodger, cousin Florrie, now had her own place. She was sixty-two years old and her health was beginning to trouble her. More and more she rested, as she was now well able to do, but it didn't suit her. She said she was plagued with thoughts when she rested. Lily asked what kind of thoughts. What was worrying her? Surely she had no worries of any great importance? None to confess, anyway. Lily imagined her mother was fretting about Nan and blamed her sister for being the cause of their mother's secret anxiety which rose to the surface of her mind whenever she rested.

Surely, though, the 'plague' was Alice? Alice, who lived so near to Bowman Street still, in Brook Street, who could hardly have failed to use the same shops as her mother, walk the same route to the town, board the same trams. And yet still, after thirty-eight years, she was not acknowledged. Unless Margaret Ann had visits from Alice without anyone knowing, or unless she didn't want to rest alone in her empty house because it made her vulnerable to this first daughter she went on spurning? There was no Tom to act as her representative, as he had done at Alice's marriage, no Tom to protect her from guilt or ease her resentment. But what kept Alice, and had kept her all these years, from forcing her presence on her half-sisters? Was she paid to stay away? By whom? Had a promise been exacted that she would make no contact? But how?

Plenty, in any case, to plague Margaret Ann's restful afternoon naps.

V

Lily's contact with her mother remained very close. She was an exemplary married daughter, visiting her mother at least twice a week and inviting her to her own home for Sunday dinner. Nearly always Arthur would be mending someone's car over the weekend and he would go to pick up his mother-in-law and take her and Lily to church in the evening. The church was St Paul's now, the sister church of St Mary's which had been demolished. Lily, with her beautiful contralto voice, was still in the choir there and Margaret Ann loved to hear her sing.

Those Sunday visits to 44 Orton Road were happy ones. Lily was so organized, the dinner always on time and well cooked. And the house had a pleasant atmosphere. It seemed light and bright after Bowman Street, which in the manner of old terraced houses was rather dark. The newly distempered walls of Orton Road were refreshingly modern compared to the heavy wallpapered rooms Margaret Ann was used to, and though Lily's furniture was very basic it was all new and added to the general freshness of everything. There was a dining-table with extending leaves (said to be oak but Margaret Ann doubted it) bought for £3 5s. od.; four dining-room chairs (9s. 11d.); a sideboard (£4 10s. od.); a bedroom suite (wardrobe, bedstead and dressing-table, all for £11 19s. od.); two armchairs (£6 15s. od.) and a settee covered in leatherette, not actually new but as good as, given to Lily by her Aunt Sarah. The whole house had been furnished for under thirty pounds, not counting the rag rugs and the strip of stair carpet. Arthur's parents had given him and Lily a china tea service as their present, and Margaret Ann herself gave them a canteen of cutlery. Everyone thought the young married couple were well set up, especially considering the times.

Those times were hard. It was 1931 and business was bad throughout the whole country. Arthur had moved from Pratchitt's to the Metal Box factory (where he worked as a fitter, maintaining machines) which was now on short time. Men came applying for work every day and were turned away. Lily didn't know how much Arthur earned – in common with most men, of whatever social standing, he didn't reveal his wage to his wife – but she knew it wasn't as much as she had been earning herself in the Public Health Department where, at £4 10s., she'd been nearly as well paid as the chief clerk himself. Arthur was earning £2 4s. when he married Lily and of that he kept only the shillings and gave her the two pounds for all housekeeping and bills and every expenditure. It was quite a shock for her to know she must manage and try also to save, all on two pounds a week – she had been used to having two pounds to herself for some time before she married, giving the balance to her mother. But she was a good manager and had seen her own mother manage on far less and never once get into debt. The rent was six shillings a week, collected by the rent man every Monday and always ready for him, on top of the rent book, and coal, gas and electricity took another six shillings. So it needed no mathematical genius to see that this left £1 8s. for everything else. Lily did sums all the time to make that amount go furthest. Bacon was 1s. 6d. a pound and Arthur was heavy on bacon. His mother had stressed that he *had* to have bacon every morning and he liked it well done but not frizzled. Lily thought this a great extravagance. She was sure other men couldn't be feasting on bacon every morning, but since she had lived her adult life in an all-female household she wasn't certain. There was the bacon and then the beef, a weekly joint of about three pounds in weight at 1s. 4d. a pound in money; eggs at 1s. 6d. a dozen; and butter at 1s. 5d. a pound. These were the staples, plus bread, but that was cheap and she baked it herself. Vegetables were cheap too – carrots only 2d. a pound, a cauliflower the most expensive at 5d. But her father-in-law gave them vegetables from his allotment and soon Arthur's own would begin producing – he was a very good gardener. Arthur's wage, then, was sufficient for the moment but the ever-apprehensive Lily always had one eye on the future and she saw clearly how she would have to give up all frivolities such as new clothes or holidays if any savings were to accrue.

Early married life was for Lily rather a sequence of giving up things. Her entire day was radically different. She had been used to rising at eight to be at her work at nine o'clock but now she rose at six-thirty and lit the fire, which Arthur had cleaned out and relaid, and put his bacon on and made his bait: sandwiches, made with thick white crusty bread and containing either potted meat or cold sausage or corned beef – Arthur had to have meat of some sort. Then she made his breakfast, the bacon and a bit of bread fried in dripping, and tea, and off he went at seven o'clock on his bike to the Metal Box factory, a good mile's ride away. When he had gone, she got washed in the back kitchen, because that was where the sink was (the bath was for weekly use and the water for it heated only when the fire had been on long enough to heat the boiler). It was a cold room, freezing in winter. The walls were painted brick, dark green from the floor up to four feet and then a dull beige to the ceiling. She hated that green, but Arthur would paint it over later. She dressed in her morning clothes – a tweed skirt, a jumper and a pinny on top and her hair in a turban – keeping her smart office clothes for the afternoon. Then she washed the dishes, swept the floor, dusted and made the bed. If it wasn't wash-day, she then shopped.

There was a butcher's across the road and a general store, but she preferred to walk to a row of shops ten minutes away, liking the exercise. Once a week she went to the market and brought the joint home and any vegetables not available from the Forster allotment. She was always back well in time to have Arthur's dinner steaming on the plate for half past twelve – or twelve twenty-four, to be precise, which Arthur always was. They had that in common, reliability, punctuality, a liking for order. Meat of some sort most days, mince or stews, and potatoes with everything, boiled, mashed or fried. When Arthur had returned to work she got changed. It was at this point in the day that she felt lost. She didn't quite know what to do. There was mending and ironing, but these could be done in the evening. She'd remember the office and all the bustle and the sense of importance and the company, and feel suddenly detached from life, marooned, a little panic-stricken. To deal with this alarming feeling she went visiting, to her mother twice a week and to her mother-in-law the same, on different days. But though this used up her afternoons pleasantly enough, as it was intended to do, she still felt vaguely uneasy and even guilty, though there was nothing to be guilty about – this was what all married women did, if they were lucky, if they had a man to support them. But she appreciated all over again how much her job had meant to her, how she'd loved the organizing and the people, loved being part of some meaningful operation.

Arthur came home at seven o'clock, at the end of a long, hard day in the noisy factory. His overalls were filthy, every bit as greasy and dirty as Nan had envisaged when warning her sisters off marrying fitters. When he'd washed thoroughly, in the kitchen, which meant she had to try to keep the food clear of the splashings and sluicings, they had tea, a sort of high tea. Then Arthur would garden or sometimes they went for a walk, up Wigton Road and down Farmer Brown's lonning. Arthur had sold his motor bike, his beloved two-stroke Enfield, to pay for the furniture which was a pity because if he'd still had it they could have gone out into the real country all around that end of Carlisle. Arthur had his push-bike, his Raleigh, and went for rides into the country at weekends. It wasn't the healthy ride he went for though, it was to bet at hound trails. Lily hated him betting but if it was only with the few shillings he kept for himself she supposed he was entitled. In the winter they both listened to the wireless, though there was some clash here – Arthur liked sport, any sport, and variety and light comedy, and Lily liked hymn-singing and plays and stories and talks.

Margaret Ann told Lily to make the most of this easy time before the children started coming, and Lily tried to but she was relieved as well as happy when she became pregnant very quickly. The baby would be born in March, eleven months after she was married, a very gratifying interval. She was going to have the baby at her mother-in-law's home, a rather odd decision but one brought about partly because of her own mother's health – the angina attacks had begun and Margaret Ann was in no fit state to nurse either Lily or any baby – and partly because Agnes Forster was so desperate to have the thrill of her grandchild being born in her house. She craved the sort of involvement she felt she would have had with the daughter she had never produced. Margaret Ann was a little sad about not being able to look after Lily, as she had just looked after Jean when she gave birth to another boy in January, but she knew she had to be sensible. Lily was near enough for her to visit and see the baby as soon as it was born and she had to be grateful for that. She rather hoped Lily would have a girl, but it was a boy, born on 20 March. Three grandsons now, and inevitably she thought of Tom and how thrilled he would have been – three fine, strong, blond boys. It was hard for Jean to come to Carlisle, what with two babies and the expense to consider, but at the end of that summer she managed a trip through and Margaret Ann had the gratification of having all three grandsons on her knee. Only Nan to be settled and then she said she could die happy. Her job would be done, another family cycle complete. She had founded her own family and seen its members do the same in turn and that was what a woman's life was about.

If memories of another member of her family, of Alice, ever troubled her at this time of near contentment she did not speak of them. Alice, whether her mother knew it or not, had just moved to Upperby. She was no longer just round the corner, liable to be met any day on the way to the shops in Botchergate, always passing the house out of which she had seen her half-sisters coming and going for the last decade. What had kept Alice from declaring herself? What kind of agreement had been reached? Margaret Ann's confidence all those years of living in Bowman Street had been extraordinary.

Having a baby changed everything yet again for Lily. Those aimless afternoons disappeared. She had Gordon to look after and for a while she was entirely fulfilled. She looked after him beautifully and didn't mind the extra washing. Mother had trained her well. She knew how to work the boiler in the outside wash-house and how to use the dolly-tub and the mangle. She had three washdays a week now, what with all the terry-towelling nappies and baby sheets and clothes and towels, and she kept everything spotless. Arthur filled the boiler with water before he left for work – it had to be carried in buckets from the kitchen – and lit it and then when the evil metal cauldron was bubbling away with the at-last boiling water she added soap powder ('a wonderful invention' Mother always said) and plunged the clothes in and left them to boil for ten minutes before lifting each item out again with long tongs and dropping them into a waiting tub of clear water and setting to with the washboard, scrubbing every-thing viciously after the whole lot had been pounded with the dolly. The rinsing was another performance. It took ages, filling and refilling the dolly-tub with clean cold water, and when it was done there was the back-breaking mangling, feeding the clothes between the heavy rollers and turning and turning the handle, constantly tightening the screw to narrow the gap between these rollers so that the maximum amount of water was squeezed out. This was the last laborious stage before the next battle, the attempt at drying, attempts often doomed to failure. Arthur had made some magnificent clothes props – she wasn't short of those – and he'd put a good, sturdy washing line up, but once the washing had been pegged out there was the weather to contend with. If it began to rain there was an agonizing decision to be made to unpeg or not. If she unpegged and carted in the heavy, still-wet washing and then the rain came to nothing, she'd wasted more time and energy, but if she risked leaving it pegged and the rain fell in earnest, then the wretched washing would get even wetter and have to be remangled and she'd get soaked herself dashing backwards and forwards. Oh, washing was such a trial. It was the event of the day every day it was done, that dreaded, dreadful washing, only worth it to keep the baby's clothes pristine. Mother said she'd warned her: this was what a woman's life was about. She and Jean, with their history of good jobs in offices, hadn't known the half of it, whereas she, Margaret Ann, domestic servant from her youth, had spent her life like this.

It would have been a comfort to both Jean and Lily to have been able to say giving up their jobs had been worth it, but they'd inherited a habit of truthfulness from their mother and couldn't. The further the two of them got into the life of a mother and a working-man's wife the more alluring their past careers became. The only real compensation was their sons. They doted on them and if they had not given up their jobs, they could not have had them, could they? Jobs were traded for children and that was that. No good moaning, no good spending even a moment's resentment wishing they could have kept the jobs *and* had the boys. That was not how the world worked, their world, the world for women in the 1930s. It was hard enough for men to keep their jobs, something Lily in particular constantly worried about, especially once she had a son's future to think about. It frightened her, hearing the tales of how uncertain all employment was becoming. Men were laid off all the time and if Arthur was what on earth would they do? The thought of the dole, the mere thought, made her ill. Arthur wouldn't have words like dole mentioned. He said not to talk about such things. He was a good worker, very experienced by now and well regarded by the management, and he didn't think he would be laid off. Lily didn't doubt his estimation of his own worth but she also knew Arthur had no paper qualifications and that younger men were coming up behind him who had studied engineering at college and that they might be given preference over the unqualified, if hardworking and technically experienced, Arthur. She didn't see her husband having any protection from this kind of possible challenge. He wouldn't have anything to do with trade unions even if he was supposedly a Labour supporter then – he feared unions, noting their activity in the factory anxiously, knowing they were pressing for an all-out strike. He didn't want to strike. He feared victimization and couldn't see how the unions could beat the management.

At the back of her mind, Lily clung on to what Dr Beard had said when she left, which was that if ever she wanted to she could come back part-time, she was so highly thought of. She mentioned this to Arthur, in one of her if-the-worst-comes-to-the-worst moods, intending it to be a cheering thought, but he alarmed her with his vehement protest that he would not have his wife working, part-time or not. He wished Lily wouldn't go on about it. He wished she would just let what would be, be. There was nothing that could be done. That was always his attitude, that nothing he could do made any difference to his future. He had no power over it and therefore the best thing was to keep his nose clean and continue to work hard and hope he'd be lucky. But it wasn't Lily's attitude, not then. She didn't like Arthur's fatalism. She feared that the consequence of it would mean they would stay poor for ever. She remembered her father and how his hard work had been backed by his enterprise and how he'd flourished and been able to benefit his family. Arthur couldn't do that. She was married to a man who had skills and used them but whose prodigious hard, physical work would never bring him the rewards he deserved unless he looked out for ways of capitalizing on them, and as far as he was concerned, perhaps correctly, there were none. She was going to have to learn to be that man's wife and not complain and meanwhile her own brains and talents were not being used.

Margaret Ann, in the last few years of her life, never stopped worrying about Nan. Exactly where and how Nan was living was still not discussed back in Carlisle, though her mother and sisters had her address. The accepted version was that Nan was doing very well in the tailoring business and happily settled in the respectable boarding-house she'd described to her mother. She saw Jack Marshallsay 'often' but no, there was still no engagement – why should there be, why did her mother go on about it so? By now, Lily and Jean both knew Jack was married and reputedly trying for a divorce but they agreed that their mother could not be told this. Divorce was a terrible word, it would bring on an angina attack for sure. So would any open acknowledgement that, although Nan's boarding-house was indeed respectable, it also accommodated Jack. The two of them were virtually living together, and in 1934 they moved into what Jack called a flat in Ashton Road, with Nan simply telling her mother she could now afford to rent a place of her own (though no invitation to visit was extended). This 'flat' was more of a bed-sitting room with a tiny kitchenette and not at all what

Nan had had in mind, but Jack said it was only temporary. Once his divorce came through, once they were married, they would have a house.

The wonder to her sisters was how Nan could go on fooling herself, never mind Mother. She still acted like a queen, still thought herself more than a cut above other women, and most irritating of all would not face the reality of her situation. She was defiant about it, she saw herself as a heroine risking everything for love. Women who had to have weddings and rings before they 'gave themselves' to a man knew nothing of true love. What was the point of keeping the man she loved at a distance until he could marry her? Lily and Jean hardly dared to mention that there was surely something fishy about the length of time Jack's divorce was taking. He'd been getting it for six years now, *six* years. The sisters knew nothing of the law but they suspected no divorce however complicated could take that long. Then there was another matter. So far, Nan had been lucky, she hadn't 'fallen', but if she were to 'fall' and have a child . . . it would kill Mother. Nan scorned such mutterings. Jack was a responsible man, he knew how to take care.

He no longer travelled in ladies' costumes. Jack was now a fully qualified optician but he also had a sideline. He was a magician, no other than 'the celebrated magical entertainer Anthony Marsh', as his self-produced publicity leaflet proclaimed. This was 'Magic in its most polished form . . . a Cavalcade of Modern Mystery', suitable for concerts, dinners and cabaret parties. Distance was no object – the incredibly good-looking (photograph as proof) Anthony Marsh would go anywhere, immaculate in his tails, and with him went Zara, his assistant. Nan loved being Zara, loved the glamour of her costume – a white satin gown, cut on the bias, with silver stars sewn into it, and a white feather headband – and loved the stages upon which Jack alias Anthony performed (though from the list of some of the venues many were less than impressive). Life with Jack was such fun, married or not, and she pitied her sisters and her mother who had never known the exciting existence she enjoyed. She was never going back to dull old Carlisle.

Recognizing this, her mother decided by the end of 1935 that the Bowman Street house was too big for her. The time had come to leave it, but where would she go? Somewhere smaller? Or to live with one of her daughters? This was what she had always imagined she would do, was what mothers did in their old age, surely. She had no pattern of her own to follow, never having known her mother, but it was one she saw around her and it seemed right and proper. What would have suited her best was for one of her married daughters to have moved in with her – she had three bedrooms and a parlour and neither Lily nor Jean did. But Dave Wallace had his job in Motherwell and couldn't just find the equivalent in Carlisle. It was impossible with the job situation being as it was, and anyway he was a Scot and wanted to stay in Scotland. Arthur worked in Carlisle, so he and Lily and their son could have moved into Bowman Street but he didn't fancy it, he liked his own home. So she decided to put her house up for sale and go to live with Jean.

It was a strange decision which surprised everyone, most of all Jean. Her mother had never liked the Buildings or Mother-well and there wasn't really room for her. Dave put another bed-in-the-wall in the living-room, where there already was one. (This is how these beds were referred to – beds-in-the-wall – though in fact they were not *in* the wall at all but consisted of double mattresses laid on broad planks, fitting large alcoves, with curtains in front.) The second room was now given over to Margaret Ann and her trappings. Arthur brought her through in a borrowed car and when he returned told Lily he didn't think it would work out. His own small council house seemed spacious compared to the Wallaces' two cramped rooms in one of which all four of them were going to have to live and sleep since Margaret Ann had the other. Arthur said he didn't see how his mother-in-law could manage all the steps either but she would have to, to get to the lavatory outside. He was right. She couldn't cope and within six weeks was writing to Lily asking if Arthur could come to collect her and let her stay with them until she decided what to do. Her Bowman Street house hadn't been sold yet, there was time to rethink.

She seemed depressed, when she arrived, about the Mother-well experience but she didn't talk about it. Jean for her part wrote to Lily that she was upset. She didn't know what had gone wrong, she'd done her best. Tactfully, Lily wrote back saying their mother's inability to settle with Jean had been due to missing Carlisle – Mother had been perfectly happy with her but was homesick for Carlisle. But, though back in Carlisle, she still seemed low. One month went by, then two. The first sale of her house fell through but there was another offer. She floated the suggestion to Lily and Arthur that she should buy another house, of their choice, and they could all live together. She would leave them any new house she bought and while living in it make a contribution to expenses. Lily was tempted. There were lovely houses going up across the road, a new private estate, but Arthur was emphatic, he didn't want 'to start that'. Start what, Lily wondered, but Arthur, as always when he couldn't articulate his feelings, took refuge in further enigmatic statements. Time went on and so delicate was the topic it was never openly discussed. Margaret Ann never asked for a decision (never having directly made the offer) and Lily and Arthur never gave one.

Meanwhile, these last months of Margaret Ann's were not happy. She'd come so far from her unfortunate start as an illegitimate child, as an orphan with no settled loving home and family but, though she knew she was much loved as a mother and would never again be outcast, there was a hint of that same sort of insecurity about her final months. The woman in the car visited and destroyed whatever peace of mind she had. Gordon, her four-year-old grandson, was her greatest pleasure and comfort. She liked to be with him, playing with him, watching over him, and it pleased her to feel that by doing so she helped Lily who was pregnant again. This time, she would be with Lily for the birth and everyone was hoping for a girl, to be called after her.

But she died before any baby was born and then Lily miscarried and there was no baby to name after her. Margaret Ann's sudden death, at sixty-six, solved the problem of what she was to do in the most brutal way. She had had nothing more to expect out of life. She'd made of it more than she had ever dared to expect even if, at this distance of time, that does not seem so very much.

There remains the problem of Alice and how my grandmother appears to have treated her. If Alice had had a daughter of her own then perhaps there would still be some chance of discovering the truth but she didn't. Alice had no children. She was on her own, apart from her husband William who, mercifully, appears to have been devoted. After her outburst, and the cruel rejection of her, at my grandmother's funeral Alice kept her bitterness to herself. She vanished from my family history never having been recognized as having any part in it in the first place. She was an untouchable. Why?

Theories, informed speculative ideas, play a part in all biography but, in the case of the Alices of this world, there is virtually nothing else left after the meagre official records have been scrutinized. The more I think about it, the clearer it seems that Alice's existence was associated with such horror in my grandmother's mind that she could not tolerate the sight or mention of her. Once born, once given a decent Christian baptism as the very least that could be done for her, Alice had to be banished. This suggests the conception of Alice may have been violent, the result of rape perhaps. My grandmother wanted her out of her sight for ever, an understandable and common enough reaction in such circumstances, if pitifully unfair to the children. But in that case why did my grandfather stand as witness to Alice's marriage? Did he do so of his own volition or as Margaret Ann's representative? Am I wrong? Was he after all Alice's father?

Then there is that puzzling visit by the woman who came in the car . . . Surely it indicates another reason why Alice was a source of anguish. I jump too easily to the theory that this first child of my grandmother's was the consequence of violation, of an act too horrible for her to acknowledge and for which Alice paid the price. Maybe there was no horror. Maybe Alice was a love-child. Maybe, in that Newcastle area Margaret Ann was so used to mentioning, she had become pregnant by someone she loved who did not stand by her. Maybe the woman who came in 1936 to tell her news that distressed her unbearably was a relative of this one-time lover, who had just died but not without making some death-bed act of contrition. The woman was in deep mourning

– all that black she wore was noted – and her news most likely to be of a death. But it was a death my grandmother could neither name nor speak of to her daughter, the death of a person whom she did not wish to identify.

So now the story would change. It would be more likely Margaret Ann would want to keep Alice instead of spurning her. Unless, because Alice's father had been the love of her life, every look at the child reminded her of him. Perhaps she hated him, though, lover or not; perhaps she fled from the place where she had known him, from that Newcastle area, once he had been told of her pregnancy and rejected her, and she never wanted to see him again. Or was it a far, far better thing she thought she was doing, leaving this lover, knowing he could not marry her, making the decision for both of them to conceal Alice's birth? So who was the woman in black in that case? Someone Margaret Ann had trusted? Another servant, the only one who had known why my grandmother left her place in the Newcastle area, so suddenly, without leaving any address? And come to tell her that her lover – the master, the young master – was dead all the same. Did Margaret Ann weep because she still loved him? Did she weep at the memory of that wretched time? Or did she weep for how she had abandoned Alice, how she had denied Alice any kind of father?

These theories, the romantic, the melodramatic, the sordid, all of them can be made to work but none of them can ever be proved. Round and round it goes, this circle of questions with no answers. Why do answers matter when it is all so trivial, when Margaret Ann and Alice were nobodies and it was so long ago? Because, somehow, my grandmother, in not recognizing Alice, in keeping her a secret from her other three daughters, was part of a pattern. Secrecy and suppression were part of the fabric of life for women who had illegitimate children then, and not to be able to know precisely why such secrecy was so vital robs me of the kind of understanding I want to have. There is so much suffering there – my grandmother's, Alice's – and it hangs, threatening and stifling, always unresolved, over what was to follow.

LILIAN

1901–1981

VI

After Margaret Ann died, and her will had been found, her house was duly emptied of its possessions. None of her daughters had the space to take her furniture, so they each took small mementoes. Lilian found handling any of Mother's things unbearably distressing – she left most of the clearing to Jean – but she took a small white china jug with an intricate double handle which her mother had used for flowers, and her rolling pin and a brooch, pathetic enough items all of them. She wasn't well enough even to think about what to do with the contents of Bowman Street and never wanted to enter the house again after the funeral. She was ill in any case. She miscarried the next week and felt nervy and tearful and depressed. Memories of her father's death haunted her and though this time there was no question of locking herself in any cupboard, or the equivalent, she felt the same panic and despair.

Church helped, going to church and praying and being comforted by the thought of Mother at peace. Throughout the previous spring she and Margaret Ann had watched the new church in Raffles being built and now that it had been consecrated, in June 1936, the month before Mother died, she went to a service there, curious to see what this church was like. Later, a Book of Prayers for the Dead was opened and she wrote her parents' names in it: Thomas and Margaret Ann Hind, the first names in the whole book. The church was called St Barnabas's and it wasn't like a real church like St Mary's, or St Paul's, at all. A real church should be old and built of stone and have a spire and stained glass windows. This one looked more like an hotel with its flat front and its rendered cement walls – it lacked dignity, it was flashy. It was meant to have a fresh, original look, in keeping with the garden-city image behind the whole concept of Raffles, but to Lily and many others the stark design and the glare of the scraped ivory-white cement was too brutal. The newness of everything about St Barnabas's was disconcerting, inside as well as out. It didn't smell like a church, it wasn't hushed and holy. There was certain pleasure in the absolute cleanliness of everything – the new, light oak wood was so smooth to touch, the shiny hymn books creaked with newness when opened – but it was not conducive to prayer. The vicar, the Reverend Bouch, realizing this, told his congregation it was exciting to be at the beginning of the life of a new church and it was up to them to make of it a place dedicated to the greater glory of God. St Barnabas's gave them the chance to make a new start in their spiritual lives just as the new houses they now lived in had given them a new start in their temporal lives. Listening, Lily was resolved to give St Barna-bas's her backing. A new start was what she must try to make, for the sake of her child and children to come. Every-thing Mother had done had been for her daughters and her example was there to follow: for the sake of the family every woman must do her best.

The money from the sale of Bowman Street was split between the three daughters, enough for each of them to put a sizeable deposit on a new house if they wished. It was a great opportunity, but Lily and Arthur missed it. The houses on the private estate opposite them, the very ones Margaret

Ann had suggested buying, were finished and for sale at five hundred pounds. Lily ached to have one of them. She went and looked round Inglewood Crescent and admired the modern kitchens and especially the all-tiled bathrooms and the space two living-rooms offered, and the temptation to put down all Mother's money, which would come to half the price, was strong. But no. It would be folly. Arthur might lose his job at any moment and then where would they be? In debt. It was better to put the money in the bank for that rainy day which sometimes felt it had already arrived. It would be there to fall back on, to keep terror at bay, since true terror was very much to do with having no money, the consequence of losing one's job.

The thought of having two hundred and fifty pounds in the bank ought to have made Lily happier but it didn't. It seemed, somehow, to underline how much she lacked, to emphasize how many times over she could have spent that sum. She wanted both to feel financially secure and to know better days were ahead, but two hundred and fifty pounds in the bank didn't give her either feeling. Arthur was lucky to be hanging on to his poorly paid job at which he worked so hard and it was impossible for him to advance. Not quite impossible, true. He came home one day towards the end of 1936 to say that some manager from the Metal Box Company of South Africa (formed in 1933) had been touring the works and had stopped to watch him mend a particularly compli-cated machine and then asked him if he'd like to come out to South Africa and work for him. Arthur snorted derisively when he related this tale – South Africa, it was absurd, the man must be barmy, imagining he'd leave Carlisle for South Africa! But Lily didn't laugh. She questioned him closely and heard the salary would be three times what Arthur was getting in Carlisle's Metal Box and there was a house thrown in. She didn't want to go to an outlandish country like South Africa either, she was as attached to Carlisle as Arthur and as fearful of travel, but nevertheless it was an opportunity.

The matter was never mentioned again, but Lily thought of what a new start in another country might have meant when she became pregnant again in 1937 – another mouth to feed and more workers laid off at Metal Box, though still not Arthur. But the five-day week was introduced, the 45-hour week with no overtime available at the moment. She felt she'd always be scrimping and saving and never have any of the things she wanted. Maybe it was wrong to want trivial things like new clothes but she couldn't help it. She loved clothes and she hadn't bought a single garment in the six years of married life. Her once-smart office clothes were almost threadbare and she didn't even have the money to buy some material to make a new blouse at least (not that she would have made it very well, and Nan was too far away to help). She needed a new coat but coats were anything between four and six pounds and quite out of the question – the cheapest was twice Arthur's wage and Gordon's shoes were more important, he had to have them. She was ashamed of how she ogled a tweed coat at £4 10s. in the window of Bullough's, of how she fingered the new artificial silk fabric in Binn's at 5s. 11d. a yard. She was tired of buying cheap this and cheap that when once, when she had her own job, she could have what she wanted (within limits, but perfectly acceptable ones). It soured her soul, the penny-pinching. She couldn't accept it the way Mother had always done.

Mother's money was badly needed in 1937. Gordon was ill so often and there were many doctor's visits to pay for and medicines to buy. He fell ill easily, with all the common childhood diseases (always with complications in his case) and then the more rare ones, like diphtheria and pneumonia. Lily was terrified when Dr Stephenson said the five-year-old Gordon had pneumonia. She wouldn't leave his side and when, the fever at its height, the child started to babble about angels she became hysterical and fell down on her knees and prayed and prayed, and in general, as Arthur put it, 'carried on'. She didn't, she said, want the baby she was carrying if Gordon was taken from her. Arthur didn't know what to do with her. He wished Jean or Nan would come. In the end, though Gordon was actually recovering by the time she arrived, Nan did come.

That was another shock. Nan was pregnant too, more pregnant than Lily herself, her baby due at the beginning of April, Lily's at the end of May. 'Are you . . .?' Lily asked and Nan said no, she wasn't married yet, and this time there were tears in her eyes and not tears of angry defiance. Thank God Mother was dead. There was a hope that Jack's divorce would come through in time for them to marry before the baby was born, but his wife was still (according to him) proving a bitch. Jack had spent a fortune on legal fees, (according to Nan), and still this awful woman was being obstructive. She even told Lily – which horrified her sister – that Jack knew 'a very eminent surgeon' who would solve Nan's little problem quite easily and painlessly for a certain sum of money which Jack was more than willing to pay but, to Lily's relief, Nan didn't want that. She was nearly thirty and after thinking she never wanted children – they were such a nuisance – she now longed for a baby, for Jack's son. She wanted this baby and hoped that its birth would make Jack's wife relent and give him a divorce. Poor Nan, after all, and perhaps poor Jack (though that rather stuck in the throat).

Nan went to Jean's in Motherwell to have her baby – what a come-down, but she had nowhere else to go, no one to fall back on except family. Jack with his ever-ready habit of solving problems by spending money didn't understand why Nan refused to go into a nursing home when she'd happily lived with him seven years pretending to be his wife anyway. Why couldn't she just pretend in a maternity home? But Nan wouldn't. She went to Jean's and suffered the indignity of giving birth in the Buildings on 3 April 1938. It was a long, difficult birth – she had a far harder time than her sisters – but she was thrilled with her son, named Michael John Marshallsay. Except he was not legally entitled to his surname. On his birth certificate, in the box headed: Date and Place of Marriage (of the child's parents), were written both Jack's and Nan's names, repeated in the next column with Father under Jack's name and profession. There was no question of Michael's parentage not being acknowledged. Once he was born, Nan's attitude to the saga of Jack's (non-existent) divorce proceedings hardened. She wanted her son to be legitimized for his sake not her own. So did Jack. He finally filed for divorce that month and though it took two years to be made absolute he could now assure Nan that his wife had relented and all would soon be well.

Of the sisters, it was Nan who was most changed by motherhood. She was taken by surprise at the ferocity of her devotion to Michael and the depth of her love for him. It was equal to her love for Jack, something she had never expected. She wanted to breast-feed her son, even though it was unfashionable and neither of her sisters had engaged in such a peasant activity, but Jack was horrified. He told her he didn't want her breasts to sag. Luckily, or unluckily, Michael failed to thrive on her milk and he was soon on the bottle. Jack was relieved. He was rather irritated by Nan's reaction to being a mother. She wasn't an instinctive mother though, and wished she was near Lily or nearer to Jean to give her confidence, instead of on her own in Glasgow. When Jack announced he had been offered a better job by Strother's, an opticians in Carlisle, she was delighted. Once, a return to Carlisle, the home town she'd thought so dull and boring, would have dismayed her, but now it would bring her near to Lily and they could be mothers together. Jack had already rented a semi-detached house only ten minutes' walk from Lily's council estate. The Marshallsays were installed in Carlisle before Lily had her second baby.

The last month of her pregnancy had been calm. Lily seemed more like her usual self now that Gordon was fully recovered and had started school. The weather that May was good and she sat in the garden, thinking about Mother. She desperately longed for a girl this time, because she didn't intend to have any more children, a girl to be called Margaret, as planned before, as planned by all three sisters whenever they were pregnant – to one of them would fall the honour of being the first to have a daughter, the first to use Mother's name. Arthur wanted a daughter too – his mother drove him barmy longing aloud for a granddaughter to make up for that daughter she had never had – but he was more interested in the actual date she would be born. At the Palace cinema a film was to be shown called *Little Miss Somebody* and the cinema was offering a Little Miss Somebody Prize to the first girl born in Carlisle after the start of the first performance at three-thirty on Monday, 23 May. The certificate of birth had to be brought to the cinema on Saturday, 28 May, when the prize would be awarded. Arthur had his hopes, being a gambling man, and when Lily went into labour in the front bedroom of 44 Orton Road early on the morning of 25 May, he felt he was in with a good chance.

It was an easy birth, a matter of only an hour long, with the midwife arriving just in time. To everyone's joy, Lily had produced a girl, a pretty, delicately formed daughter with small, sweet features. No need to ask her name (though Ann was not included, in an attempt to give her some individuality). Alas, Arthur was pipped at the post. Another girl was born on 25 May only half an hour earlier and given the Palace cinema's prize, though it was only a Little Miss Somebody cot, plus a photograph of Binkie Stuart, the four-year-old baby film star, tap-dancing on a piano, as she did in the film.

Everyone was for a while happy. The longed-for girl was born, Lily was well, the summer of 1938 was a good one, and if everyone else in the country was convinced war was coming nobody at 44 Orton Road gave a damn – all that mattered was their own family life and they didn't see it as threatened by what was said to be happening in Europe.

Arthur was not quite thirty-nine when war was declared in September 1939. When the First World War had broken out he'd been not quite fourteen and desperate to join up. He couldn't wait to be old enough. In 1917 he ran away to Newcastle to enlist, giving a false name and age, but his father followed him and dragged him out of the recruiting office and thrashed him for being a fool. By 1939 he was no longer a fool. He had no desire to be a soldier and he didn't have to be, not yet anyway. Instead, he was sent to Skelton, near Carlisle, to the power station, to work there maintaining essential services, and to various other places – factories producing plates for the framework inside Wellington bombers and machine-gun clips – in northern England. When he was at Skelton, ten miles away from his home, he cycled off on Monday morning and returned on Friday night, but when he was further away he went by train and wasn't always allowed the fare to come home at weekends.

It suited Lily very well to be on her own with her two children much of the time. Life was simpler, easier, unpunctuated by the homecomings of a man for his dinner and tea and without filthy overalls to wash. She wasn't afraid because there was little feeling of being at war in Carlisle. As in the First World War, Carlisle was hardly touched. No bombs dropped on the city and hardly an air raid siren was heard. Its citizens became so complacent that in 1942, at the height of the war, only one in a hundred was found to be carrying the regulation gas mask (for which slackness the whole city was reprimanded by the War Office). Carlisle City Council had at least paid heed by spending £27,250 on trenches and shelters for schoolchildren but these were hardly used. Except for the inevitable absence of a great many men and the presence of evacuees, Carlisle women did not suffer from the horrors being endured to the north in Glasgow, to the south in Liverpool and to the east in Newcastle. Most of the evacuees came from Newcastle but Lily had none billeted on her since she had only two bedrooms and no parlour and had two children.

Weekends when Arthur came home were difficult. He was always good with the children but they had to learn to share their mother with him and they'd protest, especially Margaret. Gordon was docile and biddable but Margaret even as a baby was neither. She was noisy and demanding and given to tantrums if she couldn't get her own way, tantrums Arthur feared would have to be beaten out of her if they went on. It gradually dawned on him and Lily and the whole family that this Margaret, far from being like the saintly grandmother after whom she was named, was like Nan. Fiery, selfish, ambitious, just like Nan. She wasn't turning out like either her grandmother or her mother except, like Lily, she was clever. She talked in long sentences at two and never stopped asking questions and wanting to try to read. It made everyone more nervous than proud, though they enjoyed listening to the infant Margaret reciting nursery rhymes and little poems as she stood on the living-room table looking adorable in a frock Nan had made for her, white double chiffon with red satin spots on it and a big sash. She was A Picture, the child, but also A Handful. Only Nan thought she was wonderful and wished she had a daughter just like her.

But she only had Michael with no sign of any others, and her life was now not so different from her sisters' even if once she'd sparkled like Lily's little girl. She was much more comfortably off, she knew that, living in a pleasant, well-equipped and furnished house (though it was only rented) and with a car. Jack certainly earned very much more than either Dave or Arthur, working as he did at Strother's – 'If It's Eyesight Bother Consult Mr Strother!' – but all the same he was hardly the very rich man of Nan's early dreams. She spent her time looking after Michael and the house (though she had a char for the rough work since Jack didn't want her hands to get coarse any more than he had wanted her breasts to sag). Nan was frequently reminded by Arthur of her once-grandiose ideas, and how they had hardly been fulfilled, which she found maddening. She insisted that Jack would be rich, when the war was over. And there was another way

Arthur needled her. Why hadn't Jack joined up? Why wasn't he a general by now with his officer-class accent? Instead he stayed in Carlisle, aged only thirty-four, and made a nice little income from operating within the black market. He offered Arthur whisky but Lily wouldn't let him accept. She was outraged at Jack's wickedness, and even Nan was embarrassed. She wanted Jack to be wealthy but not through any kind of cheating, however minor.

Sometimes Lily would accept eggs and butter from Nan, who claimed to have a surplus, even though she knew really that such largesse in wartime implied sleight of hand. Nan was generous and Lily did not like to spurn this sisterly generosity. Besides, she needed the extra food. She was a good manager but Arthur's wage was difficult to manage on now she had two rapidly growing children and was in permanent fear of having more. Being sensible Lily, she tried to be sensible about this problem, but contraceptive advice even for married women was virtually non-existent in Carlisle in the mid thirties. No good knowing Marie Stopes had opened a birth control clinic in London in 1921, or that a National Birth Control Council had been founded in 1920, or even that in 1939, the year after Lily had her second child, a Family Planning Association had been formed – nonsense to imagine the country immediately covered with Family Planning Clinics. In Carlisle, as in most other cities, there was only a Babies' Welfare Centre where babies were weighed and 'appropriate advice given to the mothers, who are served with a cup of tea and a biscuit for one penny'. The appropriate advice didn't extend to the limitation of families – with the tea and biscuit went just the advice to keep windows in the house open and drink plenty of water.

The only recourse any young mother had was the family

doctor. Lily's was Dr Stephenson, her parents-in-law's family doctor. She disliked him intensely and didn't know why she'd allowed herself to be persuaded to register with him. He was a big, fat, red-faced man, very gruff, totally lacking in any bedside manner. It was acutely embarrassing to go to him. The whole business of birth control upset Lily, but then so did the whole business of sex. But she tried to be brave and after a visit to the dreaded doctor had produced no enlightenment, beyond being told it was her husband's business to take care, she felt there was nothing she could do except try to limit intercourse. She got into the habit, when Arthur was ready to go to bed, of staying up, saying she would just finish the darning. Then she would sit close to the fire and darn and wait and listen and hope to hear him snoring when she would at last join him, slipping between the covers with the greatest caution.

It didn't always work. By October 1940 she knew she was pregnant again and was distraught, in floods of tears. 'It can't be helped,' said the fatalistic Arthur, but she thought it should have been helped. How were they to manage? How could she give three children the kind of upbringing she couldn't even give two? The level of her distress and resentment made her ill. She could hardly cope with the boisterous Margaret who wanted to be on the go all the time. Nan saw a solution. She and Jack were at last married – in May that year, five days before Nan's thirty-third birthday, an extremely quiet register office affair with Michael not present – and she wanted another baby but so far had failed to become pregnant. She would adopt Lily's baby. What could be simpler? But Arthur was outraged and so really was Lily, in spite of her general misery – it was their baby, they would keep it, they were married and respectable and, however hard up, not so poverty-stricken that they had to give in to such an extreme solution. No. Nan could not have their baby. Dr Stephenson gave Lily a tonic to buck her up, and kindly pointed out that this was only her third baby not her thirteenth. This didn't console her. She was listless, mournful. She went through all the motions of looking after her family, never defaulting on the cooking, the washing, the cleaning, but her unhappiness was a blight.

Nan was concerned and tried to be positive. Jack was doing well and money was not short in the Marshallsay household, so she insisted that when Lily's time came she should go into a private maternity home in Stanwix, Carlisle's poshest area, to have her baby, and she would pay. More objections from Arthur who didn't want anyone's charity but Nan tore into him, said this was her *sister*, this was *family*, there was no question of charity for heaven's sake. And Lily was ill, she needed to be cared for. How could she rest if she had the baby at home with Gordon and especially that demanding child Margaret around? Nan threatened Arthur with Lily's total collapse and finally, grudgingly, feeling bitter he could not afford to pay himself, he relented. Lily gave birth to another daughter in the privacy of a home on 22 May 1941. Nan, who took her in and stayed with her, could hardly bear it – another sweet little girl (and maybe this one would stay sweet). Once Lily saw her baby, her resentment vanished. She was still low and worried but the baby wasn't blamed, she was quite forgiven. Nan named her. She suggested the name Rosemary in front of Arthur who immediately vetoed it because it came from her and because it was 'fancy'. He wanted Eileen. Nan then put up Pauline, only this time to Lily first, who then suggested it to Arthur as her own. So Pauline it was, with the fancy Rosemary in the middle, as a sop to Nan, who was triumphant at having pulled a fast one on Arthur.

Three children now and life was hectic, all memories of once having wondered how to fill in the afternoons long gone. Nan came over often with Michael and already Lily could see the difference money made. Michael wanted for nothing – clothes, toys, picture-books, outings – he was totally indulged. Lily knew such material things didn't matter but she was ashamed of how much they mattered to her. She couldn't dress her children as she would have wished, especially as she would have loved to dress Margaret, the way Mother, in the good years, had dressed her and Jean and Nan. The only consolation was that in wartime no one, certainly no child (except for Michael), was well dressed. Clothes were not only costly, if you could get them in the first place, but coupons were needed. Each adult got sixty-six a year for most of the war, and a pair of shoes cost five for a start. All Lily's coupons went on her children, though Nan did make her a new dress after Pauline was born, a plain navy which cost a few for the material. It wasn't a very nice dress either, though Nan did her best – the style predetermined by wartime regulations, where even the number of buttons and width of the seams were laid down. The dress was actually as dreary as Lily felt, in spite of its white collar.

She took her dreariness to church and was comforted just by being there. She'd always liked going to church not only because she believed in God and was a devout Christian but because of the atmosphere. Even in the new St Barnabas's she felt soothed, cut off in the most satisfactory way from the real world and all her troubles. She liked the choir and the vestments and the candles (St Barnabas's, for all its modernity, was High Church) and the singing of hymns in her rich voice, and listening to sermons and lessons being read. Her mind, while she was in church, stopped bothering her. The awful scramble of discontent that was often confusing her settled down and she found some peace. Over and over again she would count her blessings and, listening to the many prayers for the fighting men, and those bereaved by the war, she knew she had many. She had what she had wanted, after all, the home and the children, especially the children, two girls, a boy – what a lucky woman. Nothing else should matter except her family and she hardly dared admit then, at the age of forty, that anything else did. In church she was humble and grateful and tranquil.

That was how the new vicar saw her, quiet Mrs Forster, such a good parishioner. He was the sort of man Lily felt she ought to have married, a professional man, educated. She could see herself as a vicar's wife quite easily (and wistfully). This new vicar wasn't married. He was a pleasant, rather lazy, kind man without much charisma but he had the common touch to a remarkable degree. He went into local pubs and had half a pint of mild and was quite at ease, which is more than could be said for the other patrons who didn't approve of the vicar joining them at all. Arthur thought it scandalous behaviour, he loathed the sight of a dog-collar at the bar, and even Lily was uncomfortable hearing about it, with her fear of drink. She had to work hard to persuade herself that if the mountain (Arthur and Co.) wouldn't come to Mohammed then Mohammed had to go to the mountain, namely the Horse and Farrier pub – or something like that. 'He has to go there to do the Lord's work,' she said piously to Arthur. 'He has to go because he's gasping for a drink, more like,' snorted Arthur.

The new vicar visited Lily at home, as he did all his

parishioners, cycling round the Raffles estate on his regular calls. She was one of his most stalwart supporters, never failing to come to church on Sundays and twice when Communion was given at the morning service. Two of her children were baptized in St Barnabas's and as soon as they were old enough enrolled in Sunday School. Mrs Forster's strong voice could be heard soaring over the mumbles of others and he told her frequently what pleasure it gave him to hear her singing hymns as they should be sung, with vigour and enthusiasm. Mr Forster, it need hardly be said, never darkened the church door and was always at work when the vicar called, as were all the husbands on the estate, at work in the factories mostly. Mrs Forster, the vicar commented to several churchwardens, did not seem like a working man's wife – she was so immaculate in appearance, in how she kept her home, in how she brought up her children. He asked her help with organizing the church bazaar and the Christmas sale of work and she did it most efficiently. This brought them together quite a bit and he gradually realized that for all her outward air of control Mrs Forster must suffer some inner turmoil. She had a facial tic, not very pronounced most of the time but there, an involuntary muscular spasm between her left eye and the corner of her mouth. Every now and again when she was privately, though not obviously, agitated the left side of her face went into this rapid, shuddering, momentarily disfiguring, spasm. Others had noticed it too but no one ever commented on it. Nan and Jean, when they met, discussed it and agreed it had only begun after Mother died, and only become marked after the birth of Pauline. Lily was under strain, they said, but couldn't really understand it. What strain? What was wrong with her?

VII

Lily went to the vicar about Margaret when the child was four and told him how worried she was because her daughter needed to be at school, she was so bright, and yet the starting age was five. Margaret could read already and tried to write and was never finished asking questions. The vicar picked up a copy of the parish magazine, not the most alluring reading matter for a four-year-old, but not at all daunted, indeed eager to show off, Margaret duly read aloud the Bishop's Easter message, stumbling over only a few words. The vicar was impressed. He suggested that Mrs Forster should take Margaret down to Ashley Street Infants School and demonstrate her ability to read and ask if an exception could be made for this exceptional would-be pupil. He would be happy, he said, to put a word in himself, to ring the headmistress and arrange an interview, which he did. Margaret was taken to Ashley Street and given a book to read and asked questions. She enjoyed all the attention very much and Lily was vastly relieved not to be let down. The headmistress said that yes, in the circumstances, she thought an exception could be made and that Margaret could start school in September though she would be only four years and three months old. It was an experiment though – if she could not cope she would have to be removed. Was that understood, asked the stern headmistress sternly. It was a privilege, letting so young a child start school, and she hoped it was appreciated.

It certainly was. It was appreciated by Lily, who now had the exhausting Margaret off her hands for most of the day, and appreciated by Margaret herself to the utmost. She adored school from the moment she began and had no fear of the huge building itself, the same kind of grim red-brick edifice built in the same Gothic style as Lowther Street School, Lily's old school. The playground was a concrete Square, the lavatories were the same kind of freezing outside horrors shared still by all the Board Schools, but inside things had changed. The Infants reception classroom was big and light and it had a chair-swing suspended from the beams of the ceiling and a small see-saw and a sandpit, and bright pictures on the cheerfully painted walls. But it was the books Margaret seized on, many of them, picture-books with easy words, too easy. Margaret zipped through them in no time. There was never any question of her not coping – when her mother came to collect her at the end of each day she was suffering from nothing more of a problem than overexcitement. It proved difficult to explain that there was no school on Saturdays or Sundays. Margaret had to be taken down to Ashley Street to have it proved beyond dispute that the doors were firmly locked.

Then, after six months, in the middle of the now happy Margaret's second term, catastrophe: she was taken away from her beloved school. She and her sister Pauline, aged not quite two, were suddenly taken on the train by their father to Motherwell, to their Aunt Jean. Their father left them with Jean and returned to Carlisle the same day. No explanation was given to the confused Margaret, torn from the school she loved. Nothing made sense to her. Pauline cried inconsolably and, when not weeping, stuck her fingers in her mouth and held her ear with her other hand, her fat little arm crossed over her body as though to comfort herself. Margaret didn't cry. She was said to sulk, her silence taken as a deliberate insult. She was A Big Girl she was told and Big Girls did not sulk. The only words she uttered were 'When can I go back to school?' The answer was always the same: soon. But soon never came. Every day she asked the same question and every day she got the same non-answer, together with the aggrieved reminder that she was having a lovely holiday and should be grateful and happy. Jean became quickly and naturally exasperated – there she was, doing her best, looking after her nieces as well as her own two boys and all she got was mutinous stares from one and tears from the other. Life was hard. Her sons slept in one of the two beds-in-the-wall in the living-room and the girls in the other, and they constantly woke each other up. Dave was on shift work and needed his sleep during the day sometimes and it was impossible to give him peace. She could have stood this if she had received some affection from her nieces in return but she didn't. Pauline wanted only her mother and Margaret her school.

In May Pauline was two and Margaret five within three days of each other. Jean excelled herself by having a party for them. She managed to scrounge an egg to make a birthday cake and icing sugar to ice it with and there were eight pink candles to go on it and orangeade to drink with it – quite a feat of organization and effort in 1943, not to mention the involvement of expense. She bought presents too, a cuddly toy for Pauline and a book for Margaret, and had them properly wrapped up in some tissue paper she'd hoarded. Other children in the Buildings were invited and within the confines of Jean's one room and kitchen games were played. Oh, how hard Jean tried! But though Pauline stopped crying for all of ten minutes, Margaret didn't smile once. She was sulkier than ever in spite of looking so pretty in a dress Nan had made and sent. Jean was furious. She came near to regretting she'd ever taken her difficult nieces, but what choice had she had? She had to help poor Lily, that was what families were for, that was what sisters did, took each other's children when necessary. Arthur couldn't look after them. He had to work to keep his job, and if there was no relative to take the children at times like these then they went into a Home. She and Nan, who had taken Gordon, had had no alternative. They didn't pause to wonder if there might be one, knowing there was not. But Jean wished Nan had taken Margaret all the same. It was true, the child was not in the least like her saintly grandmother after whom she had been so misguidedly named. She was like Nan. But Nan had taken Gordon whose schooling couldn't be interrupted. It didn't matter about disrupting Margaret's as she was only five.

In June 1943 the girls were collected by their father. Their mother didn't rush to welcome them when they got home. All the kissing and hugging was on their side, but they had enough warmth and delight between them to make up for their mother's apparent lack of it. She was very, very quiet, very still. She moved about carefully, as though she might break. And she was thin, very thin. Their father watched her anxiously and warned the children repeatedly about noise. Margaret found it very strange but at least she was home and, better still, back at school. The headmistress was cross that she'd been taken away so abruptly but as Lily frequently said afterwards, what else could she have done?

It is at this time, in 1943, when I was five, that my own real memory begins, real in the sense that I can not only recall actual events but can propel myself back into them, be there again in my Aunt Jean's room-and-kitchen, standing by the window at the back of the Buildings, staring out at the outside staircase and the tops of the wash-houses, while behind me Jean asks me what is the matter. Why am I not playing the party games, all in my honour, and she turns me round and I see her exasperated face and feel her anger and it is a triumph. I feel triumphant, though I don't know why. That is what I call real memory, not at all the same as 'remembering' being taken to Ashley Street School to demonstrate my boasted ability to read. Though, because my mother later told me about it so often, I often claimed to remember it and could easily convince myself that I did.

So I can stop now, writing in the third person, stop retelling stories I was told about the years before I was born, about when I was under five, stop splicing oral history with local history and start instead letting my own version of family lore come into play. I am there, at the centre. What a difference it makes, how dangerous it is.

Quite what was wrong with my mother in the spring of 1943 nobody in my family has ever been prepared to tell me, either then or now. Again and again I would ask my mother why I was taken away from school when I had virtually just started and it had been such a struggle to get me a place. But after the usual 'What else could I do?', there was only 'I was ill', said firmly and always followed by an abrupt leaving of the room or the beginning of some task, the making of tea, the washing, always some activity to hide behind. Nan and Jean, when in adult life I tried them, when I asked what kind of illness my mother had requiring Pauline and me to be sent to Motherwell for two months, pretended forgetfulness which was at obvious odds with their notoriously sharp memories.

Jean would say, 'Oh, you don't want to go bothering yourself about that. Dear me, it was centuries ago. What does it matter?' and Nan, who in general loved to tell things that shouldn't be told, said, 'It's Lily's business,' and resisted temptation for once. My father is still alive. He is ninety-four and his mind is as clear and vigorous as ever, but he plays dumb. He doesn't say he *can't* remember, I notice, but that there is nothing to remember, and that has to be that.

But since this is where I enter the family story as myself it matters to me that I come on to the stage in a cloud of freezing ice, obscured by that deliberate suppression of the truth which my grandmother turns out to have been so good at. Probably something is being made of very little. I suspect my mother may have had some kind of nervous breakdown and that attached to it, in 1943, was the same sort of stigma as attached to the bearing of an illegitimate child, the same sort of social pressure to find this shameful. Only medical records would prove whether I am right and they do not exist. Most doctors keep records for ten years after a patient's death and then destroy them and it was thirteen years after my mother's death that I began trying to check her health in 1943. She may only have had some sort of collapse and stayed at home, with rest the only treatment, or perhaps she was hospitalized. Carlisle's mental hospital, Garlands, only releases records a hundred years after the death of the patient, so goodbye all hope of finding out anything that way.

Still, I am convinced my mother's illness was mental rather than physical. After we came back from Motherwell my father's most oft repeated instruction was 'Don't upset your mother, or else'. Or else what? He often finished orders with this 'or else' in a mildly threatening way, but there seemed some vague extra significance about this particular 'or else'.

My mother was not to be upset, ever. We, the children, understood that, if not the reason for it. I tried to keep to myself anything that might upset her and that came to mean everything that troubled me.

Soon after I went back to school I had a finger which turned septic – I'd cut it in the garden – and my mother took me to a clinic in George Street. It was for mothers and young children and mainly dealt with routine weighings and inspections, but on Wednesdays, at nine o'clock, it also dealt with minor ailments and injuries. Why I was taken with my sore finger to this clinic, and not to Dr Stephenson or the Outpatients at the Infirmary, reflected my mother's dislike and distrust of both. She was more comfortable, less intimidated, using the clinic and that was more than a little due to the fact that it was mainly staffed by women doctors and nurses and health visitors. She was still overawed, though, by the white coats and very tense indeed, very anxious that I should behave properly and that I should understand how quiet I should be.

This was odd because the clinic was noisy. It echoed with shrieks and roars and all the staff were constantly shouting to be heard above the din. We sat on a hard wooden bench and watched and listened as doors were banged open and shut and solid shoes thumped the brown linoleum as they marched to and fro. Bowls, enamel bowls, were carried in and out of rooms whose interiors were never seen, so quick was the door-slamming, bowls often covered with muslin cloth and those cloths sometimes stained red and handled with distaste, held far away from the body. There was a lot of clattering, the harsh metallic sound of steel instruments being dropped on to trays and tables and into containers. Over everything hung the smell of disinfectant and iodine and some other strange, sickly, cloying smell. I was frightened and my mother, sitting rigid beside me, clearly nervous and worried herself, the tic in her face hardly leaving her poor cheek alone, didn't help. I wanted to go home but I didn't say so nor did I cry. My mother had explained, gently and patiently, that my finger had to be looked at because there was something very wrong with it and at this clinic it could be made better. It was my index finger, on my right hand, and it was massively swollen and painful and had not responded to my mother's careful attentions. She'd had me soaking the finger in a pudding bowl of water and salt as hot as I could bear it. She'd even tried a poultice, a revolting affair of soaked bread wrapped up in a bandage. But nothing had done any good and now, the pain worse, the swelling spreading down the finger and the fingernail black, professional help was needed. I understood all that. There was no escape.

Our turn did not come for a long, harrowing time, long enough to watch one boy of about my age be carried screaming into the room everyone sooner or later disappeared into and, after an agonizing interval of bull-like roars, followed by a silence that was just as alarming, emerge limp and white-faced in his mother's arms, his eyes closed. My heart thudded and real fear gripped me so that I began to shake. What did they do in that room? My mother put her arm round me and squeezed me to comfort me but I was beyond her sympathy. I knew she was powerless. She was in the hands of these big, bustling women who strode around the clinic in such a hurry, their white coats flapping. They could do what they liked to me and my mother could not stop them. The worst fear I had, worse than the thought of the pain to come, was of being separated from my mother, which is exactly what happened. 'Next!' one of the nurses roared, and it was my turn. My mother stood up with me but was told I was A Big Girl and it was only a finger and I didn't look as if I was going to be silly and make a fuss, so it would be better if I went in on my own. Obediently, my mother let go of my hand. Just as obediently, I trotted after the nurse who told me that I was A Good Girl, not like some. For once, praise sounded hollow even to my five-year-old ears. I wished I had the courage to behave as my insides wanted me to, to scream as the boy had done.

The doctor was busy having a cup of tea and a biscuit. She crunched the biscuit and eyed me through her wire-rimmed spectacles and repeated what the nurse had said, that I was both A Big Girl and A Good Girl, and she threw in A Bonny Girl too. When she'd brushed the biscuit crumbs off her coat she looked at my finger and said what my mother had already said, it was a cut gone septic. To my joy, she then told the nurse to 'bring the mother in'. Once brought in, flushed and trying to look dignified, though her facial tic worked against her again, my mother was treated to a lecture on hygiene – my mother, the most fastidious practiser of hygiene imaginable. She went redder and redder, but speaking in a very quiet voice said she always washed cuts and put Dettol on them and had done so in this case, and had dressed this cut finger and changed the dressing every day and – but the doctor interrupted at this point, clearly realizing at last that she was not dealing with some ignorant woman. My mother, as ever, looked smarter and neater than everyone else around her even if her clothes were old. A little battle had been fought and, though I didn't understand what it was about, I felt happier because my mother had seemed stronger. But not for long. The doctor said my finger would have to be lanced and would my mother please hold my hand steady. My mother took hold of my hand and smiled at me encouragingly but all her short-lived strength of mind had gone and, as she told me to close my eyes and take a deep breath and it would all be over in a minute, I saw that it had. I'd seen the doctor select a thin, sharp-looking instrument and I knew what was going to happen and that it would hurt dreadfully and there was nothing my mother could do about it. I began to pull my finger back and said I didn't want it to hurt. 'It'll hurt more if we don't get the poison out,' the doctor said (just as my father had done, only to be furiously reprimanded by my mother, but she didn't now reprimand the doctor). 'No,' I said, 'no,' and hid my finger behind my back. 'Oh dear,' said the nurse to the doctor, who was smiling, 'and we thought she was A Good Girl, didn't we? Maybe Mummy had better go and let me hold her.' Now I was bawling and crying and clinging frantically to my mother but it made no difference. The strong nurse prised me from her arms and I heard her say, 'Out you go, Mother!' and she went.

It was all over, as promised, in a flash, a moment of searing pain quite unlike the throbbing before, and then some cool, soothing substance was applied to the finger and a bandage put on and a leather sheath over it. The nurse told me to run along and find my mother outside. I tried, but only got as far as the door and fainted instead, to everyone's interest – five, it seems, is too young for a faint. My mother recalled the wonder of it for years, as well as the drama, this five-year-old staggering out of the room and slowly crumpling up in a heap on the shiny floor of the corridor. 'It was scandalous,' my mother always ended, 'the way they treated us.' But then the entire medical profession was always thought scandalously callous or useless. My mother saw herself as let down over

1. Lilian, aged five, Thomas Hind, Jane (known as Jean), aged two, and Margaret Ann Hind

2. Thomas Hind standing on the tram steps with Lilian, aged four, behind the driver
(CUMBRIA COUNTY LIBRARY)

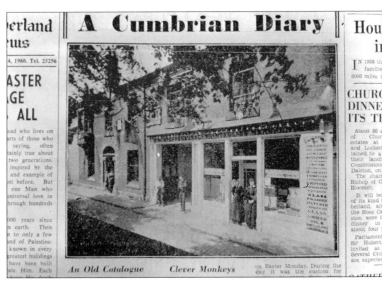

A Cumbrian Diary

An Old Catalogue   *Clever Monkeys*

3. Number 4 Paternoster Row (*left*) where Margaret Ann worked as a domestic servant for the Stephenson family. The family's business premises adjoin the house (*right*)
(CUMBERLAND NEWS)

4. The inside view of Carlisle's covered market showing traders selling flowers, eggs, butter, etcetera, *circa* 1901. Thomas Hind's butcher stalls were higher up, beyond this part
(CUMBRIA COUNTY LIBRARY)

5. Jane (Jean), aged eight, Lilian, aged eleven, and Annie (Nan), aged four. Their beautiful dresses were made by Margaret Ann Hind

6. Lilian, aged twenty-five, when she was working in the Public Health Department

7. A panoramic view of Caldewgate from the tower of Trinity Church. Margaret Ann was born in St John Street, a turning on the right at the end of this street
(CUMBRIA COUNTY LIBRARY)

8. The wedding photo, 11 April 1931 *(left to right)*: Agnes Forster, George Forster, Arthur, Lilian, Margaret Ann

9. A holiday photograph of the charabanc leaving Scarborough in 1931. Lilian and Arthur are in the second row from the back

10. Lilian, me, aged seven, and Pauline, aged four

11. Jack, looking rakish even on the beach, and Nan, elegant as ever

12. Jack and Nan, still glamorous in their early forties

13. Family group on the sea front at Silloth, 1951: (*middle row*) Michael, Jack, me, Nan, Lilian (*behind*) Dave and Arthur (*front*) Pauline

14. Lilian aged forty-five

15. Me on the set of *Georgy Girl*, aged twenty-eight

and over again, and the fear of doctors and hospitals and clinics grew with her rage and humiliation. Never, ever, were members of this medical profession seen as compassionate, kindly people. No. They had power over her but were invariably thought to have misused it. Their knowledge was admitted but their use of it deeply suspect. My mother, for all her intelligence, never let a doctor know of her contempt. She never questioned the decision of any doctor because she was much too afraid of her own ignorance being exposed and because doctors had rank and she did not. Often her demands (though never voiced) were for miracles. They were unreasonable and no doctor could have fulfilled them, but there were many times when she just craved a detailed explanation and did not have the nerve to insist on it (and it was certainly not in her experience freely offered). So the whole object in our family life became to keep away from all doctors. Forced to succumb and put herself at the mercy of one, my mother got in a state at once.

Waiting-rooms made her agitation worse, especially Dr Stephenson's. It was such a dreary, funereal place, not the slightest attempt made to supply either colour, comfort or distraction. We began tip-toeing and whispering as soon as we entered the big outer door and by the time we were in the actual waiting-room our voices had dried up with apprehension. It was a huge room, high-ceilinged, with big windows shrouded in net curtains, and in the centre was an enormous mahogany table with a glass vase (empty) on a lace mat laid not quite halfway down. We sat on leather-covered dining-room chairs, the leather stretched so tightly over the seats that it squeaked when our bottoms touched them. It felt strange, sitting on these chairs, ranged round the walls, when they were so far from the table they matched. There was no reading matter except for leaflets about such compelling subjects as head lice. The silence was intense, disturbed only by fidgeting, by the ticking of the imposing clock in the hall, and by nervous coughing, some of it my mother's. It was holier than St Barnabas's church and just as cold. But my mother would always say how lucky we were to have doctors who no longer charged for their services and that sitting in that awful room was a privilege and one her mother could have done with and would have been thankful for – bad enough being ill without the additional worry of having to pay to be better.

VIII

When the war ended, I was seven. Lily was forty-four, Jean forty and Nan thirty-six. Nothing much changed for any of them except that Arthur was back full-time at the Metal Box and Jack no longer had a nice little earner exploiting the black market (though that continued for a bit longer). The war, in my family, had meant so little. No men had been killed or wounded or imprisoned nor were they returning victorious. The war had meant rationing and that was about all, though Jean had heard Glasgow being bombed and knew it was about something rather more. The women didn't have to learn how to slip back into normal life because, in their particular cases, they had hardly had it interrupted.

Normal life for my mother was dull. This dullness was reflected in the weekly letters she wrote to Jean in Motherwell, but nevertheless she enjoyed writing them. I liked to sit and watch. It was a formal business, this weekly letter-writing and it impressed me. My mother looked so important doing it. She would spread a felt undercloth on the living-room table and put a sheet of blotting paper on top of it and then a bottle of Quink ink and a pad of blue Basildon Bond notepaper, and then she'd pick up her blue and black Conway Stewart fountain-pen and start. Her handwriting was fluent and vigorous, quite large, both up and down strokes firm and clear, and while she was writing there was no hesitation. It was all done at speed. I had to sit quietly so as not to spoil her concentration, but when she'd finished I'd ask what she'd written about. The answer would be 'nothing'. Watching her fold the four or five sheets up, written on both sides, I'd protest – how could she have written *nothing*, the paper would be blank if she'd written nothing. 'Nothing worthwhile,' she'd say, 'but Jean likes to read anything.'

So did she. Jean's letters, also about nothing worthwhile, were little events. My mother would look for her letter arriving, on Tuesdays, and the moment it came slip it unopened into her apron pocket to save for later. It was a treat, kept for the afternoons, when the washing and cleaning were done. She'd sit with a cup of tea, all nicely changed into her afternoon skirt and blouse, and read Jean's account of wash-day and how the prop had collapsed and dirtied an entire load, and about how Mary next door had had a bad asthma attack, and how Dave was exhausted what with his long shifts and then studying at night school to become an optician like Jack, and how she'd been on the bus to Glasgow but hadn't bought anything, and how cold it had been ... More or less the same prosaic account every week. My mother always finished these letters looking faintly disappointed. Jean's life was so similar to her own and seeing it described, week after week, only served to emphasize her own discontent. What on earth did either of them have to write about except what women living in a tightly structured domestic slavery always have to write about? Nothing. Nan said she didn't know why they bothered. These letters of her sisters bored her to death. She never wrote to Jean but then, apart from depending on Lily to write for both of them, she was not speaking to Jean (now that would have made a good letter but it was never written down). They had had a row, about food. Jean and her family had come to stay with Lily and had not brought any rations. Nan noticed and was furious – Lily had a bigger family to feed and couldn't afford to use her rations for Jean – and tackled her sister. Jean in turn was furious and denied she had scrounged off her sister – and so began a feud which lasted almost a decade. Lily was the go-between, constantly trying to make peace between her sisters and reminding them how their mother had loathed family disharmony more than anything. She didn't know how they could keep it up. (My father did, though – he had just begun not speaking to his only brother and with remarkable staying-power kept it up thirty years. I have still not been told the reason for this total breakdown of communication, though I ask all the time.)

Occasionally, Lily and Jean had something beyond the absolute ordinary to write to each other about. The letters were thicker and livelier when Nan moved from Carlisle to Nottingham. There was so much to comment on. Nottingham, for a start – it might as well have been the moon, it was thought of by the sisters as so outlandish. When Jean went to Motherwell it was near Glasgow, of which everyone in Carlisle had heard, but *Nottingham*? Visions of forests and Robin Hood and that was all. Nan was reported by Lily to be excited. Nottingham, wherever it was, was south and to move south was smart. And Jack was moving there to manage his own shop which, Nan said, would soon become a chain of shops. However, Lily also reported to Jean that Nan and Jack were to live above this shop at first, only at first, but still, *above a shop* . . . Michael wouldn't be with them when they moved. He was being sent away to prep school. Well, that certainly had the pen flying. It was scandalous. Poor little Michael, already an excitable child, difficult, prone to bronchial trouble and never properly recovered from a terrible accident when he was eighteen months old. He'd fallen on the doorstep and smashed a milk bottle and the glass sliced deeply into his upper lip – the horror, the agony of it. The lip was stitched up but Michael's sweet little face was disfigured for life, the stitched-up area giving the impression of a hare-lip badly corrected. And now he was being sent away, only seven. How could Nan allow it?

It was a topic for open discussion not just in letters but in our house. I asked what prep school was and why Michael had to go. Privately, I thought the idea of being at school all the time utterly desirable, but I managed not to say so out of loyalty to my mother – if I said what I felt, that it sounded a good idea, people might think I wanted to leave my mother and it would hurt her. Prep school, my mother explained, meant preparatory school, a school to prepare pupils for entry to public schools at thirteen. Jack had gone to one and then on to Worksop, of which no one had ever heard, but my mother said it was 'a bit down' from Eton and we'd heard of that, somehow. Michael had to go to a prep school or he wouldn't get into Worksop and become a gentleman like Jack. Nan couldn't prevent him being sent away because Jack was boss. This surprised me. I'd thought Nan was boss. She always seemed to be. But no, apparently Jack held the purse-strings, as it was referred to, and what he said went. Very interesting to me. Everything to do with Michael's education was interesting. While in Carlisle, he'd gone to the fee-paying Carlisle High School Kindergarten, which for reasons I'd never understood upset my mother. She muttered about wishing her children could have that chance. What chance? Michael could hardly read and I could. He definitely (at six) couldn't write properly and I could. Jack knew this. He was forever getting me to read his newspaper to him and then passing it to Michael and asking him to do the same and when Michael couldn't, laughing. Cruel and silly, but exciting when an enraged cousin Michael tore the newspaper up while I sat modestly with downcast eyes.

Nan was going to be a lady of leisure in Nottingham, so my mother said. She'd only have a flat to clean and would have the charlady she'd always had. Jack didn't want her ruining her lovely hands, remember. Lily's and Jean's were already ruined. All that washing and scrubbing with never a thought of rubber gloves; who had time or money to go bothering with those?) If Michael was away at school she would have nothing to do except cook and shop, and then only for two people and with sufficient money. Plenty of time for that forty winks she'd begun to have lately, a habit which had Lily and Jean convulsed, though I could never discern quite why. They'd laugh when they were together discussing Nan's forty winks, how she'd literally lie down with a newspaper over her face, and keep absolutely still, after lunch each day. It was to keep her young – Lily's and Jean's laughter would increase at this point and they would always end with one of them saying to another, 'Really, isn't Nan annoying?'

Annoying or not, Lily knew she would miss her. Their own mother had always longed for a sister. After a mother it was what women most needed in life and she had had neither. 'You're all lucky,' Margaret Ann evidently used to tell her three daughters. 'You're twice blessed with two sisters apiece.' It didn't matter how different sisters were in personality or abilities, they could be relied upon in a way no one else in a working-class culture could be. Not that Lily had ever relied on Nan but on the other hand she had often felt the benefit of Nan's presence. She'd been there, in Carlisle, for nearly ten years now, visiting twice a week and helping in emergencies. She'd sewed for us, making Pauline and me the dresses my mother couldn't afford, making costumes for plays at school – never had there been an archangel with wings like mine in the Nativity play, wonderful contraptions of gauze and wire – making others for fancy dress competitions (her Carmen Miranda outfit, the head-dress a miracle of felt fruits, won me first prize). She took me for picnics too, in the car to Silloth, company for Michael. In her own way, Nan had been good. 'She can afford to be,' said Arthur, but Lily jumped on him – no need to spoil Nan's thoughtfulness, her generosity. She would be missed; there was no substitute for her support. My mother had women friends, but friends were not the same. They were not *family*.

My mother had two categories of friends, those from her office days and neighbours. She very occasionally went into the Public Health Department to see those few friends who after all this time were still there and some of them visited her. One of them was a man, Leonard Oates, who had started as an office junior two years before she left, Uncle Len to us. My father smirked when Len came, which my mother hated. Len was apparently known to have been sweet on my mother, which my father found amusing, partly because he was ten years her junior and partly because – very veiled hint, this, and quite untrue – he suspected Len of being a 'nancy boy'. Len was quiet, gentle, refined, rather silent and a bit timid. My mother liked to see him. They'd have slow, careful conversations about things to do with mutual office friends, about the old days. Len went on exotic holidays which my mother loved to hear about. ('He can afford to,' Arthur said again, and was told to shut up.)

But the friends I knew more about were the neighbours.

Mrs Gillespie lived across the road in one of those private estate houses my mother had always envied (though it was only rented). Mr Gillespie worked as a railway clerk so the Gillespies were a cut above the blue-collar workers in Raffles. Mrs Gillespie – Ruby, though never called that, the prefix kept always in place, then – was a bustling, energetic figure, more important to me than to my mother. Mrs Gillespie was fond of what she called 'hikes', which sounded so adventurous and exciting even if they turned out to be the same familiar walks along the river Caldew, and she was forever changing her furniture around and decorating and making things. She had one son, Colin, my age, and encouraged me to come over to play. I went eagerly but not much playing with Colin went on. He'd open the door a crack, stare gloomily at me and ask what I wanted. I always had to have some excuse to have come over, something apart from that lame-sounding 'Your mam said I could.' Mrs Gillespie would eventually realize I was on the doorstep and bustle along the hall and welcome me in. I played with her most satisfactorily. She was a one-woman handicraft industry, always with bundles of raffia ready to show me how to make baskets and mats, always ready to get out paper and paints and let me slosh about (Colin didn't slosh, he was a good artist). I couldn't get into the Gillespies' house quick enough or for long enough. 'You'd think she lived there,' my father grumbled, and I was always about to say I wished I did when I'd catch sight of my mother's face and desist.

Noticeably, my mother had no friends on the Raffles estate itself. She was perfectly neighbourly but not exactly a friend of any woman on our side of Orton Road, the demarcation line between council and private housing. She was a good neighbour though. By the time I was old enough to realize it, she had become the one sent for in every sort of emergency, births and deaths a speciality. Any woman who went into labour and was afraid the midwife or the ambulance wouldn't come in time would send for Mrs Forster – quick, tell her to come – and my mother always answered the call. She delivered our next-door neighbour's baby one memorable day, a day of such drama I could hardly bear the ordinariness of the day that followed it. The husband rushed into our back kitchen, just as we were getting ready for school, yelling that Mary was giving birth right there on the floor and no nurse had arrived, so my mother rushed back with him. I wished I could go with her but had to be content with eavesdropping, much later, on my mother's account of the birth, and her part in it, as related to Mrs Gillespie. All she'd done, my mother said, was wash her hands and put a clean towel under Mary and a pillow under her head and then she'd concentrated on keeping her calm and urging her not to push and assuring her the doctor would be there soon. He wasn't actually there soon but it didn't matter because in spite of Mary trying not to push the baby was born quickly and easily and my mother held her up by her ankles and slapped her behind as she'd seen the midwife deal with her own babies and then she'd cleared her nose and mouth of mucus and wrapped her in another towel. My mother kept saying she'd done nothing, really, nothing, but she was the talk of the estate, the stories of what she'd done growing by the minute. It was the same with deaths. My mother laid people out. She was called in to put cotton wool in all the various orifices and to wash the bodies. For once, Arthur and Nan were in complete agreement. They were revolted and didn't know how she could. Arthur said she was wearing herself out and doing such things was not good for her. But still people came in times of crisis and my mother always responded. At Christmas the tokens of appreciation were almost embarrassing – flowers, chocolates, cakes, all from grateful beneficiaries of Lily's competence and kindness.

Sometimes she was called upon to do something much more difficult than attend births or lay out bodies. Raffles, in the post-Second-World-War period, had become a different place. It was no longer spoken of in garden-city terms but as an estate getting rougher all the time for reasons no one understood. There were some problem families now living on it and some notoriously violent men. A child would come screaming to our back door or, worse still, a woman herself, a woman already bleeding from a smack in the mouth or blow to the nose. My father, if he was there, would instruct my mother to ignore the screams and the rattling of our latch – she should mind her own business, keep out of it – but she never did. She'd go off with the child or pull the woman into her kitchen and bathe her wounds and soothe her while I watched – though told sharply to go back into the living-room and close the door at once, please. I'd hear my father say, 'Don't get involved. Now I've warned you, Lily,' but my mother didn't bother replying. Eventually, the woman would stop sobbing and going over what had happened – I could never hear the details clearly enough, to my fury, and my mother would never repeat them – and then she'd start worrying about her children, whom she'd left at 'his' mercy in her panic, and my mother would go back with her. I offered to accompany her but my services were rejected and I'd be told once more, angrily, to go inside and stay there. When my mother came back she'd be very quiet and sad and look shaken. She wouldn't answer any of my urgent questions – I wanted to know most of all why the woman had gone back to this man who'd hit her. My mother would only say that the woman had no money and nowhere to go and then I'd switch to asking why she hadn't rung the police and had this brute put in prison. 'You don't understand,' my mother would say wearily. I certainly didn't.

What I did understand, though, was that my mother's life seemed one of complete self-abnegation. And I was beginning to understand something else: I wasn't going to be like her. Everything Lily did was not only for the good and comfort of others but actually went against her own interests. It had crossed her mind sometimes, she'd admit, that she should have been a nurse. She would like to have ministered to the sick properly, to have had some proper training. Too late by the time she realized this caring instinct was so strong in her and needed a more structured and satisfying outlet. She'd made her choice and that choice was to have a home and children and a husband, and it was no good pining after alternative careers. The little bouts of being an Angel of Mercy were a relief from the drudgery of her routine. No woman exists who wants to start the day off standing in a freezing cold wash-house supervising a monstrous boiler, but my mother more than most was made wretched by this kind of hard work as a housewife. All around her, on the Raffles estate in the 1940s, women were doing precisely the same, not a washing-machine between them, but none can have felt any more disappointed to be doing it than my mother. She'd been brought up to accept her lot by Margaret Ann, but she couldn't, she just could not. She still had expectations of something else, something better in life, and she wanted it so badly. I saw – no, I felt – that wanting. I tried to work out why a woman as beautiful (to me) and clever and good and kind didn't have what she wanted even if I didn't know what

150

it was she did want. How had this state of affairs come about? I decided it was because she had made one fatal mistake: she'd got married. Simple. She'd got married and then had children, all part of being married and inevitable, I thought, and trapped herself. The very thing that had released my grandmother (though I didn't know this then) had trapped my mother. The conclusion was obvious. I would not marry and therefore would not have children. I would keep out of the trap and I'd be safe. I hadn't it in me to be a selfless wife and mother and carer. I'd escape. To where? I'd no idea, but quite early I sensed I might do it through school. I felt that somehow the secret was to stay in the school world and cut myself off from this other world my mother was so unhappy in, the home world. The circumstances of my mother's life and her unhappiness were the spur to make my own life into something different. I would not and could not be like her and nor, really, did I want to be, even if I thought she was so admirable.

As if my mother wasn't already doing enough, a great deal of her time towards the end of the forties became taken up with looking after Agnes, her mother-in-law. Agnes was suffering from rheumatoid arthritis. She was crippled with it. First her fingers grew gnarled and twisted until they bent right back and she couldn't use them and then her hips were afflicted and she couldn't walk. She lay in a bed set up in a corner of the living-room at the back of her house. It was beside a window but all she could see through it, if she could make out anything through the net curtain, was the narrow concrete yard, the brick walls, the two doors going into lavatory and wash-house. She lay in that bed propped up by pillows under the devoted and constant but far from tender care of her husband George. He fed Agnes, washed her, helped her on and off the commode (roughly, he was clumsy by nature). My mother visited every other afternoon, taking my sister and me after school. She brought cakes and scones she'd baked, and magazines – the parish magazine mostly – and she tried to make Agnes more comfortable. She took the sheets home and the nightdresses and returned them with bunches of lilac and stock and sweet-smelling roses.

They were part of the battle against the general smell in Agnes's room. It was dreadful, a stink not a smell. The window was never opened, the fire always on (Agnes was always cold) and the commode was never emptied regularly enough. My mother stayed an hour at least and tried to ease her mother-in-law's pain. She brushed her hair gently, rubbed various ointments on her wasted limbs, changed her nightdress and bedjacket, and talked to her while George took a break in his allotment. Agnes confided in Lily, she wept, she voiced her misery and despair, and my mother listened and sometimes cried herself. I could hardly stand these visits. Agnes loved to see us, her granddaughters, but we did not love to see her. We hated it. She frightened us. She was like a witch with her poor hands and dreadful pallor and moans and smells. I even found it a strain to be in the same room as her at all – there was neither pity nor sympathy coming from me for her, only horror. I'd hear Agnes call Lily an angel and bless the day Arthur married her. She was an angel, a saint. It was her role and she filled it ungrudgingly, but I was not going to do the same, never, never. It appalled me.

On Sundays my father took his turn at visiting his mother, taking my sister and me yet again. (Gordon never seemed to be included – he was nearly always off at Scout camp.) We walked the mile to Richardson Street, dressed in our best,

and sat in the back room for precisely half an hour: another
ordeal, more torment, much harder to endure without our
mother. George gave us tests, mental arithmetic tests. I
snapped out the answers and soon Pauline was just as quick
and we'd get a penny for every correct answer. At the end of
the half hour, depending on how well we'd behaved, we'd
get either two shillings or a tin of John West salmon. George
had hoarded it in preparation for the war; he had a cupboard
full of it. If we'd been 'bad', we got nothing. Being 'bad' meant
we'd fidgeted, asked too often if it was time to go yet, held
our noses against the smell, not smiled, not recited poems
when asked, touched the piano or the china in the parlour
next door when we wandered into it. I never touched the
piano but Pauline did. She longed to learn how to play it but
we had no piano at home and our grandparents wouldn't let
her play this one because it was too precious. When she could
play properly, like her mother Lily, then she could come and
play it (but how was she to learn without access to a piano —
it was a puzzle).

I preferred to touch the china. A set of a dozen of everything, fine bone china, kept locked away in a huge glass-
fronted cabinet. But I knew where the key was kept and I'd
take it out of the Toby jug on the mantelpiece and open the
cabinet and finger the china, heart pounding in case it broke.
I liked the colours — deep burnt orange and dark blue and
gold — and the way I could see light through the cups when I
daringly held them up. Agnes had said I could have it all
when I married, but since I was never going to marry, not
even to gain the Crown Derby, that wasn't much use.
Repeatedly I'd remind myself I wasn't going to be like my
mother. There she was, answering everyone's demands —
Agnes's, her husband's, her children's, her neighbours', her

church's – and getting nothing in return. Nobody, so far as I could see, lavished the same kind of care on my mother as she lavished on them. Her very goodness maddened me. It made me cross and resentful but I didn't know why. Why didn't I want to emulate her? When I tried I was a failure, to my mother's sorrow.

One way I tried was by agreeing to go alone to my grandmother's on Saturday afternoons and read to her. I made enough fuss about it but I went, to please my mother and not in the least to be kind to my grandmother. What I read to her was *The People's Friend*. I liked to read anything but even so found *The People's Friend* dreary. There was nothing attractive about this magazine to an eight-year-old – the age I started this reading aloud – but Agnes liked it read literally cover to cover, starting with the advertisement for soap on the front. I'd drone through not only the stories (her favourites were those by Annie S. Swan, scores of them) but instructions as to How to Knit Fluffy Mitts For the Cold-Fingered Brigade (though her hands were so crippled she would not knit again), or how to make new frocks 'and cheer the gloom away'. There were always uplifting letters in each issue and a special corner for children which I was supposed to find entertaining and never did. The whole magazine was written in tiny print, three columns to a page, single spacing. I used to try to persuade my grandfather to buy *Picture Post* for me to read aloud instead, but he wouldn't. *Picture Post* was twice the price of *The People's Friend* and anyway he was only going to buy what my grandmother had herself once regularly bought, no newfangled, expensive magazines. But sometimes my mother would buy, and send me with, *Picture Post* and I'd read that far more enthusiastic-ally, though what I wanted it for was the pictures of the film stars it usually had in it. There was actually a fair amount of reading matter too, long and serious articles, and my grandfather would take a malicious delight in making me read every word knowing I could make little sense of screeds on Russian foreign policy or discussions on the H-bomb. When I stumbled, he'd laugh and tell me to get back to *The People's Friend* and stop trying to be something I wasn't.

What I knew I wasn't, apart from clever enough to understand these articles, was a nice little girl which is what my mother wanted me to be. I still looked nice, true. I had long, thick, fair hair and a beautiful complexion and I was tall for my age, but I wasn't nice. I was by then already difficult, moody. I'd left behind that pretty little dear they'd all drooled over, even when I reminded them of Nan. Once I tried to strangle another girl, or so she and her mother alleged. I was scornful. I explained that I'd only been showing Angela *how* to strangle someone if she should so desire and what if there were bruises all round her neck? But my mother was shocked. She looked aghast and then sorrowful and said how upset she was. Nice little girls did not act like this, and God would be upset too. I know I laughed when she expected me to cry. But I was furious. It was stupid of her to think I'd really tried to strangle silly old Angela. If my mother wanted to believe that nonsense then I was determined to let her. 'I wish I had strangled her,' I boasted, 'then I could go to prison and get away from here.' My mother said she didn't know what to do with me, she couldn't imagine what would become of me. She said all she had ever wanted to do was please her own mother and help her. All I seemed to want to do was cause trouble.

Except at school. At school I was bright-faced, eager, absolutely desperate to please. Whenever my mother went there – not often, parents were rarely invited in – she'd be astonished by the paean of praise for both my ability and behaviour. Here, at least, I was like her. But she always emphasized that, though she was pleased, I mustn't think being clever was as important as being nice and good. She wanted a sweet, kind, thoughtful, willing-to-help daughter ready to follow in her footsteps in that respect. Instead, I was already walking away from this calling. I didn't want to learn to be any kind of carer. I wouldn't accept that my role as a female was to serve on the domestic front. My father raged against my disobedience. I wouldn't wash dishes, set and clear tables, bring the coal in, or in any other ways help my mother. He slapped me but I withstood these not-very-hard slaps easily, so he bought a leather strap with thin thongs at the end and used that on the back of my legs when I goaded him, and goading was exactly what I did. Soon, in efforts not to help in the house, I was trying to stay out all the time, mainly by going to the Gillespies. If I had to be at home I read my library books. I'd sit absorbed, hearing nothing, until my father would snatch the book away and shout, 'Get your nose out of that book and help your mam, or else!'

IX

Towards the end of 1948 'or else' took on a more sinister meaning. My mother was going into hospital. The announcement was made in doom-laden tones – 'Your mam has to go into the City General' – by my father. I didn't ask him why. I didn't want to give him what I felt was the satisfaction of realizing how afraid I was, that for once I wasn't going to say pertly, 'Couldn't care less.' I asked her, later. The answer was, 'For an operation.' What was an operation? My mother seemed so evasive, almost shifty, that I couldn't embarrass her by asking more questions. An operation. In the City General. People died in hospitals sometimes. If my mother died, what would I do? A mother was essential to life, or at least my mother to my life. It wasn't just self-interest which made the thought of my mother possibly dying so terrifying, it was because I loved her then so passionately. My poor mother, all that caring for other people and now in return an operation.

Yet on the Sunday before the Monday she was to go into hospital I was particularly difficult and objectionable. On Sundays we often had rice pudding, my father's only taste in puddings (except for ice-cream). I hated it. On that Sunday we had it, all glutinous in its oblong enamel dish, the edges of the white mess slightly burned, just as my father liked it. My mother knew she couldn't miss me out entirely, in spite of my loathing of this pudding, because my father would insist, for obscure reasons of his own, mostly to do with 'taming' me, that I had to eat some. She gave me a very small portion but even so my stomach heaved at the sight of the slippy-sloppy contents of my bowl (such a pity I'd never heard of 'Whatever's the matter with Mary Jane?/It's lovely rice pudding for dinner again'). My father ate his with enormous noisy relish and still I hadn't touched my spoonful. The usual battle commenced. He glared at me and ordered me to eat up. I glared at the rice pudding and stirred it round and round. He ordered me to stop messing about. I closed my eyes. My mother said, 'Please, Arthur, she doesn't like it.' 'She'll like what's put in front of her,' my father said. 'Wasting good food. She's spoiled.' 'Please, Margaret,' my mother pleaded, 'just one spoonful.' I shook my head. We all sat there half an hour, an hour, long enough for the rice pudding to be quite cold and even more nauseating. Finally, my father lost his temper and yelled, 'You're making your mam ill, you are! And it's her operation tomorrow. You'd better eat that damned pudding, or else! You'd better hope she comes back!'

Rice pudding – operation – not coming back. The impact of this curious logic was tremendous. It made perfect sense. I ran out of the house, heart thudding, my mother's death owing to my failure to consume rice pudding already a fact. When I had to return home, after hours of demented wandering round the estate, I tried hard to be quiet and helpful. So did my father. He'd obviously been told off by my mother and rice pudding wasn't mentioned. The evening was spent with us being given instructions as to how to manage during the next two weeks. Mrs Gillespie would come over each morning and plait my hair. Gordon, who had just started work in a chemist's shop, would leave just before Mrs Gillespie came and in between Pauline and I would organize our own bowls of Weetabix, heating the milk for them and taking *great* care with the lighting of the gas cooker. After school, we would make our own tea, just sandwiches, taking *great* care with the bread knife, and Mrs Gillespie would pop in around five, though it was not exactly clear why. We went through it all several times, together with other instructions to do with washing and changing our clothes and saying our prayers and closing the back door properly.

The whole two weeks were wretched. The house seemed lifeless, barren, everything about it cold and dismal to the point of being utterly alien. Nothing had changed but because my mother was not there everything had changed. We were silent and unnaturally polite. I started having nightmares, dreaming that everything in the bedroom that was brown – bedstead, chest of drawers, the linoleum on the floor – was blood. My father, exhausted from his long hours in the factory, and hospital visiting afterwards, never heard me as I woke screaming and sobbing and gradually calmed myself. Once, coming out of my blood-filled nightmare, I was violently sick and vomited into the bath, imagining I'd eaten rice pudding. In the morning the sick had frozen, the night was so cold, and I had to boil kettles of water and take them upstairs and dissolve the mess before it would go down the plug hole. Oh, it was a miserable time, but when, in the second week, I was allowed to visit my mother in hospital I knew I must never tell her so.

I went eager and excited but returned more scared and unhappy than ever. My mother looked dreadful. She was puffy-faced and a funny, yellowy-white colour and, though propped up on pillows, looked stiff and uncomfortable in the hospital bed. Everything about the ward she was in made me nervous – the antiseptic smells, the occasional moans from some patients, and even the nurses who, instead of being the gentle souls I'd imagined, drifting about smiling and soothing brows, were bustling and sharp and told me off for bringing dirt into the ward on my shoes. Settled on a chair that was much too low, I looked up at my mother beseechingly, wanting her to comfort me, but she needed comfort more than I did and I didn't know how to give it. She was sad, tired, she had no energy. She asked how things were at home and I lied with spirit and conviction, painting such an exaggerated picture of domestic harmony that she managed a fleeting smile. Leaving the ward, I hardly dared to look to right or left. I didn't want to register all these sick women. I couldn't bear to think what had been done to them and that they were in pain. It made me feel weak and dizzy seeing them out of the corner of my eye. I just wanted to escape, escape from women and their operations, whatever they were.

When my mother finally came home she took a long time to get back to normal, but just her presence was enough to give our home back its familiarity. I heard her telling Mrs Gillespie 'the whole thing was now out' and she was glad 'to be rid of it'. So that was apparently good news. It had to be even if I didn't understand it, but my mother didn't act as if she were glad. She dragged herself about looking weak and grey and collapsed often on the bashed-up old settee in a way she had never done. My father was understanding. He wouldn't let her get up first in the morning any more. He made her stay in bed the extra hour and took her tea before he left to cycle through the icy morning to work. His concern came out in a renewed attack on me for not helping enough in the house. He said I should be made to do more, but my mother said, 'Oh leave her alone, her turn will come soon enough.' *What?* I could hardly believe my ears. *My turn?* For what? Operations? For lying sick and weak in bed? No. I would not. I would simply refuse to take this turn of mine, I would refuse, somebody else could have it, not me.

It was such a relief when my mother was back to doing the washing and singing hymns again, neat and bright in her pinny and turban, in control of the house and us. And then something unexpected happened. A letter came for her, from the Public Health Department. It was sixteen years since she had worked there, but as Uncle Len was always telling her she hadn't been forgotten. She was being asked if she could come back just for three months to fill a sudden vacancy it was going to take time to find the right person for. My father was doubtful. He didn't like the idea at all, when my mother had just recovered, when we'd just got back to normal. But my mother wanted to take this temporary job. She was attracted not only by the money, though that was certainly an attraction, holding out as it did the possible, just possible, prospect of being able to afford a week at Silloth next summer, but by the thought of doing something other than clean and cook. So she went back, worried she wasn't smart enough, but looking transformed in some cast-offs of Nan's hastily sent: a grey pleated skirt and cardigan and a pale pink blouse with a bow at the neck, a bow tied and retied twenty times before she finally set off. She loved that three months. We didn't. I came home once more to an empty house and this time there was *no excuse*. I wanted to open the kitchen door to the smell of my mother's baking and the sight of the fire burning and the knowledge I was going to be cherished from the moment I entered. I sulked, hung about pretending I hadn't actually arrived home yet, did none of the small enough tasks I was supposed to help with. I let my mother come home to none of those comforts she regularly afforded me.

The strange thing was that she didn't seem to mind or even notice, she was so happy being back at work. We were all jealous, quite plainly so. We'd growl and stop her telling us about her day, taking no pleasure in her pleasure. Watching her spend her own money *was* a pleasure we were willing to share, though. She went to a little shop in Botchergate, but at least it wasn't the Co-op. I suggested Bullough's or Binn's for this exciting shopping expedition, but then I would with my Nan-like notions. The little shop was fine. My mother bought a new skirt, a deep blue, her favourite colour, and a twinset of almost the same colour, just slightly paler, and a silk slip to go underneath. She longed for a coat but having a big item like a winter coat would have ruled out everything else, so she made her old one do. I watched her finger the silk of the ivory-coloured slip and smile, and I saw her look at herself, wearing the whole new outfit, in the shop's mirror and smile even more at how attractive and suddenly younger she looked. The next month it was shoes, bought at K Shoes, black court shoes, very smart, and a pair of fur-lined boots (though those were bought from a stall in the market). My mother had good legs and fine ankles and in her new shoes and blue skirt looked elegant. Her final purchase was a hat, in blue felt with a feather at one side. Then it was over, the extra money spent and the miracle was that it had been spent on herself and neither saved (the Silloth week idea abandoned as unrealistic) nor spent on us.

She was offered a permanent part-time job – times had changed and married women were allowed to continue part-time – but she didn't accept it. It was too much to take on, when she had a house and husband and children to care for,

for more than a short time. It was all right to neglect her duties for three months but not for ever. Arthur wasn't happy with her working, anyway. He still thought it wasn't right when she was a wife and mother. I heard her explaining this to Mrs Gillespie and others and never once did she mention her own real feelings, that she wanted to work because she liked it. She seemed to put up no fight. Then just at this time Arthur was once more offered another job at a higher wage and with a house. Joy? No. It was in this country this time but in Liverpool. He was no more tempted than he had been before by South Africa. Liverpool? But it wasn't Carlisle, why would he want to go there? Why would he want to uproot his wife and family? Unthinkable.

My mother soon felt great guilt because she'd been 'selfish' and spent her own money on herself and not on us, on my sister and me. It upset her dreadfully that we were not, that year, going to be dressed for Easter. 'Getting dressed for Easter' was a ritual in Raffles, conferring instant status which is what this emphasis on clothes partly was – but only partly. My mother still loved clothes for their own sake – they made her feel so much better – but it was true she also thought they were actually important. They showed the world you respected yourself and had made the effort to be as immaculate as possible. They showed that however hard your circumstances, you could rise above them. Easter was the time this was most true. If your children did not have brand-new clothes to wear to church on Easter Sunday, if they were not 'dressed for Easter', then you lost face. 'Are you getting dressed for Easter?' we asked each other at school and great was the satisfaction if the answer was yes.

That Easter, the Easter following the purchase of her own

new clothes, the clothes that made her feel nothing was quite as bleak and disappointing any more, my mother took me aside and with the most solemn of expressions broke the news that Pauline and I would not be dressed for Easter unless some money our grandmother had put in the Trustee Savings Bank for us was used to buy new clothes. She said she wished she could afford to buy us the clothes but she couldn't and so we'd have to give permission for grandma's money, intended for our future, to be broken into. It was only a case of taking twenty pounds out of a hundred pounds, but she stressed the choice was mine. I agreed at once. I couldn't see why she was so hesitant and anxious about this trifling matter. I went to the Trustees Savings Bank with her and we were both completely cowed by the necessary form signings and negotiations before two ten pound notes were delivered to us. The moment we were out of the bank my mother said, 'I shouldn't have done that,' as though we'd just robbed it, but soon, aided and abetted by my excitement, she perked up and we started on the spending. We bought yards of fine grey flannel to be made into costumes for Pauline and me by a dressmaker Nan had recommended from her old days in Carlisle, and pink silk blouses with little pearl buttons and straw hats with artificial flowers, pink and white rosebuds, wreathed round them, and new black patent leather shoes, the sort with one thin strap over the foot. Heavens, the pleasure, my mother's and ours. How we strutted to church on Easter Sunday, the 'best-dressed for Easter' girls on the whole estate.

We were never again garbed so finely, but one year two 'new' dresses appeared. Since we hadn't shopped for them, they'd just appeared, laid out on our bed, I was surprised. They fitted each of us perfectly. I examined mine carefully. It was new but somehow not new enough. It didn't quite feel how new usually felt. I said so to my mother who immediately blushed and confessed the dresses had come from a second-hand shop in Globe Lane, a very *clean* second-hand shop. There was no other way of providing us with new clothes, she said, voice trembling, she was sorry. I was furious, I couldn't bear her regret – to be so upset just because we had to resort to second-hand clothes, as if it mattered. But they did, to her, and I had to struggle not to let them matter to me, because of how she'd made me think of clothes. It wasn't snobbery either. It was this conviction that clothes revealed character. They showed the world what you were, and we were decidedly not a hard-up family living on a council estate. My God no, we were always incredibly well turned out and proud of it, especially the women. My mother might not be able to indulge her love of clothes but clothes were her way of pretending life was not how it was. Women like her had to delude themselves through disguising realities and clothes were one way to do it.

Another lesson I didn't want to learn.

An important part of being a daughter was shopping. A son might be sent on messages but that was not to be confused with going 'up street' to shop which a daughter was expected to do as a matter of course. Going up street shopping always felt exciting, an event. We had to be dressed properly, we had to look as smart as possible (clothes again). It was a case of 'Go and put on your other skirt and clean socks and wash your hands and face and brush your hair, or you're not going.' We caught a double-decker Ribble bus from just outside our house. Each of us carried a bag, my mother and sister and I. I wished I had a wicker basket, baskets were so much prettier, but though she used one for local shopping, my mother would not sanction baskets for the serious stuff. She had a large leather bag, for carrying heavy-duty goods in, and ours were string bags, flimsy things which opened out to reveal themselves as surprisingly capacious but could only bear the weight of light articles.

The bus stopped at the Town Hall. Our shopping began in the covered market as shopping always had done all my mother's life and her mother's before her. We went through the big double doors and down the little cobbled hill and patronized the butchers' stalls just as my grandmother had done. We bought the same kind of Cumberland sausage and potted meat and black pudding, which I hated to eat. The rest of the family loved these delicacies, especially potted meat, which was spread on buttered bread, the jelly part soaking right through. After this meat-buying ordeal, things improved. I liked the fruit and vegetable stalls, full of produce not very artistically arranged but absolutely fresh, brought in every morning from the surrounding countryside. Nothing exotic, no pineapples or melons – I hadn't yet seen such fruits – and no fancy foreign vegetables, just huge cabbages and cauliflowers and leeks and onions and millions of potatoes, millions. My father grew most of our vegetables in his allotment but we bought tomatoes after his greenhouse was smashed in a storm. The last port of call was to the butter women who sat behind trestle tables, their butter and cheese arranged in front of them, the butter pats each with an individual crest. As in every aspect of our lives shopping in the market was carefully structured, the route between the stalls never varying – butchers, greengrocers, butter women. Progress was very slow. Plenty of time, while goods were selected, talked over, paid for, for me to stare up at the glass roof where pigeons flew about and to be aware of the echoes in that cavernous space. It was always cold, since there was no heating and doors opened on each side to the streets beyond, and the stallholders would often have a struggle weighing things with hands wrapped in two pairs of fingerless mittens and scarves dropping down and getting in their way. On the many wet days rain would sweep in and trickle down the main cobbled entrance until it became a veritable stream and puddles were hard to avoid. How I longed to get out of the market and into the warm shops.

We went next to Lipton's for tea and for sliced cooked ham, two different counters in the same shop, two different queues. I'd be put into one, my mother and sister would stand in the other. Such patience we had, fully expecting each transaction to take the ages it did. Everyone watched to see what others bought and whether any preferential treatment was being given by the assistants. These assistants had white hats on and were very quick which made all the waiting hard to understand. It was the paying which took the time, the system of putting the money in cans which whizzed overhead to the central cash desk and then back again with the change wrapped in the bill. Binn's had just abolished this method. In Binn's each assistant dealt on the spot with the money, but then Binn's and Bullough's were a cut above the rest and going into either of those large (for Carlisle) department stores was the best part of shopping.

Going into them was an indulgence, a treat. We only bought small items there, things my mother knew were the same price everywhere. Reels of thread, press-studs, sometimes stationery, never anything expensive. The whole point was just to have a reason for going into Binn's and savouring its graciousness. We never bought even the cheapest item of clothing there. Clothes meant the Co-op, where else? A long

167

walk from Binn's down English Street, wide and elegant with its seventeenth-century Town Hall at one end, and past the splendid Victorian station and into Botchergate, a long, noisy, narrow thoroughfare with ugly shops, only worth venturing into for its two cinemas. The city suddenly felt claustrophobic and dreary the moment Botchergate was entered. I didn't know a thing about architecture but I knew the buildings were different, the atmosphere something to do with the layout of the street.

Nothing was more depressing than the Co-op. It was halfway down Botchergate, set back, an enormous building with a central square inside round which balconies ran at every one of the three levels. These were reached by stone staircases which took ages to clamber up and made my mother's legs ache. The goods seemed drab and were badly displayed – no thought or care was given to any kind of arrangement since economy and value for money were the Co-op's most worthy criteria. The lighting was minimal and poor, the assistants on the whole elderly and downtrodden. The experience of shopping at the Co-op was dismal and there was no joy in our actual essential purchases – vests, knickers, socks and liberty bodices. The Co-op specialized in a particular kind of fleece-lined liberty bodice, a sort of waistcoat, worn over a vest, which did up with cloth buttons at the front and sometimes had tabs hanging down so that suspenders could be attached if desired. Liberty bodices were worn tight, that was the point of them, and though the material they were made of was soft, they were akin to a corset for the young. Washing them was laborious. They weren't really meant to be washed and hardly ever were. Washing made them shrink, however carefully it was done. But my mother placed great faith in the protective values, against cold, of liberty bodices. She had us in them all winter and half the summer and if we did develop colds it could only be because our liberty bodices had worn thin and we must get new ones from the Co-op as soon as possible. I hated mine. 'Why is it called a *liberty* bodice?' I'd ask, aggrieved. I knew what the word liberty meant and there was no feeling of freedom in this garment. My mother didn't know and saw no need to know. It wasn't important.

Last stop was for bread and, occasionally, as a reward for enduring the Co-op, cream doughnuts or chocolate eclairs. We walked back up and out of Botchergate and round the crescent and into Lowther Street, where my mother had gone to school, which was spacious if not as impressive as English Street. There was a small baker's shop halfway along where we bought a special kind of treacle loaf and delicious teacakes (round, soft roll-like bread, plain or sweet, with or without currants, and coming in three sizes). Then we cut through one of the medieval lanes and got the bus again at the Town Hall. That was it for another week. We'd been 'up street' and my mother was exhausted, mainly with the stress caused by seeing so many things she wanted and couldn't afford to buy. She would sigh as she put her bag down and then, still in her coat, sit down and close her eyes for a moment or two before she made a cup of tea. That was her way of attempting to relax. Reading was not an aid to relaxation; she never picked up the newspaper. She was on her feet again too quickly to read anything.

She didn't in any case read much – the parish magazine, my grandmother's *The People's Friend*, the Bible and that was about it. She thought magazines a shocking waste of money, full of silly pictures and articles, entirely frivolous. My love of virtually any magazine annoyed her. In the house of various neighbours I read *Woman* and *Woman's Own* and loved them, loved the sheer brightness of them however false the contents, and I bought the *Girls' Crystal* and later *Eagle*, and *Girl*, for myself. I read every word, however sentimental or trite (not that I recognized the stories in these publications were either), caring only that what was offered was a view of life quite different from the one I was seeing. I loved the fashion pages and would pine for the cheap or special offers – a red taffeta skirt was what I most wanted at ten. It looked so shimmeringly beautiful on the *Woman's Own* model. I'd lie on my stomach on the living-room floor for hours going through stacks of old magazines I'd been given, reading the same stuff over and over.

It exasperated my mother. 'I thought you had more sense,' she'd say, and when I started buying my own magazines there was no holding her scorn – 'All that money!' she'd exclaim over the sixpence I'd spent, 'And for what? Just rubbish.' My only defence was to declare I liked rubbish, which she dismissed, rightly, as an inadequate answer. I couldn't articulate what I got from trashy magazines, why the arrival of a new copy of one of them cheered me up. They didn't cheer my mother up. Life might be mundane, it might be grim, but no silly magazine was going to make any difference to her. But then no kind of reading did, she couldn't get from reading what I could. I could even read my brother's comics, though in fact she never objected to my love of *The Hotspur*, *The Wizard*, *The Rover* and *Cannonball*. It was always those women's magazines she saved her contempt for – it was almost as though they were a vice to which she saw I was addicted, as though she thought I was betraying, in my love for them, a weakness which it was her duty to combat – that way, the way of popular magazines, lay perdition.

Equally suspect was my passion for the photographs of film stars. She couldn't see the point of the glossy publicity photographs for which I sent away – they held no romance for her at all. I'd gloat over yet another signed copy of Hedy Lamarr's hand-out picture and she'd shake her head in disbelief and disgust. I had a scrapbook and pasted the photographs into it and then turned the pages slowly, hypnotized by the huge eyes and long eyelashes and luscious lips and shining hair of my favourites. But my mother, with her unyielding respect for absolute truth, knew these images were fraudulent and didn't want me to be hoodwinked. Nor did she want me to have stupid ideas. I might think that I, too, could become a film star and my head was already full of such dangerous, outlandish notions – I was *always* thinking I could be what she was absolutely certain I could never be. Once, she opened a demand for more money from a company peddling these pictures. I'd sent for a new Margaret Lockwood photograph and, when it did not come, announced I was going to write and complain. That was when my mother told me she'd opened a letter asking for two extra shillings before it could be sent, and so she'd torn it up. I was furious and said I'd have sent the extra money and I would do so now. 'Then you're a fool,' she said. 'You're letting yourself be taken advantage of. That photo isn't worth it. I was only saving you from yourself.' That had me screaming – the last thing I wanted was to be saved from myself. I wanted to *be* myself and myself yearned for those alluring, glossy photographs. I sent the extra money but my postal order was returned. The offer had closed.

I often spent my pocket money equally ridiculously but

my mother didn't always disapprove. If I gorged myself on ice-cream sundaes that was apparently all right. But what she really liked was for me to choose to spend my money on others, to be virtuous with it, to put it into the collection box at church, or into the missionary box she had at home. Sometimes I did. But though I liked the feeling of goodness this gave me, and even more my mother's approval, the trouble was that this feeling was so short-lived. In the money would go, my weekly two shillings, and almost before the collection plate had passed to the end of the row I was resenting its disappearance. I simply couldn't bear to think of having no money now for another seven days. It was preferable to try to be magnanimous but get something out of it. A perfect opportunity presented itself when an unpopular teacher, Miss Parker, retired. Nobody gave her a present. I told my mother how sorry I felt for poor Miss Parker, the only teacher ever to leave without being presented with flowers or some token of appreciation. Then I had the brilliantly noble idea of buying Miss Parker a present myself and taking it to where I knew she lived. My mother was thrilled – *this* was the daughter she'd always hoped she'd reared. I duly saved my weekly two shillings pocket money for four weeks, and then I went to Woolworths and bought a picture. It was in a gilt frame, six inches by eight, so quite respectably large to me, a print of a meadow with a little girl picking poppies in it. I thought she looked rather like me and was pleased at the similarity.

I wrapped it up in tissue paper and off I went, already anticipating Miss Parker's tearful gratitude and practising my own modest reception of it. But visiting teachers in their homes was not something anyone ever did and as I neared Miss Parker's house on the banks of the Caldew I remembered why she had been so unpopular: she was terrifying. She'd been a great caner, using not a cane but a solid wooden implement, thick at one end, narrow at the other, a sort of pointer for using on the blackboard. I was nervous by the time I rang her bell and even more so as I heard her coming to her door. She hardly opened it. Only a crack, but sufficient to see her bad-tempered expression, the glare behind her thick spectacles. 'Yes?' she said sharply. 'What do you want, bothering me?' I thrust the wrapped picture at the gap in the doorway, but it wouldn't go through. I swallowed and whispered. 'It's a present. I wanted to give you a present.' '*What?*' she shouted, making no move to open the door wider. 'Speak up, for heaven's sake.' I tried again. 'It's a present, for retiring. I wanted to give you a present because you didn't get one. It wasn't fair.' The rage on her face finally got through to me and I dropped the picture on her doorstep and ran, only slowing down when I was round the corner. Then I stopped and cried.

It had all gone so wrong, my wonderful gesture, and I didn't understand why. What had I done? What had I said that was so wrong? Why was Miss Parker so angry? My mother consoled me and said some people saw the worst in everything and I was not to be upset because God had seen and heard and knew how kind I'd tried to be. Didn't I remember the bit in the Bible about turning the other cheek? Well, this wasn't exactly the same, but it almost was. I must, in effect, turn the other cheek. She was proud of me. It had been a useful lesson in humility, she said. In fact, though I was only dimly aware of it, it was nothing of the kind. It was a lesson, rather, in what happens when you're so in love with your own virtue you fail to see you're patronizing and self-righteous.

X

Soon after Miss Parker left, I went into the Merit class. The Merit was the same examination my mother had sat at eleven, but it now controlled entry to the once-exclusive fee-paying Grammar and High Schools as well as to the two schools, the Margaret Sewell and the Creighton, created from the old Higher Grade. Carlisle, in short, had by the late 1940s a tripartite secondary education system. The top percentage of those who passed the crucially important Merit went either to the Grammar School, if a boy, or to the High School, if a girl, then the next in order went to the other two schools. Those who failed were doomed to go to secondary moderns which were much worse than secondary and modern not at all. So the Merit was a big event in our lives. Its significance was clearly understood. It settled our future, it pigeon-holed us, at eleven, as clever, quite clever or stupid.

My brother Gordon had failed the Merit in 1943 and since he was not stupid I'd always known there must be something wrong somewhere. My mother was distraught and blamed the weeks off school Gordon had been obliged to have because of illness. He'd had scarlet fever the months before he sat the Merit; he was in the fever hospital for weeks (so was Pauline, but I never caught it. I never caught anything). My mother knew the Merit was largely an intelligence test but she also knew Gordon had missed all kinds of practice tests and that, since he lacked confidence at the best of times, this was a handicap. There was still a year to go before the vital 1944 Education Act, usually known as the Butler Education Act after Rab Butler who was Minister for Education at the time. It opened the way for any child, however poor, to gain entry to the previously fee-paying grammar schools, since ability was now to be the only criterion. Universities and colleges would also be within their reach since means-tested grants would be available, as well as state scholarships, to cover all expenses. My grandfather had offered to pay for Gordon to go to the Grammar School but he refused to be paid for. He was upset and he was proud – if he hadn't passed to go, he didn't want to. Arthur thought he was right, Lily that he was wrong. Arthur was no advert for not going to the Grammar School. What job would Gordon get, a product of Ashley Street Boys? A poor job, his highest aspiration an apprenticeship in some trade, and my mother knew he was worth more than that. He was quiet, like her, and shy, like her, but he was also perfectly intelligent and hardworking and well worth educating. She felt that when he got over the poor health, which had dogged him all his childhood, he would make up for lost time and flourish, he'd be a late developer (and he was). It was maddening that I was clever and was the one never ill. I, as a girl, didn't need to be clever. It would do me no good just as it had done her no good. I would only marry and have children and share her own fate, whatever I said.

So there was not the same anxiety over the Merit when it came to my turn to take it – except in my own mind. The thought of failing the Merit made me want to die, as exaggerated a reaction to the thought of it as that. I *had* to go to the Carlisle and County High School for Girls (I loved its full title). Nothing else would do, certainly not the Margaret

Sewell School. My mother's and her family's attitudes to the High School in her day were not mine. I didn't believe for one moment that the High School was above me, or too good for me, or not for the likes of me, and if that meant I was getting above myself, too bad, I was desperate to exceed my supposed reach. But it was to my advantage in every way that the situation in 1949 was dramatically different education-ally from how it had been in 1913. The High School was no longer fee-paying. Entry was free and through the passing of the Merit only. Books did not have to be paid for and, though there was still a uniform, there were grants for those too poor to afford the expenditure. The very mention of the word 'grant' produced shudders of horror at home – grants were *charity*, and never ever would we be recipients of that – but not in me.

I took to haunting Lismore Place where the High School stood, aloof behind its fences. I'd walk along the road and if no one was about put my eye to a crack in the wooden paling and ogle the impressive building, a large country house in appearance, with grass tennis courts in front. Every time I passed a girl in the High School uniform I'd feel such acute pangs of envy – oh to be able to wear that navy gym-slip, that blazer with its rose-and-castle crest, that grey felt hat! Garbed like that I'd be straight into one of those utterly unreal but passionately desirable school stories I read so many of. I'd no longer be living in the middle of a dreary council estate having a dreary life. Then suddenly, for the first time in my young life, I became ill. The Merit was in March, and in January I contracted jaundice and was off school for six weeks. My mother was worried but I was frantic – 'Will I be better for the Merit?' I sobbed, lying there so weak and tired I couldn't even read for a while. She went down to the school and asked for the practice tests, something she hadn't known to do for Gordon, and when I was a little better I did them and she took them back to the school where the headmistress assured her there was nothing to worry about. I was absolutely certain to pass for the High School, it was impossible for me to fail.

But I didn't think it impossibile. Ashley Street didn't send many girls to the High School. Its catchment area was poor, unlike that of Stanwix School up above the Eden. They sent girls by the dozen to the High School, whereas Ashley Street only managed one or two a year. The Merit was on 2 March. I didn't return to school until 28 February, still shaky on my feet. I kept a diary that year, a little red Letts Girl Guide diary, and all it seems to record are dates and feelings to do with this wretched examination. The results of the Merit were due on 15 June. They were posted, as everyone knew, on the fourteenth to the homes of the children who'd sat it. For days before I betray in my diary the most agonizing tension, describing my nightmares, the waking up and screaming in the middle of torrents of running blood (the same nightmare I always had). It wasn't connected at all to the Merit or the High School, but when my mother woke me and calmed me she always said, 'I wish this Merit was over. This is ridiculous.' She tried to tell me it was not the end of the world if I failed. There was no pressure to succeed coming from her or anyone else. But she didn't understand, only my diary understood – 'It will be the end of the world', followed by a line of exclamation marks.

What a fuss for a ten-year-old to make (I wasn't eleven until May). No results came on 15 June. The word went round that the schools had them, and Ashley Street's were bad. I woke on the sixteenth feeling so sick and dizzy, as though the jaundice had returned. I couldn't eat a thing or utter a word. I got ready for school, with a struggle, and then stood at the window watching for the postman. My mother said nothing – I looked so pitiful and it was a new emotion to feel pity, she later said, for her always aggressive elder daughter. I saw the postman on the other side of the road. He walked up the path and put something through the Gillespies' door. Moments later Mrs Gillespie flung open her window and shouted to no one in particular, waving the envelope violently, 'He's passed! Colin's passed for the Grammar School!' I was by then on my own doorstep, anxious to take my envelope myself from the postman. He was almost level with our gate. He was level with it. He was past it . . . *past it*. My mother's hands were on my shaking shoulders. 'Just go to school,' she whispered, 'it can't be helped.' Walking stiffly, heart thudding, tears barely held back, a tragic little figure no doubt, I began to cross the side road to the bus stop. A milk float just missed me – 'Look where you're going!' the milkman shouted. I wasn't going anywhere, alas. I would be staying at Ashley Street. I heard my mother shout, but I thought she was just telling me to be more careful too, and kept on walking, one-two, one-two. Then she caught up with me, breathless, and shoved a brown envelope into my hand – 'It was a mistake,' she panted, 'the postman came back. You've passed for the High School.'

My happiness was overwhelming – I was ecstatic, such joy, such relief. It was miraculous. 'I cannot write down how HAPPY HAPPY HAPPY I feel' the diary was told. Suddenly I was sweetness and light at home, my spirits unquenchable, my optimism all-embracing. 'Getting above herself already,' my father muttered ominously, but my mother told him to let the child have her moment. She had to go down to the

178

High School to see the headmistress, to be given instructions about rules and uniform. She came back apprehensive. 'It's such a big building,' she told me when I plagued her for information. 'There's a huge hall, you'll be lost in it.' I knew I would not. 'The headmistress is called Miss Wilson. She wears a black gown. You'll have to do homework, you'll have to have all this uniform. Look, I don't know how we'll manage.' I looked at the list, savoured each item, adoring the very words, the very ordinary words – leather satchel, gym shoes, tie, V-necked pullover, navy raincoat-with-hood, obtainable at the school outfitters, Jespers.

My mother came to life. 'No,' she said firmly, 'it will have to be the Co-op. I can't pay Jespers' prices.' I pleaded and pleaded but she was annoyed and told me not to be absurd, a gym-slip was a gym-slip wherever it was purchased, and Jespers were notorious for charging twice what every other shop did. Even going to the Co-op would be ruinously expensive and I had to understand that. What I understood, and so did my mother really with her love of clothes, her sense of style, was that a gym-slip from the Co-op was *never* going to look like one from Jespers. Luckily, my grandparents were so proud of my amazing feat that they gave my mother the money for the uniform. 'Get her the best,' my grandfather growled. It was the first time I had ever liked him: the best could only mean Jespers.

My mother still insisted on the Co-op for some basic items – she would *not* spend 4s. 6d. on a pair of white socks when the Co-op had identical ones for 1s. 11d. Since my clothes snobbery didn't extend to socks I graciously conceded the point. It was enough that the gym-slip and blazer were bought at Jespers. My mother enjoyed going there as much as I did – she was haughty and dignified and her voice changed; she used her church voice to ask for 'the larger size, please' and to say 'a little longer, I think'. The room in which the school uniforms were kept had a carpet on the floor and rows of solid wooden shelves and the assistants were very superior. They wore tape measures round their necks and called my mother 'modom'. She was more than equal to the challenge of matching their hauteur. When we'd finished this exclusive shopping we went and had our tea in Binn's café as a special treat. 'I just hope you like this High School when you get there,' my mother said, 'after the carry-on you've made.'

I did. I loved the High School in a way that made my love of all school from the beginning seem a feeble thing. But I realized quite quickly that I lagged behind. I didn't know things other girls did. Who was Dickens? The teacher asked how many girls were familiar with the work of Charles Dickens. Several put their hands up. Dickens, it seemed, was an author and these girls had read *Oliver Twist* and *David Copperfield*. I'd been taking books out of the library at the rate of six a week by then for four years, but I had not hit on any Dickens. I went straight to the D shelf after school and got cracking. But there were other gaps harder to do anything about. French. Two girls could speak some French. Their parents had taught them. And geography. Some girls had a, to me, amazing knowledge of the world just through having globes and atlases at home. So I wasn't the cleverest. At the end of the first year I was only sixth in the English exam, though I was top in History, and around tenth, in a class of forty, in everything else. 'Not as good as your mam was,' my father commented, only to be told by my mother not to be so daft. This was the High School, not the Higher Grade, and I was doing very well. She'd been to an Open Day, a newfangled idea she greatly approved of, and had been so pleased at the evidence of how I was getting on. I answered most in the classes she sat in on and was the liveliest. She saw how eager and determined I was and appreciated that was how I differed from her younger self: she'd been clever, she'd loved school, she'd worked hard but she had had no determination, no ambition. It scared her slightly to see me striving so hard and for what? She couldn't see any end to it. All she could see were problems looming, a gulf emerging which would grow wider and wider. There had been no such gulf between herself and her mother, even if she had been educated far above her own mother's level. They had still wanted, and thought important, the same things: homes, husbands, children. In short, families. What was I, so keen, so expectant, going to think important? What was I going to become if not a wife and mother?

I startled her, in my first term at the High School, by saying I wanted to become a Member of Parliament. What a noble calling, I thought, knowing nothing whatsoever about it. I was carried away with having been elected to the School Council (easy enough because no one else wanted to be, in our form). Off I trotted – 'I will be late home. I have a Council Meeting, I am afraid' – and was heavily disillusioned almost immediately. Junior representatives were kept firmly in their place and, even though I was prepared to be bold and push my opinions forward, I only had to open my mouth for the headmistress to hold up a silencing palm, as though she were a traffic warden and I a particularly noisy car. It might be called a *school* council but it was the headmistress's and she made it plain it was only an indulgence on her part. She was happy enough to allow discussions on whether to have liquid instead of solid soap in the cloakrooms, but when it was suggested packed lunches would be preferable to the deeply unpopular school dinners, there was a sharp veto and that was that. Girls, we were told – all written up in the minutes – could not stand up to a busy day of mental and physical activity without a cooked meal. Girls couldn't wear shorts for games either, another constantly suggested change, because 'shorts are ugly at the waist'. I pondered that one for a long time and finally, when towards the end of the meeting I was allowed to speak, I asked how shorts and skirts differed at the waist. Didn't they have the same waistband? 'What a foolish remark,' the headmistress said. 'Any other business?' I decided I didn't want to be an MP, to my mother's relief.

Already I was worrying about what I would be. School was clearly understood to be only a stepping-stone to work. At the end everyone had to have a job. Gordon, who was seventeen to my eleven, had already had a job for three years and I didn't want to work in a chemist's shop as he did. So what would I be? I tried to analyse what I was good at. History and English and Art and that was about it. What sort of job could I get being good at those? Then I tried to think what I liked best. Same answer. Reading, that was what I liked best. Was there a job called A Reader? I had a brilliant English teacher, Miss Wynne, who was helping me to be A Reader. She gave me a list of all the authors a well-read person should have read. It was a long, long list, full of suggested titles for each author, and she told me it would take years for me to get through it. It was exactly what I needed and wanted but it irritated my mother, she saw it as creating that very gulf she dreaded. The more I read, the further away I grew. She never had read much and now she read not at all, claiming she had neither the time nor the energy (a claim I believed until I realized it was not time or energy she lacked but the interest). My father didn't read, though his claim was once to have read an Edgar Wallace. There were only the usual books in the house, usual to a working-class family, where there was neither money to buy books, in the pre-paperback era, nor space to stock them. The Bible, prayer books, hymn books, a *Home Doctor*, a cookery book, and some children's books bought for me. I was lucky there. Nan bought me Beatrix Potter books and I had Grimm's and Hans Andersen's fairy tales, and some Alison Uttley stories, so I had had a good start, good enough to launch me until I discovered the library and then Miss Wynne's list.

But I could never discuss anything I'd read at home. Trying to talk about the contents of books was showing off and there was no need for it. My reading was seen as a weapon I used against my family, a way of absenting myself from their company. 'All she does is that damned reading,' my father complained, and it was true. It made me strange to them. I even took to going to bed at six o'clock to have peace to read. I had to get into bed to do it because for most of the year the bedroom was freezing cold, but I didn't mind – light nights, dark nights, cold nights, warm nights, it was the same to me. It made no difference, I was in bed with my books. Downstairs, in the one small living-room, the wireless blared away, meals were eaten, everyone talked, but upstairs it was quiet. My family, especially my father, hated my retreat. When he objected, when he shouted at me to come down this minute, I'd shout back, asking what was wrong with going to read upstairs. He never had any answer but 'Do what I say, or else.'

I just stayed where I was, feeling triumphant.

XI

Even though I was so happy at the High School I was greatly preoccupied then with the subject of death. My mother seemed to me almost to like death. She was always talking about people about to die, or having died, always attending funerals and not looking too miserable about it. 'Your mam likes a nice funeral,' my father would smirk and she'd be furious with him, but for once I felt he was right.

I had never been to one but as my grandmother Agnes's was reckoned to be imminent I lived in hopes. What I hadn't been prepared for was visiting her, with my mother, in the geriatric ward of the City General Hospital. I'd never visited anyone in hospital except for my mother on that one occasion and I was a little nervous at the memory of it, but I was given no choice. My grandmother wanted to see me in the full glory of my High School uniform, a treat which could not be denied. I hated entering the hospital – it all came back to me how frightening hospitals were – but this dislike was nothing compared with the terrified revulsion I felt as my mother and I walked into the geriatric ward. It was a Nightingale-style ward, rows of beds on either side of a long aisle, with windows so high up nobody could ever look through them and they had to be opened by a cumbersome method of pulling strings. The noise was incessant, wailings and screechings, howls and sudden piercing screams, and the constant calling of names. My grandmother was in the bed

184

next but one to the end of the ward. She was huddled under the sheet, her crippled hands on top of it, her head to one side at an odd angle, eyes closed and mouth open revealing a sludgy-looking cavern without teeth, her thin white strands of hair falling over her yellow-looking face. She was crying softly, a high-pitched keening sound, constant and curiously rhythmic. My heart started to thud, my stomach to churn, but it was the woman in the very end bed who grabbed my attention. This old woman wasn't lying still at all. She was halfway out of her bed, struggling to get fully upright, her nightdress rucked up to expose thin lard-white legs and her hands clawing at the wall. These hands flailed at the wall again and again and each time left marks, dirty brown marks, and then they went under the nightdress and emerged to smear more brown on the wall . . . I hardly realized she was plastering the wall with her own excrement, but my mother did. 'Stay here,' she said, pushing me to the far side of my grandmother's bed. 'Don't move.' I stayed, trembling, while she ran off and came back with a nurse who roared at the demented woman, yanked her nightdress down, lifted her up bodily and carted her off. 'Poor, poor soul,' my mother murmured.

I never for one moment thought 'poor soul'. I was still staring at the brown streaks on the wall and gagging at what I had at last worked out it was. I couldn't speak a word during the whole of the visit, not even when begged by my mother to tell my grandmother about my beloved school. I was dumb with fright and I couldn't understand how my mother could act so normally, as though she'd already forgotten what had just happened. When finally we left the ward I felt dizzy. My steps slowed, even though I longed to run and escape, and looking down at me my mother saw I was colourless and about to faint. She sat me on a stair and put my head between my legs and soon I felt well enough to go down the staircase and out into the fresh air. 'I don't know why you should faint,' my mother said, puzzled. 'It isn't as if you'd been hurt.' But when we got home and my father heard the saga, he said my mother should never have taken me to that damned place. It made *him* feel sick, it made *him* feel faint. 'Someone has to go,' my mother said.

It was another unmistakable sign to me that I wasn't going to be able to emulate my mother. I wasn't fit to do women's work. My mother blossomed in these situations – she was so calm, so gentle, so capable and kind and cheering. But I panicked, I felt faint, I was useless. The tradition of being a carer, with what it implied, would not be carried on by me. I was hardly my mother's daughter at all, although I still prayed to become like her. But praying was just on the edge of ceasing. Throughout my childhood I'd said my prayers on my knees at bedtime. When I was very young, my mother knelt with me, gently placing my hands together, fingertip to fingertip, precisely so, palms as flat against each other as I could make them. I liked pushing them together, feeling my prayers would be pushed to heaven by the very pressure I was exerting. I loved praying. I did it with great intensity. I loved the very words of Gentle Jesus / meek and mild. I was in love with Jesus and pleased my mother with my devotion. I made up my own prayers after Gentle Jesus had been said and talked to Jesus (rather than God) with great passion, explaining and justifying at length whatever rigmarole I came out with. Even my mother's patience was tried and she'd urge me to stop now. Jesus had other prayers to hear.

I liked a bit of martyrdom too. My mother would suggest that as there was ice on the inside as well as the outside of the unheated bedroom window, Jesus wouldn't mind if I said my prayers lying in bed, but I would insist on doing the praying properly, knees stuck to the shockingly, searingly cold lino. A touch of shivering was very satisfactory, I felt. I was trying hard to be worthy of Jesus (and my mother). This was proof of my intentions. Yet another was my decision to become a missionary. At seven, this had seemed my destiny. I told my mother and asked if she would like that. I watched her carefully, knowing it was a trick question. But she was up to it. 'If Jesus decides he wants you to be a missionary then I do too,' she said, 'but He won't decide until you're grown up, so I don't have to think about it yet and neither do you.' I was glad because I didn't really want to go to darkest Africa and hoped Jesus would pick me for something else, so I didn't have to renege on my promise.

The prayers went on until I was nearing twelve. Then, one night, having got to the stage of mumbling Gentle Jesus, and certainly no longer on my knees, I suddenly started thinking about the meek and mild bit. If Jesus was so meek and mild how come He had all this power? Meek and mild began to seem code for feeble and useless. It was awkward that I'd begun to question religion in general because I was still a stalwart church-goer and was soon to start confirmation classes. When I did, the curate at St Barnabas's gave me a booklet, *My Confirmation Day at Home and in Church*. It told me that 'on first waking from sleep' I should remind myself that 'when I go to bed tonight, if I live to the end of the day, I shall have been confirmed'. It had never occurred to me that I might not live to the end of the day. Was confirmation life-threatening, then? Then the booklet instructed me 'Do not let your thoughts be taken up with what you are going to wear.' Good heavens, that was surely the whole point of it – the yummy white dress – the romantic veil – the delicious white lace gloves . . . It was better than being 'dressed for Easter'. I knew I should not agree to being confirmed. It was a cheat. I was only doing it because my mother expected and wanted me to.

I had a new white dress, sure enough, but it didn't prove worth selling my soul for. It was badly made and the material was a cheap rayon which creased instantly it was put on. But I paraded up the church aisle with everyone else and went through the whole ritual. The service seemed mumbo-jumbo, but afterwards my mother was so pleased. I was safely in the Church, my rebellious instincts curbed before any real harm was done. Except they weren't. Hardly was I confirmed than the real questioning began. 'Look,' I would say to my mother as we walked back from church on Sunday evenings, 'if Adam and Eve were the first man and woman on earth, where did they come from?' She said God made both of them and put them on earth. 'Then who made God?' She struggled valiantly to explain God was not actually a person. 'How do you know?' Then I'd switch to speculating about infinity and the solar system and wondering where heaven was. 'How do you know there is a heaven?' I'd say. 'Nobody can know, nobody comes back after they've died and says so.' It was a series of really quite short steps from this kind of simplistic challenging before I made the big jump to declaring that confirmed or not I no longer believed in God.

My mother said she'd pray for me, pray I'd come back into the fold where God would be waiting for me and would welcome me. A life without a belief in God was to her insupportable – she needed to believe some supreme authority was ordaining everything, that her fate was *meant*. It gave her such comfort to believe this. 'Ours not to reason why' was a motto of great appeal. She couldn't see how I was going to be able to cope without a religious faith — it was what had got her and her mother through their hardest days. They believed, and it made their lives tolerable, and afterwards they would get their reward in heaven where they would meet and have the wonderful time they hadn't had on earth. It was her turn now to ask me awkward questions: if I didn't believe in God how did I account for the start of the world? I had a smart answer, learned parrot-fashion from something I'd read: we have finite minds and therefore cannot comprehend the infinite. My mind couldn't grasp the true scientific explanation, just as my eyes couldn't see round corners, but that didn't mean there was nothing round them. I was content, for once, to admit ignorance, even to claim it as adequate and definitely better than any faith in heaven and angels.

But it wasn't anything like adequate at first. I missed the security of believing in God. God was such a neat solution to all the problems that scared me. I'd lie in bed, imagining myself looking down from the ceiling at my own body, then further away in the sky looking at our house, then out in space looking at the world turning, then . . . Then what? My heart would thud when I got to that bit and I'd rapidly bring myself back from space, from the sky, from the ceiling and into my own body again as quickly as possible. No God, so no answers, no life after death. I wished I could see a dead body just to be sure they were nothing. My chance came at last with the death of Florrie, my mother's cousin. I knew I couldn't ask to see her body in any spirit of scientific inquiry so, looking suitably sentimental, I said I'd like to say goodbye to her. My mother should have seen through this straightaway. I was notoriously squeamish and sensitive. Why should

I want to see a dead body? It was enough, surely, with my record, to make me faint. And I'd never felt a thing for Florrie, a miserable little woman who lived on her own in a tiny house in Denton Holme. Visiting Florrie was part of the weekly torture of visiting my grandparents – half an hour with them, fifteen minutes with Florrie, then home for Sunday dinner. Florrie never said much. We just sat there and were looked at. My mother always referred to 'poor' Florrie, and when I asked why she was to be pitied I was told she had no one. My mother's greatest sympathy was always reserved for women living alone who had *no family* – it horrified her, the mere thought.

Florrie died suddenly and wasn't found for a whole twenty-four hours. It was my mother who found her. She'd had a heart attack and fallen on the bedroom floor and lay there until my mother called in on her regular Wednesday afternoon visit. 'What an awful death,' my mother kept saying, 'awful, awful, no warning at all.' This didn't seem at all awful to me, but I had the sense to keep quiet. I went upstairs with my mother to see Florrie in her coffin. They were very narrow, twisting stairs and I wondered how they would get the coffin down. The curtains were drawn in Florrie's bedroom and it was quite hard to see anything clearly but there was no missing the coffin. My mother beckoned me to the bed. 'There you are,' she whispered. 'Poor Florrie. Isn't she lovely? Doesn't she look at peace?' I looked, relieved to find I didn't feel like fainting, that I had none of the familiar physical symptoms of fear. Florrie didn't look lovely or at peace, whatever that was. She didn't look anything to me, she didn't even look asleep. I put out a finger and was about to touch her cheek but my mother stopped me, scandalized, and hissed, 'You don't *touch*!' I stared at

Florrie a bit longer, feeling suitably chastened. Her face was puffy. Her fingers were lumpy-looking, arranged in an awkward-looking clasp. The nails seemed black, the skin of her hands mottled. My mother took a green pottery rabbit from the mantelpiece and gave it to me as something to remember Florrie by. It was hideous, and anyway I had her dead body to remember her by, quite memorable enough.

My father was angry after Florrie died. It was to do with Florrie's will or the lack of it – I wasn't allowed to know the details. 'The only one who did a damned thing for Florrie,' said Arthur, 'and she gets nothing.' My mother said she had neither expected nor wanted to inherit the little poor Florrie had, but while my father went on ranting away I noticed an expression of what I interpreted as a consciousness of her own virtue on her face. 'The times you've gone down to Florrie's,' my father stormed, 'in all weathers, making yourself bad with it, getting things for her, having her for Christmas, and for nothing, all of it. It's always the same. They've a damned cheek, that's what.' Who 'they' were and what had been done that was 'a damned cheek' I could never discover. It was something to do with Florrie's one-up, one-down little house. So far as I could make out, some very distant relative whom no one had even known existed had come forward and claimed the house and its contents. If there was any meeting with this person I missed it but the repercussions of what my father called a swindle lasted for months. We weren't even allowed to walk down Florrie's street now, the very paving-stones were tainted with ingratitude. But my mother put flowers on Florrie's grave, which, as my father triumphantly noted, was more than 'they' did, and she was remembered and missed by her. It was one more family responsibility off her list yet for a while she was bereft.

My mother seemed to need these female relatives to whom she was so kind but I could never work out why. Why she looked after all the aunts and cousins who became semi-dependent on her mystified me. Maybe I was wrong and she didn't actually like the task. Maybe they wished themselves upon her and I hadn't the wit to see the situation as it really was, but she never once voiced or indicated resentment. Aunt Jessie, my father's aunt by marriage to his uncle, was another needy soul as Florrie had been, though not visited as frequently because she didn't live in Carlisle. She lived in a remote cottage over the Scottish border near Eastriggs. When we went to see Aunt Jessie we went by bus, changing three times. My mother didn't know how Jessie, a widow now, could live in her dark and cold cottage on this desolate Solway coast and shuddered every time she thought of her there alone with no family near by. She tried to persuade her to move to Carlisle to be near us so that she could be properly looked after, but Jessie stayed put. She came to us for Christmas but otherwise never left her cottage. When she in turn died, not long after Florrie, I expected similar outrage from my father, but to his astonishment Jessie had made a proper will and had left her cottage to my mother – no 'they' materialized to snatch it away, to cheat my mother of what he saw as her just reward for her devotion. The cottage was hard to sell but the four hundred pounds my mother eventually received seemed a huge amount. Once more, like my grandmother's money, it was put in the bank for a rainy day and, spread over many years, it covered all kinds of expenses which otherwise would have been disastrous.

Some of it was spent on what my mother always spent windfalls on: clothes. But by now I was old enough at thirteen not to want the clothes she tried to buy me so that I would look smart. Smart was the last thing I wanted to look. Our ideas on how a teenage girl should look naturally differed radically. My mother liked to see me in frocks, preferably in pale colours with full skirts, cap sleeves and Peter Pan collars. When, over a series of months, during which I'd saved Christmas and birthday present money, I bought a black polo-neck sweater, black trousers and a camel duffel jacket she was appalled. 'I don't know what you look like,' she said, to which I replied, 'I look how I want to look.' But what did I want to look like? Different. Simple as that. Different from my mother, different from most girls and women in Carlisle then. Since to my mother clothes were serious, and certainly not anything as frivolous as an expression of personality, she had no sense of humour about my choice of garb. It hurt her, actually hurt her, to see me looking, she said, like a tramp.

There was nowhere in Carlisle in the early fifties that stocked the sort of clothes I wanted. Teenage boutiques didn't exist nor did street markets and we were even woefully short of chain stores which catered for the would-be trendy. So I pored over pattern books in Binn's, page after seductive and misleading page of *Simplicity* and *McCalls*, and selected things I liked the finished look of, then bought material, from a limited selection, to make up the patterns. Disaster. My mother looked on in horror as I butchered yards of black poplin and then screamed and roared at my own mistakes. 'You're like me,' she said helpfully, 'useless at sewing, not like Nan, not like your grandmother.' I hated her saying that. It made my fury at my own ineptitude worse. So I struggled on, determined not to be beaten, yet never achieving the knack of pinning the fragile tissue-paper pattern on to the material, never mind learning how to sew the stuff properly.

All those stupid little black darts, meant to indicate where a cut should be made outwards and I always cut straight across, so that there was then nothing to match one side with another. I couldn't work the sewing-machine either. It had been my grandmother's (not the one Mrs Stephenson gave her when she married, but a later model). Even threading the wretched needle was a job I found difficult enough and then, when I did get started, ramming the material under the cruel little needle, I jammed it within seconds. When finally I'd managed to free the garment I was trying to stitch and proceeded slowly and carefully along a seam, my stitching was always hopelessly zig-zag. 'Good job you don't have to earn your living this way,' my mother said.

My latest ambition was to be an actress. How did one become an actress though? Was it a living? Who knew? None of us. It was totally outside our experience. But we went to Her Majesty's Theatre in Lowther Street and saw a repertory company called the Salisbury Players, presumably earning its living, so why could I not become one of them? I was good at acting. I'd already appeared in school plays. My mother couldn't understand it. Acting wasn't in the family. Where had it come from, this dubious exhibitionism? It was pure showing-off and therefore not to be encouraged. In her opinion going to the cinema, as well as the theatre, only made me worse. Forget the Salisbury Players, why could I not be a film star? Margaret O'Brien – I could easily be her. That, at least, made my mother laugh. 'Oh, yes,' she agreed, 'be a film star and go to Hollywood.' I didn't see why not. Week after week I queued to get into one of Carlisle's five booming cinemas and week after week had a greater love for motion pictures. In the smoky, pitch-black anonymity of the cinema it was possible to escape from myself, my home, my town, completely and to be sucked into whatever world was up there on the screen. I had to have the money to pay for the ticket, but I was good at handling my pocket money and any other money I earned or was given. My mother, naturally, had never had this newfangled thing called pocket money – the idea of children having a regular sum of money given to them for nothing, to spend on themselves, was fairly outrageous, and my father, from whom this money had to come, was not ever going to allow pocket money as a right. Sometimes he agreed to give it, sometimes not. But mostly he did, though he had little enough of his own. We were fortunate though, in that our grandfather also gave us a weekly sum, just as long as we answered his mental arithmetic questions, and on top of that I did messages for a woman across the road. I went shopping for her, with a list, and got a shilling in return. Then there were presents from relatives, not just at the usual times but whenever they came to the house – giving children a couple of shillings was part of the visiting pattern. I saved my money diligently, never buying sweets (as long as rationing lasted I'd sold my sweet coupons), and then I worked out how I could spend it. The cinema came first, the shilling for that automatically set aside, and always every week a certain amount also set aside to accumulate until there was enough to buy my mother a present.

I had always loved, all my childhood, buying her presents. It wasn't the self-sacrifice that appealed (though in my religious phase it did) so much as the hope of delighting her by giving her something I'd heard her yearn after. Pearls. She longed for pearls. Nan had pearls, she had never had pearls, so pearls it would be. I once saved every penny, even my cinema pennies, for three months so that I could buy her a pearl necklace for her birthday. I was intimidated by the mere sight of the jeweller's shop windows but for my mother I was brave enough to do anything. I went in and asked the price of a pearl necklace. The assistants were kind, probably amused, but even kindness could not bring a pearl necklace down to the thirty shillings I had. Seeing my face, it was suggested I should try the market where there were some very nice, really remarkably pretty, artificial pearls and these days everyone was wearing them, it was so hard to tell them apart from the real thing . . . I went to the market where thirty shillings was ample to buy a pearl necklace. The stallholder gave me a box lined with blue velvet to put them in. I gave them to my mother on her birthday in an ecstasy of pleasure and watched her open the box. Her expression remained composed, though she smiled and said the necklace was lovely. 'You shouldn't have,' she said, 'it's too much.' But she seemed so sad. My pleasure somehow was not matched by hers.

Later on, it became easier to please her. My sister and I, when we were thirteen and ten, used to take her to the cinema on the last day of the holidays and then to Binn's for tea, paying for everything ourselves. We went to see pictures like *The Blue Lagoon*, which she loved, and then for tea she had a waffle, drenched in syrup. We sat in the window of Binn's café on the top floor, feeling so exalted as we looked down on English Street. There was a white tablecloth on the table and proper napkins and white china with gold rims round the plates and heavy silver cutlery – it was very grand. My mother loved this treat from the moment we stepped out of the lift and threaded our way past the ornate hatstands across the red patterned carpet to the choicest table – she was regal, gracious, with her two daughters, one either side. Once seated, she'd invariably recall her own mother and shiver as she remembered her working here, when Binn's was Robinson's, and say how times had changed. But she didn't allow herself to become depressed by the thought of her mother's hard times. Instead, she tucked into her waffle and wiped her fingers and mouth daintily afterwards. She liked sweet things. She'd deny it sometimes – she somehow felt it was sinful to like sweet things – but never very strongly. Her love of anything sweet was on a par with her love of clothes – eating a waffle, stroking the silk of a new garment, I'd see a spark of buried sensuality otherwise never visible or believable. Watching her eat a chocolate eclair oozing cream, or spread Cumberland rum butter on a hot scone, I'd see her face momentarily lose her Quaker look. Her eyes would narrow, a languor would steal over her, a little moan of satisfaction escape her lips . . . heaven. This love of cakes and pastries made her a good baker but not a good cook. Her day-to-day cooking was bland (though of course heavily circumscribed by the lack of money to buy good ingredients).

I liked Nan's food best. Jean's was like my mother's. Her griddle scones were sublime, but for the rest very ordinary, mostly potatoes, chipped and mashed and baked and roasted (once a week with the precious joint). Nan, on the other hand, didn't like baking. It wasn't good for the figure to eat all those cakes and scones, and she and Jack always watched their figures. But otherwise she cooked well. She had the money, the time, the interest, and the experience of eating in hotels and restaurants, which her sisters didn't have, and her food was different as a consequence. She served fish I'd never heard of, like halibut, cooked in a way which seemed exotic (wrapped in tinfoil and baked in the oven with herbs and butter). Her vegetables didn't have the hell boiled out of them, and at Nan's I found a salad didn't necessarily mean a lettuce leaf, half a tomato and a piece of beetroot. The best food of all was her cheese. I loved cheese but only knew Cheddar. At Nan's I tasted Stilton and adored it. ('Do you know how much it is a pound?' my mother asked when I suggested putting it on our Co-op order.) The rest of the family, when they stayed with Nan, always complained of being hungry afterwards but the Marshallsay fare suited me fine.

I was always glad to get home though. It puzzled me. I loved the way Nan lived but still I was glad to get home, back to the shabbiness, to the cramped conditions, and all because of my mother. There was nothing motherly about Nan, or what I thought of as motherly. My mother was thoroughly maternal and I was proud of this. She never shouted or lost her temper as Nan did, and even more important, she always put us, her children, first. Everything she did was for us without consideration for her own needs. Nan, on the other hand, frequently put herself first, much as she adored her only son Michael. What *she* wanted often mattered more than what any child wanted. No wonder Michael loved to come to stay with us. My mother and indeed my father put him first all the time, throughout his whole stay, and he naturally lapped it up. His Aunt Lily had infinite tenderness for this nephew with his disfigured lip and bronchial wheeziness and a father who seemed permanently irritated by him. Her strong maternal instincts went out to him and I watched, satisfied, knowing my mother was what a mother should be and never once stopping to query this belief.

XII

Everything to do with money in our family was handled by my mother. She paid the bills, she did the budgeting, she decreed when money could be spent and on what. My father earned the money and gave it to her (always excepting that ever-undivulged small amount he kept back so that his exact wage would not be known), but she said what could be afforded. Answer: very little. Certainly not a new bicycle for me. It was out of the question and I knew it. Every Saturday I'd torture myself by going down to T.P. Bell's, the bike shop in Abbey Street, just round the corner from where my grandmother had worked for the Stephensons, and looking at bikes. I felt my desire to have a conventional black Raleigh was modest – nothing flash, no yearning after a sports model with dropped handlebars.

I didn't blame my parents for not being able, as the parents of my new friends at the High School were able, to buy me a bike. I knew they would have done if they could and never once mentioned the subject. But I didn't have to. It was apparent when they saw me eyeing the bikes of others and swearing I'd rather walk than cycle any day. Then my father suddenly suggested I could buy a bike on HP. What was HP? 'It's wicked,' my mother pronounced immediately and, to my father, 'Don't go putting ideas like that in her head. It's scandalous. HP indeed! That's for fools wanting to get themselves into debt and for a bike, ridiculous. You should be ashamed.' But my father wasn't in the least ashamed. He was quite prepared to stick up for this wonderful thing called HP and explain it to me. It was Hire Purchase, generally known as the never-never. 'And rightly,' as my mother was quick to point out. If I signed an HP agreement with T.P. Bell I could have a new bike there and then. They'd give me a card and every week I'd go and pay five shillings until the bike was paid for. There would be a deposit of £2 10s., which I already had, and then I could manage the weekly payment if I gave all my pocket money plus the extra I earned from doing messages and any birthday and Christmas money I was given, usually a fair amount.

It seemed a brilliant idea to me, until my mother pointed out scornfully that in the end I would have paid very nearly twice what the bike cost originally and also that if I defaulted on the weekly payments T.P. Bell could claim the bike back and wouldn't have to refund the money already paid. It was how people got into a mess, my sensible mother said, and she would have nothing to do with such schemes. But the temptation was irresistible. My father went with me to T.P. Bell's and the dastardly deed was done. I rode the gleaming new Raleigh home hardly able to balance on the seat for excitement. Every Saturday, without fail, I went to the shop and paid my dues and never once regretted the long time it took until the debt was paid off. I loved that bike. My mother, who had never owned a bike, couldn't understand what it meant to me. It transformed weekends and holidays, meant I could roam all over Cumberland, to the sea, to the lakes, huge bike rides of thirty miles and more. 'She's getting her money's worth,' my father would say, pleased. To which my mother would riposte, 'She'll need to, the price she's paying.' She was so afraid he'd started me off on the road to ruin, given me the idea I could have anything I wanted on demand and pay later. But he hadn't. The weekly trips to T.P. Bell's rubbed the economic lesson in efficiently. I knew quite well what I was doing. There was no danger of the experience turning me into a spendthrift.

My father longed for a car as much as I had longed for a bike, but there was no hope of that. He didn't dare suggest getting a car on HP. My mother would have had a fit at such a crippling debt. So he filled the football pools in every week and hoped and hoped, and we hoped with him. She hated those Littlewoods coupons, hated the intensity with which the football results were listened to on *Sports Report*, hated the despondency that followed. 'A mug's game,' she'd mutter. My father ignored her and shouted at us if we made the slightest noise while he was checking his coupon. He believed in luck the way she believed in God, and for both of them there was no alternative. All over the Raffles estate there were women terrified their men would lose what money they had on some form of gambling – football pools, horses, dogs, whatever. My father had a fling on them all in a very modest way. He was best on horses. Carlisle had regular race meetings and when Jack came through he'd drive my father there and they'd bet together, Jack depending on Arthur's expertise. Jack would put twenty pounds on a horse, my father two shillings. My mother was furious with Jack for encouraging my father and even more angry with Nan for condoning this betting. Nan actually went with the men sometimes, enjoying the dressing-up and social side of it, but my mother never set foot on a racecourse. She loathed everything that went with any kind of gambling – the excitement, the tension, the euphoria of winning, just as much as the depression of losing. But my father always played his best card when she raised her regular objections. 'The Queen gambles,' he'd say, 'and the Princess gambles, thinks the world of her racehorses. What's good enough for the Royal Family is good enough for me.'

This was a low blow because my mother was a great royalist. She was all for King and Country. Everything the Royal Family did was of great importance and interest to her and she held up Princess Elizabeth and Princess Margaret Rose as role models for my sister and me. I loved Crawfie's book, *The Little Princesses*, bought for my twelfth birthday, even though I was on the edge of rejecting the Royal Family in the same way I was about to reject any belief in God (they were closely connected in my mind as a result of my mother's reverence for both). The lives of the princesses seemed to me complete bliss. I wished my own mother could live the life of the Queen – it seemed to me she could fill the role perfectly; it would suit her to wear beautiful clothes and ride in carriages and smile graciously. I looked at the photographs – pages and pages of them – and I could quite easily see myself on Lilibet's pony, cuddling Lilibet's corgi, playing in Lilibet's and Margaret's 'little' house which looked bigger than our own. As I read the book (many times), one thing puzzled me. Again and again Crawfie stressed how Lilibet 'longed to be ordinary' and did everything possible to seem so, insisting at camp that she washed the dirtiest dishes, asking to wear the drabbest clothes, being thrilled at secretly going on a bus instead of riding in a Rolls-Royce ... It was baffling. She could swap with me any time; she could have my ordinary life and I'd be royal instead. When I'd finally drained the book of every ounce of information I realized I didn't understand what the Royal Family was actually *for*. 'What does the King do?' I asked my mother. She tried to

explain that it was the Prime Minister and the elected government who ran the country and that the King on his own
didn't have a great deal of power, but this led on to needing
to tell me what a democracy was and where the Crown fitted
in, and though she was perfectly capable of outlining this, she
said she was sure teachers at the High School would be able
to explain, better than she could.

It so happened that there was a general election soon after
this discussion and it was decided that there should be a mock
election at school to teach us how real elections worked. I
came home full of it. We would all have a vote and there
would be four candidates representing the Conservative,
Labour, Liberal and Communist Parties. 'What's a Conservative? What's a Communist? Who do you vote for?' I asked
my mother. She said she was a Conservative, a True Tory,
but when it came to saying why, she could only do it in a
negative way, by saying Conservatives were not trouble-
makers, they were for the maintenance of law and order, they
didn't want 'everything upset'. A Conservative was not a
firebrand, a Conservative would run a mile from riots and
strikes and violence. My father wouldn't say how he voted.
He said it was his business and muttered mysteriously that
telling children how you voted was dangerous 'because that's
how Hitler got at people'.

But my mother told me that my grandmother, Margaret
Ann, used to get very upset with my father's loudly voiced
political opinions back in the 1920s. My father as a young
man had been 'red hot for Labour' and was for the status quo
being upset and established again to his and all working-
men's advantage. He didn't join the Labour Party, having a
deep suspicion of such organizations, but he went to some
political meetings and thought the Labour chaps spoke sense.

He'd voted Labour always, she knew he had, but apparently he was now disillusioned and wasn't going to vote because Labour hadn't benefited him personally and they were all the same these politicians, out for themselves. My mother wasn't sure if he was right in this verdict or not. She hoped after our school election I could enlighten her.

I came home every day with wilder and wilder interpretations of the political wisdom offered to me by the different candidates, who were all sixth-formers. It was obvious from the beginning that the appearance and popularity of these candidates were going to count more with us schoolgirl-voters than anything they said. The Conservative candidate was the most attractive but she wasn't a good speaker. She was very pretty, with long, blonde hair, beautifully brushed, but her voice was rather squeaky and her manner solemn. She went on about Winston Churchill and how he'd saved us from the Nazis and how ungrateful we'd been not to vote him in after the war. The Liberal candidate wasn't much better as far as the content of her speech was concerned, but she had a much louder and more forceful voice. She was very sporty too, in all the school teams, and made her party seem very healthy, the party for fit people who were not 'stuffy' like the Conservatives. The Labour candidate was just too emotional. She actually wept when she read out some newspaper report on how the poor were living in our big cities. This was, it seemed, the fault of the Conservatives even though they were not at the moment in government – Labour had done what it could but had only made a start and needed many more years in power to carry on the good work. Then there was the Communist candidate – small, ugly, bespectacled, scruffy, but what a brilliant speaker. Our entire system of government, she bellowed, was a farce. The rich got richer, the poor got poorer and nothing would change until outdated democracy was swept aside and replaced by the people as the state and the state as the people, one for all and no more class divisions, no more inequality . . . I went straight home and announced I had no doubts, I was a Communist.

It was hard to decide who was more shocked, my mother or my father. Both of them said Communists were evil, wicked people who wanted to take everything away from everybody and make the rich poor and the poor poorer. When I attempted to correct this false summary by relating what the candidate had said I was shouted down by my father – he hadn't sent me to that school to learn this kind of rubbish. I said he hadn't sent me anyway and got walloped for cheek. I tried to argue with him, pointing out that as a worker at the bottom of the heap he should be *for* Communism. But no, he wasn't. He knew what had happened in Russia and that was enough. So what had happened in Russia? Never you mind. My mother, as ever, was calmer and had a better reason for hating Communism. Communists didn't believe in God. They made the state into their own God. Since I was almost ready to declare I didn't believe in God either, this sounded quite attractive but I didn't yet dare say so.

I ended up voting for the Labour candidate but not with much conviction and with only the vaguest idea still of what was the difference between Conservative and Labour. The Conservative won with the Liberal a close second and Labour a poor third. The outstanding Communist candidate got only three votes and I was ashamed not to have voted for her. Meanwhile, outside school, the real election was going on. Posters appeared in some windows but not many, and in Raffles they were all for Labour. In Carlisle, the Labour candidate was returned but in the country in general the Conservatives triumphed. My mother was mildly pleased; my father said he didn't care. I wished aloud we had politics on the timetable as we did History and other subjects and my father said the day 'they' started 'that' it would be a bad job. Politics were trouble, politics were not for the likes of us and the sooner I learned that the better, 'or else'. But I went on feeling intrigued and even anxious about my lack of political knowledge. After we'd done a bit about nineteenth-century history at school I'd learned something about the importance of the right to vote. I knew about Keir Hardie and Ramsay MacDonald and I'd heard of Nye Bevan – I'd heard him on the wireless too before my father switched 'that rubbish' off. And I'd been influenced by the Gillespies across the road who were staunch and active Labour supporters and not afraid to say so – Mr Gillespie had stood as a Labour councillor which impressed me but not my father, who complained I was 'getting tarred with their brush'.

I said he was quite right, I was and I was glad I was.

XIII

Pleasure in general didn't feature very noticeably in my mother's life. Her sisters would hurt her by alleging she didn't know how to enjoy herself as they did, but she in turn annoyed them by clearly not rating what they called their pleasures. Jean's love of a drink and a sing-song mystified her – fancy liking pubs and noisy group outings to Blackpool. It made her shudder, all that (to her) enforced jollity, all that raucous carousing. 'Let yourself go, Lily,' Jean would urge, and be treated to an expression of bewildered outrage. My mother saw neither pleasure nor sense in any kind of abandonment. It was alien to her nature. She liked to think quiet pursuits suited her best, walks in the country, that kind of thing. But on such walks she was restless and bored, it seemed to me. 'We've sat here long enough,' she'd complain, when we'd been perched on a log in Wetheral woods above the river for only a few minutes, and we'd have to move on even though my father was absorbed watching the salmon leap and we children were happily floating bits of wood. She didn't like getting her shoes wet or dirty, or her clothes caught in brambles and even at Silloth, walking along the pristine concrete sea wall, she'd find the wind too strong while we found it exhilarating. She was hard to please, as my father constantly said, though he always said it admiringly, proud of her high standards, and the difficulties they caused.

Sometimes, in an effort of my father's to treat my mother,

we'd go to a café on our outings, but that was never a success, never gave her pleasure. There was never a cheap café fit for my mother and of course it had to be cheap or we couldn't patronize it. 'Not *there*!' my mother would cry, horrified, as my father proposed entering some shack. He'd ask why not, we only wanted a pot of tea and some lemonade. What was wrong with it? 'Everything,' my mother would snap. She was always right. I saw, with her, how dirty the tables looked, how sleazy the whole place. So we'd tramp round Keswick or Pooley Bridge, or wherever we'd gone for the day, on the bus, and eventually tempers becoming frayed, café after café rejected, my mother would agree to go into some place that at least looked clean. Then trouble would start in a different way all over again. Sometimes it would be about where we were to sit. My mother would say she didn't care but then wherever my father plonked us was hopeless – 'Not right by the door, Arthur.' More often it was over what to order. My mother would fancy a scone but they'd have no scones, or else the scone produced would be pronounced not fresh. Her critical nature couldn't let anything go and, while I felt like her, I hated the atmosphere this carping caused. If only she'd been proud of her own trenchant criticisms, if only she'd laughed at how utterly dreadful the scone or anything else was, but no, her disappointment was deep and never, ever, funny.

I knew what kind of café my mother wanted to eat in. She wanted to be in the Ritz or the Savoy in some palm court place, sitting in a chiffon dress with a white straw hat on, being served with delicious thin sandwiches and exquisite pastries on delicate china plates. Like clothes, surroundings mattered, they told you what you had become, and my mother was never going to be reconciled to a red formica table, thick chipped white pot cups, a smell of used fat and no elegance or artistry anywhere. Our outings could never give her the kind of pleasure she craved. Often, she didn't come with us at all. She said she was too tired, and she was, but she wasn't only physically tired, she was tired of disappointment. She enjoyed herself no more left at home, except for listening to *Mrs Dale's Diary* in peace. She loved Mrs Dale's life because it was the life she felt she should have had – the life of a doctor's wife, perfect. In her mind she leapt the class gulf effortlessly; she was Mrs Dale, the middle-class professional man's wife. At least she had some imaginative ability and could enter that wireless world easily.

This was where pleasure did come for her. She loved the theatre, and Her Majesty's Theatre in Carlisle, not far from where she was born and in the street where she went to school, was a very lively place right up to the end of the fifties. My mother went to see whatever the Salisbury Players were performing on Friday nights. She went with a friend, a neighbour, and sat in the gods and though she would have much preferred the dress circle she for once overcame her longing for better things and never complained about the cheap seat. But as well as going to see plays at the theatre proper she also went to all the performances given by the thriving St Barnabas's Amateur Dramatic Society. I went with her from a very young age, never for one moment thinking this was a substitute for the real thing, and my mother never suggested it was, whatever she thought. She let me be thrilled and seemed to share my excitement as we walked through Raffles to the church hall. The plays the church society was fond of were J.B. Priestley's and Terence Rattigan's, and my mother was as immersed in them as I was. We loved *Time and the Conways* and *I Have Been Here*

Before – there were lines in that one which my mother seemed to find highly significant, about people repeating their lives over and over with just small but crucial differences. She'd sigh and afterwards I'd ask why but never got a satisfactory answer. I hated the play to be over and so did she – we didn't want the main overhead hall lights to go on, or the not nearly wide enough curtains to be finally closed.

There were plays on the wireless to be enjoyed too, but listening to *Saturday Night Theatre* only led to complications. We had a wireless, a blue Bakelite thing, which could be plugged into a light socket. This was rather grandly referred to as a portable. I'd take it to bed to listen to *Saturday Night Theatre*, my favourite play of the week, so I could listen in the dark and withdraw all the better into whatever the play was about. Gordon was always out and my mother and sister didn't object. But I never heard the last ten minutes or so of any play. My father would come back from the pub and he had to have the wireless on. So just before he was due back my mother would come up and unplug the wireless and take it downstairs for him. I never even attempted to protest. That's how it was. The breadwinner had to have the wireless on while he ate his supper. My mother always said, as she did the unplugging, 'I'm sorry, but you knew it would be needed,' and she was right, I had. I had accepted the unwritten but absolutely rigid rule.

My mother, of course, had accepted many more. She had conformed throughout her life and expected me to have to do the same. When I didn't she became upset out of all proportion, as she was when I cut off my hair. This was seen as a major act of defiance, an act which would bring about retribution as surely as the shearing of Samson. Girls and women should take a pride in their hair, especially if it was like mine, long and thick and wavy, a great mane of cascading fair hair, braided and ringletted over the years by my mother. It took hours to dry. She'd wash it when I was a child and towel it as dry as possible, and then I'd sit on her knee, facing her, and lean backwards so that my hair hung like a sheet in front of the fire. 'She has lovely hair, Lily,' one and all would croon, and my mother was gratified – the cleanliness of my hair, the shine upon it, the state of it, was a credit to her.

But when I was thirteen I made my mind up. I was sick of my hair. It was a nuisance and I wanted it cut. My brother cut the end of one pigtail off and my mother was furious – 'Spoiling her lovely hair!' – but she wouldn't let me cut the other pigtail too. She said it would soon catch up, I wasn't to touch my hair. But now I wanted not just a couple of inches off but the whole lot. So I made an appointment at Binn's and went and had it all cut off – cut really, viciously short, even shaved up the back. It looked terrible, a harsh, brutal chop. I was afraid to go home, especially as I would have to pretend I loved this haircut when what I actually wanted to do was cry over its ugliness. My mother looked stricken when I edged uneasily into the house – her hand went to her mouth and her eyes widened. 'You've ruined yourself,' she whispered.

My aunts were in complete agreement. I'd ruined my looks which, in their opinion, were well on the way to ruin by now anyway. Nan in particular was appalled when, some weeks later, she came through and saw me (though by then my hair had grown a little and wasn't quite so shocking). 'You shouldn't have let her, Lily,' said Nan. 'I wouldn't have let any daughter of mine do that, ruining herself.' I jumped in to say it was nothing to do with my mother whether I cut my own hair or not. It was *my* hair, my decision and I didn't care how I looked, as if looks mattered. 'Of course they matter,' said Nan sharply. 'You'll never attract a man with hair like that.' And so we were back to the same old battle and I screamed that the last thing I wanted to do was attract men. There was more to life than that and it was a pity Nan hadn't learned it ... Uproar. My approaching two weeks' holiday at Nan's was cancelled. It was no loss. I didn't like going to Nottingham any more; the Marshallsay set-up had lost its attractions, Stilton cheese and all. It meant I wouldn't be going anywhere – almost our only holidays were visits to the two aunts, to Motherwell or Nottingham – but I was resolved not to care.

Holidays were always such a torment: the thought of them, the planning of them, the inevitably unsatisfactory nature of the ones that did happen. It was almost preferable having none, to go back to having 'days': a day out at Silloth, a day at Keswick, and so on. But we did twice go away for a whole week, all of us except Gordon who was, as ever, at Scout camp. When I was eight we had had a caravan holiday at Allonby, on the Solway coast a few miles west of Silloth. We went by train to Silloth as we often did on 'days', only this time we were important, we had luggage, we were staying. The train was, as usual, crowded and we had to fight to get on. My father barged his way to the front of the three-deep crowd standing on the platform and was one of the first into the carriage which stopped abreast with him, but he could only secure one seat before others jammed themselves into place. My mother had hung back from this unseemly pushing and shoving, but now she took the seat he'd captured – it was all like a war – and my sister sat on her knee while my father and I stood.

It wasn't a long journey, only about forty minutes, and

seemed even shorter because we knew the stations off by heart. We caught the first glimpse of the sea at Burgh-by-Sands and excitement grew until at last the tower of the church opposite Silloth Green came into view. The crowds exploded on to the platform at once, one mad panic of arrival, children shouting and running, eager to get to the sea, with buckets and spades. We had to catch a bus next to get to our caravan which involved quite a wait. My mother sat on our case and my father went off to get us ice-creams at Mr Brown's. We adored these cornets of swirly soft ice-cream and so did our mother, but since she thought they were messy things to eat she often denied herself one in order to keep her blouse spotless – a lick from ours would suffice. But on this, our first proper holiday, she'd agreed to have a cornet and my father was delighted, such willingness to be self-indulgent was a good sign and augured well for the coming week.

In my mind's eye I had seen what our caravan would be like. I'd seen it in picture-books. It would be a Romany caravan, colourfully painted, intricately carved, with cunning little windows and giant wheels, and there would be a chestnut horse between the shafts who would pull it along the seashore with us sitting up in front of the door and my father holding the reins . . . The bus we'd caught in Silloth stopped at a field gate just before Allonby. We were deposited there with our case and two bags of food. I stared. This must be a mistake. There were forty caravans parked in rows. None of them was of the Romany variety. There was not a horse in sight. The caravans were like tin boxes, ugly, squat shapes painted dirty cream or blue. No carvings, no big wheels. The field was muddy and as we walked to our caravan, called (heartbreakingly) Sea Rhapsody, we could smell the latrines. My father attempted cheerfulness but was as usual defeated by my mother's inability to pretend. 'Is this it?' she said. 'Is *this* what we've paid all that money for?' She could hardly bear to open the door and look inside our home for the next seven days. Inside there were two lots of bunks, either side of an excruciatingly narrow gangway, and the most makeshift of kitchen arrangements at the end. We couldn't all get into the caravan at once and it was clear that, if we wanted to, those first in would have to crawl into the bottom bunks. My mother didn't weep, but her rage was worse than any tears – her face was quite contorted and the tension unbearable. My father bundled us out and took us off to the sea at once, mumbling to my furious mother that he'd leave her to settle in.

Everything then depended on the weather. Miraculously, the sun shone the next day, diluting some of my mother's bitterness, and we were out of the awful caravan from eight in the morning till ten at night. My father dug for worms and then sat fishing, and my sister and I made sandcastles and paddled and wanted to swim, but our mother said it was too cold, we should give the water time to warm up (though whether the Solway Firth ever warms up is doubtful). She sat on a rug and rested, her back against the wooden supports dividing the beach into sections and breaking the force of the high winter tides. This was her holiday, the first in ten years, and a large part of it was spent reminiscing about other holidays at Silloth and Allonby when she was a child. She said how wonderful holidays with her father had been. I asked which caravan they'd stayed in and she was scornful. They had *not* stayed in a caravan, her father had rented a whole house, they had stayed in comfort, they had had their meals made for them, it hadn't been like *this* at all. I turned this over in my mind as I went looking for shells (hard to find and only ordinary varieties). It was dawning on me that my mother considered she had come down in the world and the caravan was part of this unpleasant realization, the corned beef sandwiches we were eating for our dinner another. When I returned to where she was still sitting, her face raised to the sun, her eyes closed, I thought she looked so sad in spite of the luck of a lovely day. She did say 'this is pleasant' quite often but I wasn't sure if this constituted happiness.

We only went into the caravan to sleep and my sister and I slept straight away. My father went to the pub and then I suppose he came back and slept straight away too, the bunk situation and our proximity being what they were. For five whole days the sun blazed down, a record, and we lived on Allonby's wide and empty beach, our only company the horses from the stables exercising in the shallow waves at the edge of the sea, and the other caravanners off to livelier Silloth. My mother tanned beautifully. Off came her stock- ings and her cardigan, though she never ventured into any kind of bathing costume – she said she was too old. Old women shouldn't degrade themselves by what she called baring their flesh (she was forty-five). My father took his shirt off and went red and put it back on again and my mother said she should think so, but she smiled. This real holiday was doing her good. It had been worth it, wretched caravan or not. But on the sixth day, the day before we were to leave, we woke to grey skies and a stinging cold wind scudding straight towards us off the sea. 'I knew it couldn't last,' my mother said, triumphantly, but she was quite philo- sophical about this change in the weather. We put jumpers on and took raincoats and went into Silloth to the funfair and had a ride on the donkeys, even though by then it was raining. It had been a successful holiday, whatever the final day was like.

We had two others in the next decade before I left home. Three years and much saving later we had another caravan, this time parked in a field the other side of Silloth, at Skinburness. Another tin box, though bigger and better equipped and with a curtain between the bunks. But this time we had no luck. It poured with rain the entire week. The whole holiday – 'so-called holiday' as my mother put it – was a disaster and argument raged the entire time between my parents as to whether we should give up and go home. My father was forever expecting the sun to come out, so he wanted to hang on, whereas my mother knew it wouldn't and wanted to cut her losses. We stayed. We marched along the sea wall to the shelter and delights of a storm-battered Silloth and got soaked both going and coming back and there was nowhere to dry our clothes. My mother then stayed in the caravan moping while we got changed and went back to Silloth – another soaking – to the cinema, then cowered in a café before braving another return home. 'Never again,' my mother vowed, 'no more caravans.' So after that she turned to trying to get lodgings in various holiday resorts. The *Cumberland News* had loads of adverts – 'AYR. Board. Good Food. Homely' and 'BLACKPOOL. Central, Board 12/6. H and C'. (H and C was greatly prized, meaning hot and cold running water in your room.) She wrote off to boarding-houses in Keswick, Morecambe, Rothesay and many other places, but they were either fully booked for the week my father had to take his holiday, or else too expensive. In the end we went – where else? – to Silloth.

But at least we were not in a caravan; we were in lodgings, right opposite the Green. I didn't want to go at all. I was by then fifteen, and Silloth had no appeal, I couldn't bear the thought of it. Every day I stalked off by myself, endlessly walking the sea wall to Grune Point, the wild little peninsula on the marshland past Skinburness. The weather was blustery but it didn't rain and an evening meal was provided at the boarding-house and my mother was reasonably content. She was having a rest and said that was all that mattered, she hadn't expected anything else. My father was quite happy, as he always was at Silloth, though in my mother's opinion he rather overdid the odd pint on the grounds that he was on holiday. But then she couldn't bear alcohol of any kind. She regarded drinking as evil. We were all enrolled in the Rechabites, we children, and their philosophy, if it could be called that, was hers: never touch a drop. Pubs, she thought, were by definition wicked places and she was afraid of them. I was afraid of them too, especially the Horse and Farrier, the pub at the end of our road in Raffles. At closing-time men would spill out roaring and laughing, hordes of them, staggering home by clinging on to hedges. We slept at the front of the house and the noise on weekend nights was terrifying. It sounded as if hundreds, not dozens, of men were hurtling past our house and they sounded violent and out of control. My father would stand at the window worrying about his hedge and shout at those being punched into it in some fight, but his protests weren't even heard, the passing of the inebriated just had to be tolerated.

It was only at Christmas and New Year that my mother sanctioned drink in our house: a bottle of sherry and a bottle of port, for visitors only, to wish them the season's greetings in the accepted manner. I liked the sherry and port glasses she produced. They'd been her mother's. The sherry glasses were fluted, on long stems, and the port glasses had ruby-red flowers painted on them. Sherry or port was only ever offered in minute quantities, with thick slabs of cake or several fingers of shortbread, never on its own. But when our relations came, the Marshallsays and the Wallaces, sherry and port were spurned. They brought their own whisky, as a present, and opened it and drank it in significant quantities. Nan didn't have any – she preferred Dubonnet, she said, to eyes raised mockingly to the ceiling behind her back – but Jean did. She was annoyed at my mother's quite unconcealed look of disapproval. 'A tot of whisky never harmed anyone, Lily,' she would say, but my mother didn't deign to reply. To her whisky was not just wicked, it was an unfeminine drink and that was that. If Jean was going to drink whisky, she wished she would do it somewhere other than in our house.

Though the drinking would begin at our house on these occasions, it would be quickly adjourned to a hotel bar where there was more room (as well as more drink). We had so little space and squashing six adults and sometimes six children into a room twelve feet by ten and giving everyone a seat was tricky. It was even worse if the Wallaces stayed overnight, which they usually did because they couldn't afford an hotel like the Marshallsays. Then, they were given my parents' bed and my parents slept downstairs on the settee, and we children slept end to end, feet to heads, in one double bed. As we grew older and bigger this proved impossible and my mother would agonize over sleeping arrangements for days, trying to work out the best way to make everyone comfortable – there was certainly no jollity about it, no we'll-all-muck-in-together-somehow. Even without relations staying, there was a lot of agonizing going on after Gordon came back from doing his National Service. If he was given back the second bedroom, where would my sister and I go? At fourteen and eleven we were too old to return to our bed-in-the-wall in our parents' room. My mother was distraught thinking about it. She wrote to the council, asking to be moved to a house with three bedrooms, and preferably one off the Raffles estate which was becoming rougher all the time. Nothing happened. She scanned the *Cumberland News* every week, looking for swaps: families on council estates wanting to exchange their houses for bigger or smaller ones (which was allowed by the council if you could find someone agreeable). Then she put her own advert in – 'Exchange two-bedroomed house Orton Road for three-bedroomed-parlour-type, any estate considered'. The Orton Road bit was to denote we lived at the better end of Raffles, since its garden-city image had vanished. There was some response but people lost interest when they discovered we had an outside lavatory and no proper bathroom. Our house was not desirable even though it was in immaculate condition, regularly painted and papered by my father and kept spotlessly clean by my mother. What were we to do?

I had a solution I thought very obvious and neat. My grandfather was a widower now and still living in his privately owned three-bedroomed-and-parlour house in Richardson Street. He only used one room. We should move him into our council house and take over his. Simple, surely. No, not simple. My mother told me not to be so silly, you couldn't just uproot old people just for your own convenience. And, anyway, our house was not ours and Grandad's *was* his. It wouldn't be fair. In any case, she didn't like his house. It was too big, too cold, too ugly, too old-fashioned. My turn to say she was silly: it had three bedrooms and a parlour, didn't it? Well, then, that was enough, the space it would give us. Nothing else mattered to me. But at that moment a swap did come up: a three-bedroomed-parlour-type council house with – oh, joy – a proper bathroom and indoor lavatory on the Longsowerby estate, the oldest and best of Carlisle's council estates. It overlooked the cemetery. My father didn't like the idea of this at all, but my mother found it a major attraction. She thought the cemetery a lovely place, more like a park, and it was true, it was like a park. It had been built in 1855 and had beautiful old trees lining its avenues which led from the main gates to the two chapels. These avenues were tarmac'd and straight but there were also narrower gravel paths connecting up with them, some following semi-circular patterns. The whole cemetery was magnificently maintained and in the summer a show place for bedding plants – hundreds and hundreds of geraniums and dahlias and other violently coloured flowers laid out with regimental precision.

But the state of this house when we moved in was appalling. My mother wept when she saw it and was perfectly justified. It was filthy, absolutely infested with every kind of dirt and bug. Every room needed to be stripped and cleaned and painted, every surface scrubbed and disinfected. For once, I helped. I scraped walls, scraped paint, even scrubbed the floors and the black-leaded range, though this proved a waste of labour. Grandad was paying for it to be taken out and a modern fireplace put in. He was becoming more generous in his old age and, on his own initiative, hearing my mother express her loathing of this range, he bought something called an Osborne All-Tile fireplace (price £10 15s. od.), complete with a heavy steel grate and coloured vitreous enamel front to match. How we loved it. I could hardly wait to get home to see this wonderful artefact replace the old range, caring only that what seemed black and dirty, and hell to clean and maintain, had given way to what seemed light, bright and labour-free by comparison.

The house took many months to transform. My father could only do the decorating after work and on Sundays – he was doing overtime to pay for the paper and paint – so progress was slow. He'd come home around seven o'clock after his twelve-hour day and have his supper, then climb a ladder and start stripping the staircase and he'd be so exhausted he'd have to come down to be sick – it was too much. My mother was left day after day in all the mess and if there was one thing she could not stand it was disorder, the horror of nothing looking tidy or attractive. She was depressed but then so was I, and it was her life that depressed me most and the fear that in spite of my efforts my life, too, would be like hers. It wasn't a new realization. I'd seen ages ago her life was drudgery of one kind or another, but I was more frightened by it than I had ever been. Why go on for this, my mother's existence, the existence of those women I saw around me? She talked often of how hard her mother's life had been, without giving any details, but I couldn't see hers was any easier. When she said, in exasperation, and these were exasperating times, 'What a life!' I would burst out with, 'Why did you choose it, then?', she'd say she didn't choose it, it happened. This would lead to my refusal to accept this. I'd say she shouldn't have got married because it was getting married which had surely led to the life she had. The worst moment, after I'd asked her why she got married, was when she said she had wanted children, that was why. It was such a rotten bargain to have made. *Children*, in exchange for what? Giving up work she loved, condemning herself to drudgery.

Never once did she say it had been worth it, that she had three children and nothing else mattered.

I knew I could never make the same deal. I wasn't even sure I could make the same deal, a different one only on the surface, that Nan had made. Nan didn't have my mother's hard life. She now had her pleasant house, her car (well, Jack's), her lovely clothes and jewellery, but I had begun to see her life was dreary too, if soft and easy, and it was repellent to me. Nan did virtually nothing. She still had her char (devoted to her, of course) to clean her already clean house, a house with only two adults in it most of the time and so the work was light. She got up about ten, after lolling in bed having her breakfast, brought to her on a tray by Jack before he left for work, and then she had a bath. Then she dressed and did her face. This took up a huge slice of time – doing her face was a lengthy ritual involving the use of many creams and lotions and powders – really, quite exhausting. She looked terrific, always. The char left at lunchtime and Nan had a snack, then her famous forty winks before taking her Pekinese dog for a walk of all of a hundred yards. After that, the highlight of the day ... shopping. For clothes, for herself. People told her she looked like a mannequin, to her delighted gratification. 'I should have been a mannequin,' she'd murmur, smiling, and I'd say, rudely, 'What for? What a stupid, useless thing to be. Just a clothes-horse, horrible.'

No, I didn't want Nan's life, even if it was obviously preferable to Jean's or my mother's – except for one aspect of it. Nan loved Jack and was loved by him and I had a new interest in the whole business of love. Ask Nan why she married and the answer was that she'd fallen passionately in love with Jack. So much more cheering to a fifteen-year-old, that answer. And she was quite willing to go on about the

222

passion too. Nothing she liked better than to describe the 'bliss' of being in love, the 'ecstasy' of being in Jack's arms . . . 'Oh!' she'd shudder. 'Oh! It's heaven, wonderful. You wait.' Then she'd add the bit she shouldn't have done. 'Your mother doesn't think so, mind,' she'd say, with such a heavy significance I'd feel embarrassed, without quite knowing why, and defensive on my mother's behalf. But I didn't doubt the truth of what she said either about herself or her sister. I could see the evidence of Nan's and Jack's passion. They were quite old to me but they touched each other all the time — kisses, cuddles, arm-strokings — and sometimes Jack would come home for lunch and say to Nan why didn't she have her forty winks upstairs with him, it would be more comfortable, and she would at first demur and say what about the children, and he'd say the children could go out into the garden and play, and she'd disappear with him, giggling, and reappear an hour later looking flushed. It was reassuring, really, to know at least one woman had married for passion and had stayed passionate after so many years. I didn't know (and neither did Nan) that Jack spread his passion around. He had many affairs, one of them with his young secretary with whom Nan was very friendly, but it wasn't until later that these became common knowledge and even then he argued they didn't make any difference to his passion for Nan.

Nan started asking me if I had a boyfriend when I was only thirteen and kept up the questioning from then on. It used to worry me at first that I had to say no, I hadn't. It seemed such a sign of failure, but then I began to get irritated by this harping on boyfriends and would snap at her when asked. It was so insulting to be judged according to whether I had a boyfriend, and the worst thing was not to be believed when I said I didn't want one. But Nan's curiosity, and her belief that a boyfriend was vital if a girl was to have any status, was shared by almost everyone. Certainly everyone at school thought as she did. By the time we were all fifteen practically the whole of our class had boyfriends, and what was done by and with these boys was the major topic of conversation. Above us we had a terrifying example of what having a boyfriend could lead to. For weeks nothing else was talked about except the pregnancy of one of the cleverest and prettiest girls in the fifth form – she was going to have to get married and argument raged over the rights and wrongs, the delights and horrors of this. The girl was seen every lunchtime standing at the school gate in a clinch with the boy she was going to have to marry and we'd go and stare, fascinated by her boldness, her lack of shame, until a teacher would come along and order the boy to leave at once.

I thought this girl was mad, quite crazy. I shivered at the mere thought of being trapped with a baby at sixteen. Why had she done it? Why hadn't she taken care not to get pregnant? But the minute I'd wondered that, I also wondered how that was done. How was care taken, how was pregnancy prevented? Some knowing sort of girls would claim to have access to methods of prevention, but they were always self-important about it and not prepared to share their mysterious knowledge. I didn't see how anyone could have sex if they ran the risk of becoming pregnant and even though I had absolutely no need to know about contraception then, I felt an urgent need to find out long before it was in the least necessary. Books were the only way. I looked at medical books in the library – furtively, though I was ashamed of being furtive – but they weren't much good. I did find one of Marie Stopes's books which, though not nearly explicit enough, gave me hope. Somewhere there were Family Planning Clinics, somewhere there were devices that could be fitted which would prevent babies. Good. When I needed to I was resolved to find them. No boy, no amount of passion à la Nan, was going to impregnate me and spoil my ambitious plans. My mother, my aunts, they had made the fatal mistake of being trapped by children, and I wasn't going to.

The vital thing was to be independent, to be single-minded, to have a goal and allow no distractions.

XIV

There was, at last, an actual goal. I wished that this goal was also an actual job, a career. I wished I could say I wanted to be a doctor or a lawyer, something definite and recognizable to stop the background murmurs at home that education was a waste of time for girls. But I couldn't. All I could say was that my goal was to go to university, Oxford or Cambridge if possible.

University was naturally not a goal I thought up myself but was put into my head by teachers long before I had any real idea what it was. As far as I was concerned it was an extension of my beloved school, only better because you could be there all the time and in a sense get paid to go there. Miss Wynne, my English teacher, gave me booklets about Oxford and Cambridge and I was spellbound by the photographs – they looked literally like fairy-tale places to me, so beautiful, so utterly desirable, so worth having no boyfriends for. It was tantalizing how near escape from home and my mother's life suddenly seemed – all I had to do was work hard and do well in examinations and I could go off to this amazing place called university. It could be felt, it was solid, this route out of Carlisle, it wasn't a vague dream any more. A hop, skip and jump and I'd be there. Again and again I checked that having no money would not bar me, and was always reassured that even without scholarships I would qualify for grants that would cover everything. My mother didn't believe it, and neither did my father, but I was finally convinced.

I was saving hard, though, to equip myself to go when the time came. On Saturdays I worked in Marks & Spencer, in the Christmas holidays on the post, and in the other holidays in the Steam Laundry. The work in the laundry showed me there was a life far worse than my mother's as a hard-pressed housewife, a life I should dread far more. I got up at six-thirty, at the same time as my father had always done. I couldn't believe how cold the house was. I stood and shivered as I watched him laying the fire and lighting it as he had done ever since my mother's operation, so that we would all come down after he'd cycled off to work to find it burning cheerfully. He made his own fried breakfast, but I left before the smell of the frying could make me feel sick and got my bike out of the shed and set off across Carlisle to the Steam Laundry. We had to clock in – pay was deducted for every minute late – and then it was straight into the huge, draughty room where the dirty clothes were sorted, which opened off the laundry-room itself. The noise was such a shock, a great, tearing, thumping and hissing and clanging, making all talk impossible (though I could see the women around me talking all the time and somehow being understood). I hated the noise more than the smell: a hot, stuffy, cloying smell of soap and disinfectant which clung to the overalls we had to wear and to our hair, theoretically completely covered with caps. I was put first to sorting the in-coming dirty clothes before I graduated to making up the out-going parcels. The clothes arrived in bags which were tipped on to the ground and then every item was tagged before being sorted for different kinds of wash. I could hardly bear to lift some of the filthier items. My fingers plucked at blood-stained knickers disdainfully and the other women had hysterics at my Lady Muck expression. That was not the way to do it – they did it scornfully, jokingly, day in and day out for meagre wages and were immune to the stains and stench. They seemed immune to their entire surroundings, but then how could they be? How could I tell that they were? The lavatories were disgusting. It was an ordeal using them, slipping on the cracked concrete floor swimming in foul water leaking from the broken basins, and barely able to look at the dark brown scummy lavatory bowls, never mind the overflowing sanitary towel bins. It was even colder in the lavatory area than in the factory but the women huddled against the walls and smoked and tried to extend their tea break.

Marks & Spencer was like heaven compared with the laundry. The pay in the laundry for a gruelling eight-hour day, six days a week, was ten shillings, whereas at Marks & Spencer it was almost twice that for a job where the only hardship was utter boredom. It was easy standing behind a counter selling socks – a clean, undemanding, even pleasant way to pass the day and get paid for it. For one day, anyway. After that the boredom grew and grew, the endless suppression of yawns, the disbelief that surely against all the evidence only half an hour had gone by. But the perks were good. Cheap meals in a proper canteen, a special discount on clothes, and a hairdressing salon available in lunch-hours. The women working there were lucky and they knew it, but though I had the laundry to measure it by I still couldn't grasp how this job could be done for life. You could be on autopilot all day since only the smallest amount of brain power was needed to ring up prices and pop goods into a bag. But I knew none of the women could afford that kind of luxury, the luxury of analysing what they did and labelling it boring. Boredom didn't come into the reckoning. To live, they needed money; to earn money, they had to work; to work, they took what they could get; if they could get work in Marks & Spencer, they were privileged.

I didn't want my mother's life, but I didn't want life as a working woman in the laundry or even in Marks & Spencer. I didn't want to be condemned to a routine, dull job. Ambition was still fuelled by what I saw around me and I couldn't understand why everyone else at school didn't feel the same. Why weren't they all, as I was, raging and burning to have lives other than those of the women we knew? Yet most expectations were low. There were plenty of girls who wanted only some kind of pleasant job for a few years until Mr Right came along and claimed them. They saw no need for the kind of panic to escape that I was in. To *want* so much, as I did, was to be hard and selfish and strange. It was not normal to be so rampantly restless, to be so demanding. Aiming at Oxford or Cambridge was showing off. I even thought that myself and dreaded public failure. I couldn't speak about my lack of confidence when I knew that to everyone I seemed so absolutely confident. At home, my father was hostile to the whole idea of any university – daft, I was a girl, I'd just get married. I'd be better off working and contributing to the ever-low family exchequer. My mother was not hostile but my ambition confused her. It was unsettling, disturbing, having a daughter wanting to stay at school (which was all university was) for ever. She was proud of my puny achievements so far, my little academic successes, but where would it lead? Only to her own situation, she thought, to a defeat-by-marriage. What had been good enough for the women in the family so far would in the end have to be good enough for me. If, by some fluke, I moved on to another kind of life it would only be at the cost of separating myself from her – it would be a kind of rejection and the thought of this hurt in advance.

Nan and Jean asked constantly when I was going to start work and make myself some money. Nan especially, on her quite regular visits, was persistent. 'Eighteen?' she'd exclaim, 'You're eighteen, and still at school? Good heavens, I had my own business at eighteen.' I'd say nothing, knowing what was to follow. 'And I knew how to enjoy myself. What are you doing tonight? Oh, I loved Friday nights. I'd be off to dance all night when I was eighteen. Where are you off to?' I'd say the Garret Debating Society. She almost choked with contempt. 'Debating? *Debating?* A young girl like you? On a Friday night? Whatever is the world coming to?' My lack of response only spurred her to further efforts. 'Where's your fun?' she'd ask. 'Where's your pleasure? What's the point of being a girl if you spend Friday nights debating, eh?' I'd feel bound to extol the delights of a vigorous discussion on the H-bomb over her remembered bliss of dancing the Charleston, but the more pompous I sounded the more she shook her head. I never let Nan suspect it but her scorn made me miserable. She painted such an enviable picture of her social life as an eighteen-year-old in the twenties, whirling around in a constant dance, a glittering, beautiful girl who knew only too well what fun was. She made my kind of fun suddenly seem what in fact it was – staid, solemn, too leaden to come under the heading of fun at all. 'If I'd had a daughter,' she would always finish, '*she* wouldn't have been doing any of this debating on Friday nights. She'd have been a real girl.'

But she didn't have a daughter, and how she pined for one, and so did Jean. My mother had the daughters. She'd ended up the lucky one, to their dismay and surprise. Attacking me for not being a 'real' girl was a crude way of attacking my mother and I vaguely understood that. Nan was somehow jealous. She wanted to recreate in me what she had been at the best stage of her now disappointing life. But I was no good as a substitute daughter any more. She and Jack couldn't dress me up and take me around as once they had done. Jack was sure I was a Communist. My truculence upset him, all my loud talk of things not being fair. His daughter wouldn't have turned out like that. She'd have been a clone of Nan but with the advantages Nan had never had, and it would have been fun, fun, fun. Watching me go off to my ludicrous debating society quite distressed him.

It was fairly ludicrous, too. The Garret was exactly that: a very small attic room at the top of a rickety staircase in one of Carlisle's medieval lanes. By the late fifties these lanes were in a dilapidated state and the houses crumbling. In this garret there was a Youth Club, set up by the sixth forms of the boys' Grammar School and the girls' High School soon after the Second World War. It was also supposed to be a place where students could go to study, but all they did was study each other and plan as many socials as possible. Every now and again there would indeed be a debate, just for the look of the thing, but so much jeering went on that by the time a vote was taken on the evening's proposal nobody could remember who had said what. I was good at debating, which was how I allowed myself to be persuaded to go to the Garret, but long after I'd discovered what a farce the debating was I went on going. There was something secretive and even hopeful about entering the narrow lane and walking down the cobbled passage to the dark little Garret entry. The whole point of the shabby room was that it was a meeting place, a hanging-about place, and those were otherwise unknown in a Carlisle where, after five o'clock, there were no coffee bars unless the Milk Bar was counted. I liked having somewhere to go and it was wonderfully convenient to pretend the Garret Debating Society was a most worthy, intellectual institution. My mother was impressed, even if Nan wasn't. Other girls went to dances and parties but I went out to debate and for once she was gratified. I came home and kept the illusion intact, never mentioning the socials. These were held in a larger room across the staircase and consisted merely of records being played (until the arrival of skiffle). I didn't care about the music. It was all noise to me, and nor did I dance. There would be so many teenagers crammed into the room nobody could tell who was dancing and who was not, and there was no room for anyone to be such an obvious thing as a wallflower. Nan would've been wasted in the Garret.

Some of the boys who went to the Garret were clever but not intimidatingly so. I liked trying to best them in argument but that was as far as my interest went. I wasn't going to be distracted, I had a purpose in life. I still didn't care in the least that everyone else had a boyfriend and I didn't.

In December 1956 I was summoned for interview at both Oxford and Cambridge. The journey itself was an adventure since I'd never been further south than Nottingham and even then never on my own. My mother worried about – what else? – my clothes. Lately, I'd developed such weird habits. I wouldn't wear nylon stockings. I said I hated suspender belts. They were like harnesses and I wasn't a horse. So there I was, eighteen and either bare-legged or wearing socks if it was very cold. My mother thought this shocking. She'd worn a corset, never mind a suspender belt, since she was sixteen and considered this an inseparable part of being a woman – it proved you were a woman when you got to that corset-wearing stage. It appalled her to see me at eighteen wearing my silly socks and flat shoes. That was another thing. I wouldn't wear proper court shoes or any shoe with a high heel. Other girls couldn't wait to get into high heels, they were a coming-of-age rite, but I loathed them. Then there was the continuing disgrace of my hair, still cropped short. Socks, flat shoes, butchered hair ... and the black clothes to which I was devoted. She was in despair.

She didn't know what to say when I set off for these interviews. Good luck, she supposed, but what in this context did it mean? That I would be offered a place at Oxford or Cambridge? Well, she could hope that for my sake, because she knew how much I wanted it, but not for her own. She wished aloud that she could envisage where I was going but she couldn't, in spite of the photographs she'd seen. She couldn't imagine Girton or Somerville. She couldn't imagine what the women dons could possibly be like except that they would not be like her, that was for sure. They'd be spinsters, she supposed, clever, single women dedicated to learning and knowing nothing of wash-houses or cleaning out grates. A cut-off-from-reality life, very nice, very pleasant, and yet she still could not truly imagine it.

Nor could I. Girton was the first shock. It was so ugly, so vast and chilling and gloomy. Arriving there on a December afternoon in the rain I felt I was entering a prison. The corridors seemed endless, the closed doors forbidding and, though there was a grandeur about the main hall, it repelled me. The interviews themselves were fine, the interviewers quite unterrifying and I had no bother with any of the questions. But back in the dreary room I'd been allocated I wondered how I could successfully pretend to want to come to this place should I be accepted. Oxford was better. It was the next morning I went on to Somerville and the rain had stopped and by the time I was walking up St Giles the sun was out and the place sparkled. Somerville was not prison-like, it was merely disappointingly modern-looking but at least quite unthreatening. There wasn't much difference in the interviews but there was in the surroundings and food. Everything here was lighter and brighter. There were flowers and paintings everywhere, the mood was cheerful. If I go anywhere, if I get in to both, I'll come here, I thought, even if for all the wrong reasons, and that was before the final persuasion, the interview with the Principal, Janet Vaughan.

By the time I came to be sitting outside Janet Vaughan's room I was beginning to think there must be something the matter with me. I didn't seem able to communicate with any of the women who'd so far interviewed me. I could reply to their questions but I didn't seem able to connect with the questioners. These dons were so remote from the sort of women I knew. Their voices were different – accents, vocabulary, intonation – and so were their clothes and rooms. They weren't even akin to the teachers at school but an entirely alien breed to me. None of them seemed interested in me but only in what I knew. But Janet Vaughan *was* interested. I recognized her curiosity at once. She sat at the end of her long room and it seemed a test of deportment to get to the chair opposite her which she indicated, but once there I felt for the first time quite comfortable. She was a slender, fine-boned woman with dark hair parted in the middle and drawn back into a bun. She wasn't beautiful but she had a vitality, an alertness, about her which was attractive. Her eyes engaged and yet there was something nervous about them, and her smile flickered on and off making her seem shy. She was wearing a brown tweed suit and cream silk blouse with a large cameo brooch at the neck. Elegant, in an understated kind of way, a woman maybe as interested in clothes as my mother.

My History teacher had told me a bit about Janet Vaughan. I knew that she was almost the same age as my mother and that she was married and had two daughters a little older than me. She was famous for having done some kind of medical research in Belsen when it was liberated and I was in awe of this. This wasn't a woman who'd been shut in any kind of ivory tower – she'd seen the world at its worst, she'd witnessed horrific events. My mother, when I'd passed on this meagre information, had said, sadly and enviously, 'A woman who's made something of herself then.' I respected her before I met her and now I was in front of her was thrown by her very ordinariness. But her eyes were sharp, shrewd, when they did settle down and rest on me. She spoke in an odd, rather abrupt fashion. She asked me why I wanted to come to Somerville and I said I wasn't sure that I did want to. I blurted out some rigmarole about Oxford and Cambridge having been such a goal for so long I hadn't even thought about what it would be like once I got there – the getting there was everything. I just wanted out of the life I was born into and university was the best exit from it. She asked me what kind of life it was that I wanted to escape and I sketched in my mother's fate. I didn't know, of course, that her own mother had been a frustrated woman, for quite different reasons, and that Janet Vaughan's own ambition had been fuelled as much by her mother's melancholy as mine had been by my own mother's. Nor did I know that she was a Socialist determined to help bring about changes in society, structural changes. I was in so many ways exactly the kind of working-class girl she wanted at Somerville. The only other question she asked me was what I thought I might do after university. I said I wanted to write biographies and we had a discussion on the worth and nature of biography in general. She asked me whom I'd most like to write about and I said Christabel Pankhurst. She said, 'What a good idea,' and that was that.

It was hard to know what to say when I returned home. Not the truth, anyway. So I said very little. A full five days went by. It seemed obvious I'd been rejected by both Oxford and Cambridge. My mother was upset for me – I'd tried so hard and in the end my ambition had been for nothing. Pushing my bike up the hill in the dark and rain of the December Friday afternoon I felt like my mother, pessimistic and weary and hopeless. But when I got to the gate, the front door opened at once and my mother stood silhouetted against the hall light holding out two telegrams. It was reminiscent of the wretched Merit exam, only this time I had more control. Somerville offered a History Scholarship, Girton an Exhibition. I found it hard to credit and what was awful was that mixed up with elation there was so much doubt. Did I really want to go to Oxford (for it was Somerville I'd choose)? If so, why? Just as an escape route? Was that a good enough reason?

The sudden uncertainty blighted the joy, but I kept it well hidden.

In March 1957 I left home, as I'd always wanted to do, not to go to Oxford but to Bordeaux as an au pair girl, something forced on me in an effort to make my excruciating French better. I couldn't see why bad French should be a handicap for a History scholar but Somerville thought otherwise, and anyway going to France would fill in the long months before Oxford.

The au pair post was fixed up by my French teacher through some university newspaper. My mother was bewildered. What was an au pair? I hardly knew myself. A sort of servant, I said. She didn't like that at all – servant to servant in one generation. I tried again, not exactly a servant, more a kind of mother's help, a member of the family looking mostly after the children. 'But you don't like helping, you don't like children,' my mother protested. Too true. But it wouldn't have to matter, being an au pair was just a means to an end. The family I was going to join sent a snap of themselves. '*Five* children!' my mother exclaimed. 'They'll be RCs,' my father said, shaking his head. The mother said she had been a teacher but now ran a bookshop and the father was a university lecturer. Sounded good to me. All that bothered me was getting there.

It was such a simple journey from Carlisle to Bordeaux – I wasn't off to the Amazon – but it was daunting. Nobody in my family had ever been abroad. The most daring journey ever made was by my father when he went as a young man to London for the day. He went to King's Cross station, walked round it, thought nothing of it, and came back, to boast forever he had been to London. I bought a new case.

Nan said good luggage was important, it would last a lifetime, and for once I listened to her. I bought a large, real leather case and it became the curse of that trip. It weighed a ton, empty. Full, I could barely lift it and certainly couldn't carry it more than a yard at a time. It looked splendid though, its tan-coloured leather burnished, its straps and buckles so secure. I looked quite good too in, to my mother's joy, a new blue suit – she'd been terrified I would set off in my horrible trousers and duffel jacket (which would have been a much better idea). 'You're as cool as a cucumber,' my mother said admiringly as we waited for the taxi to arrive. I wasn't. Confident I looked, confident I was not, but she would have hated to realize that.

My inner panic was spotted by a suave Romanian, who talked to me on the boat train. I was in a state of near collapse after a disastrous race across London – I'd gone to Waterloo instead of Victoria Station – and nearly missed the train. This Romanian had probably seen me staggering down the plat-form hampered by my 'good luggage', but he didn't speak to me until we were nearly at Dover. 'Going to Paris?' he asked, and I said no, to Bordeaux via Paris. 'Ah,' he said, 'my train too.' He was very handsome, very un-Carlisle. He took charge of me when we got to Calais. When he whistled, a porter came and included my 'good luggage' with the moun-tains of the stuff belonging to him. In Paris he said that as we had four hours to put in, perhaps I'd allow him to show me a little of the city he knew so well? We whizzed about in a taxi, then walked along the Seine and on to the Ile St-Louis. We had lunch, outside, and then coffee somewhere else, outside. My life had begun, my mother's was already left behind.

We got the night train to Spain, which is where he was

going. At first we talked, my history, soon told, and his, a long business. His Christian name was Serge and he spoke fourteen languages. He dreamt in French. He was a business-man – no business named – and he was going to Madrid. It grew dark and he pulled the blinds of our carriage down. I was so, so tired. Five hours to London, another five to Paris and then the excitement of sightseeing – I was exhausted. He wasn't. He watched me yawn and said I needed a shoulder to lean on and crossed over to sit beside me. His arm went round my shoulders, the train rocked, the lights dimmed – and I sprang up and sat where he had been sitting before. There were only the two of us in the carriage, the old-fashioned sort opening on to a corridor. No one had even looked in on us since we left Paris. But I'd had not the slightest awareness of any danger and still hadn't – I was just irritated. I glared at him and said something about being disappointed in him, that I'd thought he was a friend and now he was being silly. Sud-denly he burst out laughing, roared and roared, said I was wonderfully naive, so sweet, but that never, ever, should I travel with strange men again, because they might not be as understanding and amused as he was. Then he told me to lie down and he covered me with his elegant fawn overcoat and lay down on the other seat himself and we both slept until Bordeaux.

I was still tired, and aching, when we arrived there at six in the morning. The station platform when I got off was bitterly cold and it was quite deserted. M. Blanc was not there to meet me, as promised. There was no porter. I lugged my stupid case, by degrees, to the exit. Still no M. Blanc. I sat on my case – at least it was good for something, it made a very stable seat, room for a family to perch on it – and waited. I thought about home and its warmth and familiarity. I wondered if M. Blanc was perhaps having trouble with his car, but then I saw a thin, a very thin Picasso-type (in his blue period) man walking towards me, a photograph in his hand. He checked me against it and then introduced himself.

No car. M. Blanc had no car. We got a bus. I couldn't lift my case on to it and neither could he. He coughed, put a hand to his chest, apologized. A workman helped me. Luckily, when we got off the bus, we didn't have far to go. The Blanc family lived above a shop, their shop. Mme Blanc was at the entrance to it, waiting for us. She looked as emaciated as her husband, but she had a beautiful smile and she embraced me, welcomed me most fulsomely. She took me up several flights of stone stairs to their living quarters (the case remained sulking below). These were a shock. Two rooms at the front, overlooking the street, and two at the back which had no windows except for skylights. My room was one of those at the back. It made my council house bedroom in Carlisle seem a luxury pad. Mme Blanc showed me the lavatory. To think I'd once despised our outside one ... This was merely a little compartment, quite windowless and airless, and the system itself was that all the waste dropped down a pipe without any flushing. There was no bath. In the kitchen, there was a sink with a curtain round it. Why had I ever thought we were poor? Why had I ever thought my mother had a hard time? If my mother could only see how this woman lived ...

Lived, and coped magnificently. Everything rested on Marthe Blanc's fragile shoulders and she never complained. She ran the shop — a stationery shop rather than a real bookshop — and also a laundry, belonging to her father, and looked after her family without any help but mine. I was 'the

Little Gift from Heaven' sent by the good God to make her days easier. As this Little Gift, I got the five children up, fed and dressed them, and took the two eldest to school, pushing the twins there with us but leaving the baby in his cot. When I returned, the twins had a nap and I got the baby up and took him shopping with me. We had lunch, then I had two hours off before repeating the walk to collect the school pupils. After school it was pandemonium until the children's very late bedtime. Marthe's Little Gift found it hell.

I could have gone home. I should have done. I soon discovered other au pairs had left within days. But what made me stay was not only pride, and admiration for Marthe Blanc, but the realization that I was programmed too well. For all my adolescent fighting talk of *not* being prepared to endure whatever came my way, I found it hard to act according to my beliefs. I believed women should not allow themselves to be made into drudges yet here I was becoming a drudge myself, putting up with all the hard work for five shillings a *week* plus my keep. But it was only for six months. Anyone could endure six months. Marthe had to endure her lot for life. Her husband was useless. He had lost his job just before I arrived and now did private coaching, a matter of only three pupils, an hour each, leaving him plenty of time to smoke and look miserable. He was depressed and depressing, whereas Marthe was sunny and singing. She loved her children, her little angels, and was not dismayed that she was once more pregnant. I simply couldn't understand her good humour and optimism. Never, never could I be like Marthe. The idea of having five children and being committed to caring for them was horrific.

Halfway through my stay we all went to Salaunes where

Marthe's father owned a cottage in the pine woods. It was a ramshackle, primitive place but the situation was lovely. The cottage had a cherry tree outside the door and when we arrived it was laden with cherries so huge they looked like dark red plums. We ate our meals under this tree, using a rickety, rough wooden table and a bench. Water had to be drawn from the well and the woods were used as a lavatory. I slept with the five children, though I had my own canvas bed. After a couple of days Marthe asked if I'd like to stay on with four of the children. She and her husband had to go back to Bordeaux and would take the baby if I could manage the others. I agreed at once. The weather was glorious and all I had to do was keep an eye on my charges. Easy. Easy but also boring. Mothers must get so bored, I thought, unless having your own children makes the tedium bearable. The feeding and washing of the children was nothing, that kind of organizing and supervising I quite enjoyed, but it was the endless squabbles and demands for attention which drove me frantic. The eldest, a boy of seven, was the most demanding, but he was also his mother's favourite. Mothers, they were blind.

When I went back to England the entire family were lavish with their regret. I wished I could reciprocate but I couldn't – I was just so glad to leave. I had never been cut out to be a Little Gift from Heaven. The whole experience had been like a test run for the worst possible prospect: becoming a mother of five in difficult circumstances with a useless husband. If my own mother's life had made me think of marriage and motherhood as a waste of opportunity, Marthe Blanc's made me think of it as an absolute disaster. Marthe had a degree, she'd been a teacher. She ought to have known better in my tough little opinion. It was religion which had surely trapped her most – as a devout Catholic she told me she practised no form of birth control except abstinence and in her case it hadn't worked very well.

What a fate, what a life.

XV

My room in Somerville was on the ground floor of the library block, a large, square, high-ceilinged room with a mullioned window overlooking a lawn shadowed by a huge cedar tree. It was easily four times the size of any room at home and the sheer space thrilled me. There was a bed, a table, two chairs and a bookcase. The cover on the bed was a washed-out beige, the curtains, limp and long, were a patterned fawn and white. I rushed out and spent the first instalment of my grant on cushions and material to make new curtains and then I sewed furiously and badly in my usual fashion in an effort to transform the colourless room and make it mine. I wanted to impose my own taste and I did. It was just a pity that my taste then was what it was. I'd moved on from black and now thought only in primary colours, especially blue and yellow. I'd brought a Picasso print with me and my idea was to echo the colours in it. Great swathes of startlingly blue cotton now obscured the curtains – far too hard actually to make new ones, so I'd just tacked the new material to the old – and there was more blue stuff draped over my bed with the violently red and yellow cushions lined up along the wall on top of it. Nothing could have been more unsuitable for that mellow old room, but I was deeply satisfied: a room of my own at last, my mark upon it.

But it was a strange feeling beginning to live in that room.

There was something about it which made me restless. It felt good to walk in, close the door, sit at the table and feel alone and private and cut off. It felt good just to walk around, loll on the bed, make myself coffee. I liked the silence, I liked the emptiness, I liked not having to put up with other people. But that was also what felt not quite right, what made me still tense: the other people in their rooms around me. I'd always thought I would love boarding-school, love living in such an institution, but now I discovered I did not. I couldn't stay in my room all the time and when I came out of it – to eat, to have tutorials, to go into the common room to read newspapers – I didn't like it. Rapidly I found group-living as bad as family-living – so many strangers to whom I had to be polite, so much awareness of other women laughing and talking and being busy. It was oppressive, I hated it and I wasn't going to fit in.

I wasn't going to fit in as a scholar either. The work bored me to death, though I did it conscientiously. How could women, or men for that matter (but women more so), spend their lives writing essays about medieval history? It was such an unreal task, so removed from my mother's life or Marthe Blanc's, and, though it was the very unreality I had craved, now that I'd got it, it seemed unbearably cowardly and sterile, a form of gross self-indulgence. But wasn't it what I had fantasized about? A life using my brain, of being as far as possible from acting as a slave to men or children. Curious, then, that it felt so wrong, significant surely that I couldn't work out why. I began to shun college life, either retreating into my room or escaping the building altogether.

The moment I stepped out of the college doors into the street I felt better. Sometimes I'd just walk around Oxford, but often I went to my friend Theodora Parfit's house in

Northmoor Road. Theo's mother, a doctor who worked in London during the week (for the LCC), fascinated me even more than Janet Vaughan. Jessie Parfit was clever, quite outstandingly so, and she had a high-powered job, but she was also a mother with three children, and a wife who, though not domesticated in the conventional sense, ran her husband's life and looked after her home. Janet Vaughan's children were grown up and I never saw her in a family setting, but Jessie's were young and I saw into hers with wonder. She was the first woman I ever knew who appeared to have everything – marriage, children, career – and made it work. Her house was chaotic but it functioned. She liked to cook and to sew and was totally involved with the lives of her children (though it did not escape my notice that they had been sent to boarding-school). Jessie gave me hope. Maybe the straight choices I'd envisaged as inescapable need not be made after all, maybe a woman could have a career without marriage and children proving insuperable obstacles. Jessie's success, as opposed to my mother's failure, was to do with class but even more was to do with money. Money to pay for help, money to send children away to school, money to smooth the rough path of doing everything at every turn. I began to say to myself that maybe if I earned enough money I, too, could have it all, I could enjoy every aspect of a woman's life if I found I wanted to.

I met the mothers of other Somerville friends and found examples even more reassuring than Jessie's. Jessie's juggling act, of career and marriage, wasn't as successful or happy as I at first thought but other women's were. Many of these professional middle-class intellectual women I now met were excellent housewives as well as career women and, even if they did employ a small army of cleaners to keep their homes shining, there was plenty of evidence of loving care, of the sort my own mother bestowed on her house, every sign that having a high-powered career did not mean indifference to surroundings. What I'd always lacked and wanted were convincing role models and now I had them. They'd come my way just in time because the lure of love and sex had, to my own alarm and amazement, begun to tempt me.

The best thing about arriving in Oxford was being in touch with girls who knew about birth control and abortion. Oh dear, how funny it was, how sweet, to have their little north-country friend so ignorant. In no time, once I'd confessed my secret passion, they had me making an appointment with Helena Wright, a gynaecologist in London. I hated going to her consulting-rooms even if half Somerville had already been and made fun of the experience so that it should have held no fears. Dr Wright didn't seem any less intimidating than old Dr Stephenson back in Carlisle and she was certainly no more friendly. She was brusque and businesslike and a bit hearty, and I was glad to get out of her surgery with a prescription for a Dutch cap which I had to take to a nearby Family Planning Clinic. In my innocence, I hadn't realized I would have to pay her and I hadn't enough money. The moment I got back to the flat where I was staying, she rang me up and reminded me to put the fee in the post. But at least the Family Planning Clinic did not charge. The woman asked me when I was getting married and I was triumphant as I replied, the contraceptive now safely handed over, that I wasn't. I didn't have to. I had found the secret of preventing babies so why would I get married? It wasn't necessary any more. I could have as much sex as I wanted and not face the often fearful consequences which had been the lot of the women in my family up to now. No illegitimate babies for me (as there had been for my great-grandmother and my grandmother); no extra babies I didn't plan (like my mother had); no babies precipitating me into marriage (as my aunt had been hurried into it). Why, I wondered as I went back to Oxford, did everyone stress the importance of the vote for women when control over their own bodies matters so much more?

In my second year Theo and I moved out of Somerville into two rooms on the first floor of a tiny house in Winchester Road. Below us lived Mrs Brown and her sister Fanny, and up above us, in an attic, was an old man called Reg, the lodger. There was none of the space there had been in my Somerville room – our two rooms would've fitted comfortably into it – but the freedom was liberating. Theo and I could come and go at any hour in an era when there was a ten o'clock curfew in Somerville and all men had to be out of the college at seven. My boyfriend, Hunter Davies, came down from Durham University whenever he was able to hitch a lift and we could spend the whole weekend in my minute room in front of the coal fire . . . My mother would have had a fit. She'd practically had one anyway when, the summer before A-levels, I had started to go out with Hunter thereby smashing the high ideals I'd set myself and in which she'd come to believe herself – maybe I *was* different, maybe I *was* so single-minded I could ignore the entire male sex. But no. My father broke the devastating news first. He came home in a rage one day and said, 'I've seen her, that lass of yours, behaving in a disgusting fashion on a public highway and he looks *foreign*.' It took my frantic mother ages – since, of course, a straightforward request to know what my father was talking about was too simple – to discover that this disgusting behaviour was no more than hand-holding and embracing, as Hunter and I parted company at the corner, but even that was a blow. I'd let her down, I was going the way of all flesh.

True, I was, but on my own terms and with no risk, something she wouldn't have understood even if I'd tried to explain. I could hardly tell her, after all, that just as my Oxford friends knew where to go for contraception, so they knew where to go for an abortion. In 1957 it was illegal but they were quite blasé about it. If, in spite of Dr Wright's efforts, I became pregnant I'd have an abortion. Oh, it was wonderful being at Somerville, wonderful to be in touch with this vital knowledge, worth enduring any amount of tedium over essays. My new friends, not just Theo, were from such a different world and I loved being pulled into it. They were Socialists and members of the Labour Party. This confused me greatly. I'd thought political allegiances were according to class and money but now I saw they could not be – it was as odd that my working-class mother voted Tory as that my Somerville friends voted Labour. They were all upper middle class, all from wealthy (to me) homes, and yet they all passionately wanted to align themselves with the working class. I was working class and didn't even belong to the Labour Party. I joined it sharpish. I went to Labour Party meetings and was bored to death and couldn't share the excitement of my friends. I proved a lazy, lazy member, only good for acting in Labour Party plays and little else.

My mother didn't like hearing, in my letters, about this play-acting. I wasn't supposed to have gone to Oxford to fool about dressing-up – another way I'd let her down – and especially not in any political organization. The play I acted in in my second year was Brecht's *Caucasian Chalk Circle*.

They wanted an authentic working-class girl to play the peasant Grusha and I was she. The production was a bit of a shambles, lacking the professionalism of OUDS (scorned as establishment), but it was to be seen to have a political point and was acted by committed Socialists which was intended to give it greater glory. Dennis Potter was the judge and his friends were director, producer, everything. We performed in the Town Hall and the Gaitskells came to watch which got us publicity. The play seemed leaden to me – I just stumbled about being the producer's idea of a peasant girl while Dennis, rantingly magnificent as the judge, upstaged everyone. Afterwards, Dennis and I were presented to the Gaitskells. Mrs Gaitskell looked at me sternly and said, 'Yours is not Brecht's interpretation of Grusha, I'm sure. I don't think he'd approve.' Never mind Brecht, neither did my father, not that he ever saw the play. Hearing who I was associated with was enough. 'You want to be careful,' he warned me, 'mixing with pinkos. Barmpots, the lot of them. Keep well away.'

My main object, in this new life, was to keep well away from home even in the vacations, especially in the vacations. Subterfuge, on a complicated scale, was necessary. I had to protect my mother. It wouldn't be kind to flaunt my love life; it would distress and frighten her to discover I was doing a Nan and living in sin (even without the added horror of the lover being married). She would never agree, either, that sex without marriage was morally permissible. So, as the long vacations came up, I always laid careful plans. I went to live with Hunter, first in Manchester, where he was training as a journalist, and then in London when he took up his first job, but from all over Europe came letters home to my mother describing the wonderful time I was having. My supposed trail took me through France to Spain one year, through Germany to Italy another, depending on where my Somerville friends were going. I got guidebooks out and wrote lyrical descriptions of the places I had never seen and made up anecdotes about the people I was with. It kept my mother happy and saved her from imagined shame. I saw no harm in it, only sadness that such deceit was necessary, that my relationship with my mother dictated these lies.

Landlords also had to be lied to. Since I didn't in the least mind telling these people the truth, I'd gone ahead and done so when we looked for a flat in Manchester. The result was disastrous. We were always asked if we were married – we both looked very young at nineteen and twenty-one and when we said no, the door was closed. So in the end it had to be on with the Woolworths ring and the pretence I was Mrs Davies which I detested. I didn't like the sound of it nor of the words 'your wife'. And yet, by the time the end of my Oxford days approached, it had suddenly begun to be not worth the lying. If we were going to live together for ever, as we were, how could we go on pretending we were not, for the sake of our mothers? It was ridiculous. If marriage was nothing to us but everything to our mothers, why not just get married? So we did.

We got married, on 11 June 1960, the moment I finished my last exam, but we didn't have a wedding. I cheated my mother out of that without a qualm. The marrying itself was for her sake and I didn't see why I should also have to subject myself to the sort of occasion I saw not just as an ordeal but the height of hypocrisy. She wanted a church wedding, the white dress, the flowers, the reception with all the family there, and I couldn't bear the thought of the whole charade. No wedding, then. Just the two of us, with

Theo and another friend as witnesses, popping into the register office in St Giles. When I told my mother about this plan she said she'd spend the morning in church on her own praying for me. My father relayed through her the news that he was washing his hands of me. I'd apparently made a fool of him by marrying, by *just* getting married. It was a betrayal. I'd proved no different from any other girl after vowing I would be. No presents anyway, that was for sure. My hole-in-the-corner marriage didn't deserve any and people would assume one thing only. The wider family was thrown into consternation: presents or not? Much agonizing went on before tablecloths and pillowcases were sent by the kinder relatives, quite enough in the circumstances — as if I cared. But I cared that my mother was so upset because she had no money of her own (her little legacies from her mother and Aunt Jessie long since used) with which to defy my father and give me a present. She saved out of her housekeeping and six months later bought me a Denbyware dinner service which I never could use without appetite-ruining pangs of guilt.

The evening of the day I was married it had been arranged that my mother would go to my brother's house (he was now married) and I'd telephone her there (she had no telephone still). It was a dreadful conversation punctuated by heavy sighs on her part and sudden silences on mine. Had the weather been good? Quite good, sunny but very windy. What sort of dress did you wear? Surely you wore a dress, surely you bought a new one. Yes, I did, a white cotton dress. Not very short? Well, quite short. Not bare legs? Yes, bare legs. And Hunter, did he have a new suit? Not a new one, no. His cheapo-Italian job. It looked fine, but he did have a new shirt and tie. And afterwards, after whatever they do in that office place, what did you do? We had lunch at the

Bear in Woodstock and then we walked round Blenheim grounds and sat on the grass. Sat on the grass? In your white dress? No, I'd put a skirt on by then. What time did you get to London? About an hour ago. Well. Well then . . .

Well, indeed. She was depressed but at least I had got married. And I had a home, a flat in the Vale of Health, Hampstead. But I didn't have a job yet, though curiously that didn't seem to bother her – I was now a married woman and married women didn't need jobs, remember. I said I was going to get a job in the autumn, when we were settled, but she wasn't interested. She'd accepted that I'd wasted my splendid education, just as my father had said I would, being a girl. She'd faced up to that. I wasn't going to tell her I was giving myself three months to try to write a novel. It was too embarrassing. I wasn't willing to call myself a writer until I'd had something I'd written published and had proved writing could be a job, a way of earning my living and justifying myself. I was determined to show my mother that marriage was not the end of ambition, that it in no way need impede my progress, that I still intended to have a very different life from hers and her mother's.

She came to stay that first summer of married life, an uneasy guest in a flat with only one bedroom. The flat was strange to her – a little like Jean's rooms in the Buildings in Motherwell, but not like them at all, she realized that. Only two other people lived in the house where we had a flat, Mr Elton, the owner, on the top floor and Mrs Woodcock, an elderly widow, in the basement, with another room on the ground floor. We shared a bathroom with Mr Elton which worried my mother at first until she became reassured by his dependable habits. She was more put off by the emptiness of the flat. There was nothing in our sitting-room except two single beds. These were arranged end-to-end along one wall and covered with some purple material, just flung over. My mother didn't think of these divans even as beds – beds had headboards and footboards and were made of solid wood. We had only a cooker in the kitchen when she arrived but soon got a wooden table and two stools. Then the refrigerator came. My mother was there on the great day itself, the day the shiny Electrolux arrived with its smoothly rounded door and its pale blue interior fittings. I loved it at once. It wasn't at all an inanimate object, it was loaded with significance. Solemnly I explained to my mother that having a fridge would mean I need not shop every day as she had always done. I would shop once a week and the darling fridge would keep everything fresh. My mother was silent. Finally, she said the bags would be too heavy to carry if they were loaded with a week's food, and the shops as far away as they seemed to be. I said I wouldn't be carrying bags. They would go into our car. I'd give Hunter a list and he'd do the shopping. There was an even longer silence. I added that as well as doing the shopping Hunter would take our washing to the launderette at the same time – and then she exploded, said it wasn't *right*, a man shouldn't be shopping and going to launderettes, whatever they were. The world had gone mad.

In a way, it had. Her world had gone mad. The more my mother saw of my life as a newly married woman, the more amazed she was. It was mainly the ease of it which she marvelled at. What did I have to clean, for a start? I pushed a Hoover over a fitted green carpet, I pushed a squeezy mop over smooth linoleum, I wiped my precious fridge and my equally pristine cooker – there was no labour, no scrubbing and huffing and puffing, desperately waging an eternal war against the filth of open fires. And as for the monstrous burden of washing, it had quite gone. No wash-house for me. I might not have a washing-machine of my own but I didn't need one with the new launderettes. Playing housewife – because it was like playing – gave me such pleasure, and as she watched me flick switches and squirt cleaning substances my mother's envy grew.

But the madness of this new world was more than a matter of mechanical appliances and the having of money to afford cars and launderettes. My mother was most perturbed by the equality of our marriage. By the time she came to stay I'd just begun, in September, to work as a teacher. This pleased her tremendously (she knew nothing of the novel-writing, now finished for the moment and the novel rejected by an agent). She saw that since we were both working, Hunter as a journalist and myself as a teacher, we should both share in the jobs which needed to be done. Monday was Hunter's day off so he did the shopping and washing, Saturday was mine so I did the cleaning and iron-ing; Sunday we were both off so I cooked and Hunter washed dishes. My mother observed this and admitted the fairness of the arrangement, but she seemed unable fully to approve. Was her air of faint disapproval really a regret that these changes had come too late for her? It wasn't talked about. She went back to my father reluctantly, though, back to what she saw as her duties, the making of his meals, the cleaning, the washing and the other jobs still hard for her, with her poor equipment and facilities, and nothing to me.

But what she really didn't want to return to was her leisure time. She had plenty these days, with all of us grown up and gone. Pauline, my sister, was now training as a teacher in Liverpool and my mother felt her departure far more than she had done my own. I was always difficult whereas Pauline was affectionate and domesticated and sweet – much harder to accept the absence of that kind of daughter. She wanted interests now which she didn't have. All she had, really, was the church. This was St James's now, since she'd moved away from Raffles and St Barnabas's. St James's was much more her sort of church. It looked as a church should look, with its spire and stained glass, and, though it had been built in the 1860s to serve the industrial suburb of Denton Holme, it was situated above the industrial part with a catchment area which included several well-off residential streets. My mother liked attending St James's in a way she had never liked St Barnabas's and what she liked best were the Women's Fellowship meetings.

This Women's Fellowship was a devotional meeting, not remotely like any Mother's Union or Women's Institute affair. Every Monday between sixty to eighty women gathered in Blencowe Street Mission Hall where they sat in rows, six deep, and sang hymns and choruses. They all had a booklet of these choruses, CSSM Choruses 1, 2 and 3. The letters stood for Children's Special Service Mission, a branch of the Scripture Union, and the booklet was a kind of religious commonplace booklet full of 'choruses' which derived from the Psalms and the Bible and well-known prayers. There were 709 of these choruses, helpfully divided in the index into categories ranging from Forgiveness to Strength. My mother's favourite was number 406, which came into the Assurance and Certainty division.

> Thou wilt keep him in perfect peace, whose
>   mind is stayed on Thee
> When the shadows come and darkness falls

> He giveth inward peace;
> Oh, He is the only resting-place,
> He giveth perfect peace;
> Thou wilt keep him in perfect peace, whose
>   mind is stayed on Thee.

A lady worker led the meeting, the only one ever to stand up. First she welcomed everyone, then an opening hymn was sung followed by a prayer – extempore – before they all got cracking on the choruses. A Bible passage was read, another hymn sung, and then the speaker-of-the-day (a visiting missionary perhaps) spoke for forty-five minutes. Tea and biscuits followed.

It sounds dull enough but it was the highlight of my mother's week. She had a real feeling of fellowship with the other women, but there was also a spiritual excitement about the meeting and she would come home quite flushed and exhilarated, still singing some chorus. Otherwise, her social life was limited to meeting Ruby Gillespie in Binn's café. I pointed out to her that there was no reason why she shouldn't go to stay with her sisters to break the monotony and she did go to each of them occasionally for a week. Nan and Jean were both in Nottingham now. Dave, who'd finally qualified at night school as an optician, was offered a job by Jack and took it. Jean wasn't exactly happy about this – she had many friends in the old Motherwell Buildings by then and none in Nottingham except Nan with whom she often argued. My mother found her little holidays with these sisters a bit of a strain, with the need always to be keeping the peace. It was also a strain dealing with their opinion of me. They, as well as my father, never let my mother forget how I had disappointed everyone after all my years of fine words. I might now be respectably married, I might now be respectably teaching, but I had just turned out like the others and they tried to make my mother feel I'd somehow failed her.

XVI

Soon after we came back from Sardinia, where we had our honeymoon, I had to find a doctor. I'd contracted dysentery, or some kind of food poisoning. How did one find a GP? With memories of Dr Stephenson in Carlisle I was determined to start off in London with someone more sympathetic but I didn't know how to go about it. In Carlisle doctors, even if they were detested, just got handed on in families. I didn't know anyone to ask so I staggered to Hampstead Post Office and asked for a list of local doctors and picked the nearest, in Thurlow Road, a Dr Day.

The waiting-room looked encouraging enough. Nothing funereal about the comfortable chintzy armchairs, or the cushions on the window-seat, or the fresh flowers, or the pile of newish magazines – my mother would have denied this was a waiting-room. The doctor herself was a surprise too. She was young, attractive, friendly, and chatted away with the greatest of ease. ('But is she a *proper* doctor?' I could hear my mother asking suspiciously. Quite proper, cured me rapidly.) Nor was there any need to dread calling her out. I called her at six in the morning after Hunter had spent all night struggling with a violent asthma attack and she not only came at once but said next time to call her immediately, whatever the time of night. I'd finally shaken off fear of doctors, the fear that had dogged my mother throughout her life. Even before I had children I now knew they would not need to grow up watching their mother subservient before any domineering doctor and resentful of his power. It was about class again, and education, but also about times having changed, about my doctor being a young woman, a mother herself, and this not being the rarity it had once been.

My mother was waiting for these as yet mythical children of mine to arrive. At first she waited nervously, but when nine months were up from when I married and she could be sure I hadn't had to get married (the worry had lurked in spite of scornful reassurances), she began to wait in a different way. My sister-in-law had had a son, Paul, and this one grandchild had given her own life a point again. Feeding Paul, bathing Paul, taking Paul for walks, putting Paul to bed – she loved it. Shirley, Paul's mother, didn't work. She was a proper mother. She knew her place was at home and she was very happy in it. My mother had clearly decided that my easy life as a working wife had not yet been put to the test. What would happen when the babies came? Goodbye equality then, surely. I would yet again become just like every other woman, stopped in my tracks by maternity, forced to concede only surface things had changed for women. But no babies appeared, even after three whole years. I said I didn't want them yet, but there was doubt in her expression when she heard this. How could she be sure? Maybe I wasn't going to be able to have children and that would change everything. If a woman didn't have children not only was she not, in my mother's opinion, a 'real' woman but she had never been seriously challenged. No wonder my life was easy.

In fact, it wasn't by then so easy. I'd started another novel, writing in the evenings after teaching. It was exhausting, the teaching. I seemed to be given the most difficult and unruly classes in Barnsbury School (in Islington) and the effort to conquer them wore me out. The girls were all eleven-plus failures with low expectations and I spent my time trying to raise them. I'd crawl home at the end of each day thinking that if my mother could see me it would shatter the image I'd given her when she visited. But I had to keep going, and write only in my spare time, because we needed the money to buy a house. I wanted a house passionately. It seemed incredibly important to own our own place and not to live as our parents had done in council or other rented property. I fantasized about having a whole house, walking every day to the station painting and papering rooms which didn't exist, choosing furniture, hanging pictures . . . All my salary went into the House Fund and we lived, perfectly well, on Hunter's. It never even entered my head to think about having babies until I had a home for them and I didn't care in the least if anyone thought such an attitude woefully practical and soulless.

We moved into our house (where we still live) in March 1963, a late Victorian house in Dartmouth Park, close to Hampstead Heath, but on the opposite side to Hampstead proper where we'd had our flat. It cost £5,200, freehold, but it had a sitting tenant on the top floor and was in an appalling condition. We didn't care about that. The elation of moving in was terrific – so many big rooms, such a long south-facing garden, even if it was a wilderness. We lived for six months in one room and now the exhaustion doubled, the added exhaustion of scraping walls and painting and enduring filth and mess on a grander scale than my mother had ever known. But it was all worth it. It was such a joy to come home eventually to the cool rooms painted in pale colours, to the sanded floorboards and pretty rugs, to the grey-and-white checked kitchen floor, to the big pine table – I loved every yard of the house, every scrap in it. Having my own house fulfilled me in some strange way I'd never quite anticipated. It even meant more to me than Jonathan Cape accepting my novel soon after we moved in.

It wasn't a good novel but at least it got me started and it gave me the courage not only to stop teaching and turn to writing as a career but also to have a baby. A curious connection, but a true one. I felt brave and daring just thinking about choosing to have children. All those years spent successfully preventing babies and now this dangerous urge given free rein – dangerous because I'd be wilfully creating another human being and accepting the responsibility that entailed. Children had been wished upon my grandmother and mother, they had little option, but I was deliberately, knowingly choosing. Was it right to have a baby? Why was I doing it? Because I wanted to. But what kind of reason was that for an intelligent, liberated woman in 1963? It wasn't a reason at all. It was pure self-indulgence. I didn't even think I'd make a good mother. Oh, I'd do the looking after splendidly, but what about the rest? Knowing myself as I did, how could I dare to have a baby?

My mother was delighted to hear I was pregnant, the baby due in March 1964. 'Everything will have to change now,' she said, 'no more working.' She couldn't, or wouldn't, see that the writing would be the work. Nonsense. Writing was a *hobby*. Even if I had been paid a £150 advance, it wasn't serious. She wondered if it was good for the baby I was carrying to be 'all hunched up scribbling' and wasn't impressed that the scribbling produced a second novel before the baby's arrival (for which I got £250 and rumours of film interest). Once my baby was born she had no doubt this writing would have to stop.

She seemed right at first. The very moment Caitlin was born writing seemed nothing. I could feel puny ambition drain away and watched it go happily. There my baby lay, a real person, a marvel of another far superior sort of creation, our creation, and so utterly helpless, so heartbreakingly vulnerable. I could hardly bear to have her taken away for a moment, so strong was my protectiveness. How could I be sure anyone else could be as tender and loving as I was towards her? Once we were home, I spent every moment alert to her needs. My mother, who had come down to see her first granddaughter, smiled triumphantly: it was as she had always known it would be. Babies changed women. Obsessed with my baby, I was reverting to the pattern of ages. Nothing had changed in spite of outward appearances.

For quite a time I agreed with her. I didn't want to write or have any kind of career. The baby was so much more important than anything or anyone, even Hunter. He loved Caitlin too – he was a modern father who changed nappies and wheeled the pram with pride – but he was working hard and our partnership wasn't as equal as it had been. He didn't do the shopping any more. Why should he, when I was the Wife at Home now? I trotted every day to the shops, just like my mother, and never mind the glory of the fridge-keeping-food-fresh-for-a-week. It was a chicken from the butcher, green beans from the greengrocer, bread from the baker, and this shopping fitting in so neatly with pushing Caitlin around. I had a washing-machine, so no need to patronize the launderette, and at least I didn't have to be like my mother (still doing everything with the dolly-tub and mangle) in that gruelling respect. I was perfectly happy being a mother and wife that long summer and then the winter came and Caitlin slept longer, and suddenly, to my own surprise, it wasn't enough to look after a baby and cook and shop. It wasn't boredom I felt, it was restlessness. Not the restlessness of discontent but of energies not being used, as simple as that. So I started to write again, in the evening at weekends, though one cry from Caitlin and the pen was put down at once. I wrote two novels very quickly, both light affairs but acceptable enough. I was fond of saying it was like knitting, really, just something I did to amuse myself, quite effortless. But, even if the result wasn't up to much, I knew the writing was important. It made me different from my mother. It made me something other than a wife and mother. I noticed I often started to write feeling tired and yet, strangely, finished feeling refreshed.

It was unfortunate that I was asked to write the script for my second novel, *Georgy Girl*, when I was already four months pregnant with my much wanted second baby, but on the other hand pregnancy saved me from more involvement than I could ever have stood. One thing writing for myself, at home, quite another writing to orders, other people's orders, and having to have meetings. What a disaster I was as a team worker. How clearly this episode showed me the limits of my own energies. Being a novelist fitted in with motherhood, being a scriptwriter didn't. The film people expected me to put the film first at all times – fools. It made me realize what I'd already suspected: any career taking me out of the house would be unmanageable. It would present impossible choices, impose unacceptable strains. It would show I was, when it came to the crunch, exactly like my mother and grandmother: family first, no argument. Being a wife, mother and writer was a balancing act and, though my balance was good, one push, one demand too much, and I'd fall off the tightrope. It was a lesson learned just in time. The script was handed over to Peter Nichols. The meetings stopped. The relief was great. Lumbering round the film set some months later, just before Jake was born, and meeting the star, James Mason, I had no regrets. Exciting to be involved in the making of a film but disturbing too, making me feel for that short while like a split personality, unsure who I really was.

Charlotte Rampling, who in the film played a woman who has a baby she doesn't want and feels nothing for it when it is born, came to see me. She didn't understand this Meredith character and wanted some insight. There I was, submerged in motherhood, feeding Jake while Caitlin played at my feet, and she didn't see how I could have imagined a woman with no maternal feelings. I tried to explain that Meredith had motherhood forced on her, that she hadn't been satisfying any maternal urge, and that it was perfectly possible in those circumstances for women to resent a baby who had caused them so much trouble and pain. Maternal feelings were not automatic after giving birth, I said. Charlotte herself had at the time no liking for babies, whereas Lynn Redgrave, playing Georgy, did, but Charlotte had assumed once a baby was born everything changed in a magical way: I am a mother therefore I feel as a mother. Before she left, she gestured at Jake and Caitlin and said, 'But you love this, right?' I said right. 'So you're Georgy, right?' Wrong. For Georgy, children were her all, her very reason for existing. Georgy was my mother in a different time, a different setting, with different looks and personality – but still my mother, trading everything, if necessary, for children.

★

I had my second baby, Jake, at home. I thought my mother would approve but she didn't. She said surely hospitals were safer and what was I doing, putting the clock back. But I hated hospitals and was sure I'd get on much better giving birth at home. It was an easy birth, with Hunter practically delivering his own son, which shocked my mother. It made her feel queasy thinking of husbands even watching a birth. It wasn't decent somehow. Even less decent was what she thought of as the appalling habit of taking photographs of the birth. A friend who had her baby a few days before I had mine turned up at our house while my mother was with us (down, traditional style, to look after me, though I didn't want to be looked after) and asked if we would like to see some photographs taken when Jason was born. My mother, expecting shots of a baby in its mother's arms, all creased from birth and looking adorable, peered eagerly at the snaps and then gasped. The pictures shown of the baby emerging from between its mother's legs seemed to her pornographic – the legs apart, the bloody vagina gaping, the head a black blot bulging obscenely, and all in glorious Technicolor. She was speechless, couldn't hide her revulsion. Had women really come to this?

Some things, she felt, should remain private. Modesty was being lost sight of. Since she'd said often enough that in her day giving birth was shrouded in mystery, and the shock of the reality was profound, I tried to persuade her that surely films and photographs of births were ways of properly inform-ing both men and women. No. She didn't think so. It was going too far, no need for it. She wasn't entirely approving of my breast-feeding my babies either. She was never comfort-able with the sight of my doing this and thought I should always do it in my bedroom 'where it's quiet'. She'd bottle-fed all of us. Breast-feeding was associated in her mind with poverty and she couldn't understand how any educated woman could do it. It was another backward step, further proof she didn't understand the modern generation.

Feeding on demand made no kind of sense to her either. She'd never heard of Truby King, but she had always believed in and followed a rigid routine. She'd watch me breast-feeding for the second time in three hours and say she'd always waited the 'proper' four hours between feeds and seen I got the 'proper' amount of milk. Only my babies thriving and putting on weight, even if they did cry a lot and Jake hardly slept, consoled her. But there was no growing closer between my mother and me because I now had two children. Becoming a mother myself had forged no new bond. Rather the reverse. How, when I realized the passion with which I cherished my babies, could I ever get to that state of polite affection which my own mother and I enjoyed?

Motherhood had become more mysterious, not less so.

When my mother returned to Carlisle after Jake's birth she said, 'You'll have your hands full now, you won't be able to keep up that writing.' Almost true. Family first, writing a very poor second. This time, when winter came, there was little respite from sleepless nights and the old trick of sitting down to write exhausted and getting up refreshed didn't work. How could I be as tired as my mother had been when she had young children, yet my life was so easy? I had no excuse for exhaustion with my central heating and washing-machine and never a worry over money. It was ridiculous to feel so drained and I reminded myself over and over of my mother's much harder life at the stage I was now until it became like a horror show. Everyone around me had what was called 'a little help'. This consisted of women to do the cleaning and au pair girls, or nannies, to look after the children. But I didn't want either and not just because I hated having to have people in my house with whom I would have to have relationships – it was also because I *liked* to do everything myself. I enjoyed the routine housework everyone else seemed to find tedious.

But something had to be done. It was no use wailing I had no right to be worn out when I so clearly was, silly to berate myself for my own feebleness. So a plan was thought up. On Mondays, Hunter's day off, he would take charge and I would be free the whole day. On Saturdays and Sundays he would bath and put the children to bed and I'd write from six to nine. This worked, after a fashion, though I soon learned I had actually to leave the house on Mondays to keep it as my day off and to pretend to leave it on Saturday and Sunday evenings. It seemed a miracle that anything I wrote even made grammatical sense, but I was grateful to get words on to paper at least.

What we needed, by the time Jake was one, with him still waking six times a night, was a holiday. Our hearts sank at the prospect of spending it in Carlisle but there seemed no option. So constant were cries from both mothers that they wished we would come home, it would have been cruel to deny them. Once in Carlisle, we stayed in different houses. There wasn't room for all of us to stay in either parents' house and besides there was the jealousy factor. Hunter and Caitlin stayed with his mother, Jake and I with mine. It didn't make for a happy family holiday. Then the weather, though it was June, was dreadful. Outings to the seaside and the lakes, four of us plus three parents crammed into our car, consisted of trundling around in torrential rain looking for places to eat. The visit didn't make the mothers content either – 'Only *two* weeks?' they chorused. Carlisle was still full of adult children settled with their own families round the corner, like my brother Gordon was with his. 'We'll never get to know your children,' the mothers said sadly. 'We'll be strangers to them.' We pointed out that they could come to us whenever they wished, but apart from a two-week visit to match our own to them this was never taken up. And, anyway, it wasn't held to be the same. They wanted their grandchildren *near*, all the time.

My mother especially wanted it. She was filled with dread that Gordon's firm would move him south and she'd lose Paul (which eventually happened) and then her life would be empty again. She told me of how, lately, if she wasn't looking after Paul, she'd taken to going for walks in parks on her own. My father, retired now and in spite of his gardening at a bit of a loss himself, said he'd go with her. He was the one after all who loved walks, but she told him she didn't want his company, she wanted an activity for herself. So she went on the bus to the city's various parks and walked about, then sat on a bench and felt stupid. She was as restless and frustrated at sixty-five as a teenager of fifteen, half-despising the church organizations to which she belonged, the bring-and-buy sales she helped at, the refreshment trolley at the Infirmary she helped to run. 'I've done nothing with my life,' she'd frequently say, and when I replied she'd reared three healthy and successful children she was dismissive.

It was such a relief to get away, back to our own lives. Sometimes, many times, I wished guiltily that I was much further away from my mother's unhappiness so that the feeling I was failing her might not be so strong. It might fade if thousands of miles and several oceans and a few mountain ranges were between us. The chance came in 1967. Hunter was to have a sabbatical year after writing a biography of the Beatles. We were going to go off and spend it in the Mediterranean and live like the Swiss Family Robinson. Breaking this news to my mother was hard. She saw this year as a further reminder that for her such opportunities had never been offered, that I was a different species, one with all the luck to whom hardship was quite unknown, one of a new generation of women for whom being a wife and mother meant something she'd never known.

XVII

We decided, stupidly, to go to the Maltese islands for our year in the Mediterranean, a woefully feeble decision made partly because we were so hopeless at foreign languages and wanted to go somewhere English-speaking. Gozo looked interesting and it was near enough to a hospital. This was important because both children had had accidents which left me terrified to be stuck in some part of the world where treatment wasn't near and immediate. Brought up under the permanent cloud of my mother's pessimism I was always expecting the worst.

The worst hadn't nearly befallen us, nothing like the worst, but the small taste of disaster we'd had seemed to justify my mother's dark forebodings – 'you never know the minute', as she put it. When Caitlin was two she swallowed a whole bottle of baby aspirins, and at the Royal Free casualty department they decided that to be on the safe side she had to have her stomach pumped out: I said I wanted to stay with Caitlin, whatever was done. They said no, it was better, they found, if mothers weren't present. I insisted and they shrugged and said I'd regret it. I went with the solemn but quite calm Caitlin into a room where I was to have one last try to get her to drink some vile-tasting concoction which would make her sick and avert the need for the evil stomach pump. She sat on a table, fat little legs swinging, great dark eyes looking up at me with absolute trust, and slowly shook her head. 'Make her,' a nurse urged. Make her? How did I do that? I'd talked and talked, offered bribes, explained why the liquid had to be drunk, and what would happen when it was, begged and pleaded when persuasion failed. But I couldn't *make* her, short of using brute force. My own stomach contracted with fear when the nurses, two of them, clicked their tongues with impatience and produced the stomach pump. I might as well have been my mother after all, utterly powerless, utterly craven and obedient, except that I *was* there with my child. I held Caitlin tightly, talking to her, smoothing her beautiful black hair over and over, while the tube was pushed between her pretty little teeth and down, cruelly down, into her tummy and she wriggled and became frantic and gripped me tightly in turn, and panic and fear and pain transformed her tranquil expression. The saline solution was poured down, the tube withdrawn, and she vomited and vomited. 'That's the way,' a nurse said.

It wasn't the way but I didn't know what would have been. 'She'll be all right now,' they said, but they were wrong. She didn't 'bounce back' as they said she would. All night she sobbed, all the next day she was like a zombie, and for weeks and weeks we only had to pass within a hundred yards of the Royal Free for her to start to tremble. And I wondered if I'd been wrong to insist on staying with her – maybe she now thought of me as one of her torturers. 'These mothers,' I'd heard one nurse say, in a tone of exasperation, 'think they always know best.' They would have loved my mother, only too willing to accept she didn't.

Jake's accident was just as frightening, more so because of the blood. When he was eighteen months old he'd almost cut his thumb off, falling on a sharp-edged tin box. Hunter was at home and we rushed off once more this time to the

272

Whittington, Jake screaming, blood spurting everywhere, his thumb hanging off. Now it was Hunter who insisted he was staying with his son and he did, sitting talking to him while the thumb was stitched back on. Told of this accident, my mother said – after the obligatory 'you never know the minute' – 'and you're going to take that child abroad? Is it safe? What if anything happens?'

So it was Gozo, English-speaking, near an excellent hospital (though actually a long way from the farmhouse we rented, but fortunately we never needed to go there). Before we left England, we bought my parents a bungalow. My mother moved out of her council house, with its small dark rooms, its freezing kitchen, into this brightly painted bungalow with its big windows, the first home she'd owned. But the move was more than just a matter of exchanging one house for another, it was heavily symbolic. She felt she was moving into a different world, to a position she'd always wanted. The bungalow was quite near Longsowerby council estate, but it was on a pleasantly landscaped private estate and in status it was far removed. It meant leaving the garden and starting all over again. My father wondered if the roses and shrubs he'd planted and nurtured belonged to the council because they owned the soil but he decided to take the risk. He dug up his favourites and transported them at dead of night to his new garden.

We left my mother content for a while, happily setting her new home, one that was actually hers, to rights. And she had a telephone now, a wonderful new toy, so she could speak regularly to Gordon (in Twyford, meaning the beloved grandchild Paul had been taken from her) and to Pauline, married (a lovely white wedding, making up for my own disgraceful affair), living in Cornwall with two children. If we had to go abroad for a year it was a good time to go and my mother's letters reflected the pleasure she was getting from the change of address. There was suddenly so much to do and homemaking activities had always been her favourite. She wrote one week, I wrote the next, my own letters full of descriptions of the Arab-style old house in which we lived, of how we spent half of every day on the beach, of what an adventure it was shopping in the markets. What I had hoped would happen had happened: the weight of my mother's dissatisfaction with her life had lifted from me and in any case she wasn't quite so dissatisfied. It was easy to pretend, to take her letters at face value, and think of her as a contented 67-year-old woman fully occupied with her new home and her church, blessed with three children and five grandchildren. I couldn't see her face, I couldn't catch the nuances in her voice.

We arrived in Gozo at the end of March and my parents came out to stay in the middle of May. I had never actually thought they would come when I wrote so gaily inviting them, but my mother never hesitated – this was the chance she'd always wanted, the chance to do something she thought of as bold. My father was appalled. What had got into her? It would mean getting on an aeroplane, it would mean getting to an airport in the first place, quite daunting enough. He said he couldn't leave his garden, it would be folly, not in May, not with his sweet peas just sown. My mother said very well, she would *go on her own*. Out of the question, at her age, he would have to accompany her. He was being forced into it, anything could happen. My mother was in an ecstasy of anticipation. She had practice packings of her suitcase, wrapping each item in it in tissue paper, arranging everything so beautifully, so cunningly, that the result was a visual poem. She loved telling her sisters, Nan and Jean, that she was going abroad, flying to Malta. Neither of them had ever flown and though Nan had been to Paris, Jean had never left Britain. 'I can hardly believe it,' my mother wrote, 'to think, at my age, I'm going in an aeroplane. It's marvellous.'

In retrospect, I'm not sure this trip was marvellous. It was the knowing she was going on such an adventure that was marvellous, not the experience of it, not for her. My father was the one who found it truly marvellous. He came off the plane raving about the sunrise over Mont Blanc and was into his specially bought white Marks & Spencer trousers and his Panama hat in a flash. He played on the beach with the children, admitting it was perhaps just a little superior to Silloth, and the water warmer, no question, and when he discovered every shop was a bar and every bar open all day he was converted to abroad immediately. But my mother? She didn't care for Ramla beach too much. Too hot, too uncomfortable with no wind-breaks to lean against. She didn't care for our farmhouse, too dark, too many insects, no proper furniture. She loved the children but being with them all day she found tiring – they were so wild, allowed to do whatever they wanted in her opinion, and what they mostly wanted was to run around shrieking. They didn't take to sitting quietly, her preferred occupation for children. The shops horrified her, especially the butcher's. Her father would have had a fit, she said, at how the meat was hung and she didn't recognize any of the cuts.

The truth was she felt uneasy most of the time and half this uneasiness was due to the literal discomfort of her clothes. She felt overdressed and too fat, and it wasn't surprising. She still wore her vest, if a fine cotton one, in a temperature of 90 degrees and her corset and her long knickers (though they were silk as a concession to the heats) and her full-length slip and her stockings – she wouldn't remove those because of her legs being what she called 'unsightly', and they were the most uncomfortable garments of all. Nothing would persuade her that on the beach, where there was rarely any other family except our own, it was surely permissible to uncase her poor legs from this torture-by-nylon. No. She hated her legs, they were full of horrible veins; she wasn't going 'to make an exhibition of myself'. So she perspired away, relieved when it grew a little cooler some days, when a breeze wafted in from the sea. Often we'd be swimming and I'd look back and there was this rigid little figure, so correctly dressed, hunched under a beach umbrella, and it seemed ridiculous that she should be imprisoned in those clothes, clothes belonging to another era. I hoped I would never wear a vest or a corset, or long knickers, or stockings even, when I was no longer young and slim and happy to wear virtually nothing except a bikini and shorts.

Next door to us – except next door wasn't actually next door – lived a retired gentleman who was very kind to my mother. A little further away lived two other male friends who were also kind to her. They were homosexuals who had escaped Britain's absurd laws before these were abolished. My mother thought them charming and had no idea what had brought them to Gozo in the first place, but my father muttered on about nancy boys and that they were not nice at all, especially with children around. My mother ignored him, as we did (though it was cowardly of us not to attack his prejudice) and enjoyed the refined teas 'the boys' invited her to. 'They make their own cakes,' she exclaimed, and to my father, 'Catch you making cakes, Arthur.' She missed entirely the significance of his 'Aye, catch me in an apron playing mother.'

It was a weird set up, my mother commented, living on this rocky island in the middle of nowhere, swimming the day away, lolling in the sun. It was like playing, she thought, but could not decide on the exact nature of the game. Living? And if mere living was a game, was it enviable? Did she wish that at thirty she, too, had been playing this way? The funny thing was that no, she didn't. Roots and routine were her watchwords, not this floating about without serious intent. She told me that she shut her eyes when we were on the beach sometimes and tried to see herself at thirty, my age then, and she couldn't believe the contrast, but she said this without her usual tone of envy, more in a tone of a curious *doubt*, doubt that what seemed to be true was indeed true, that things were what they appeared to be.

One of the biggest puzzles for her was her son-in-law. Hunter was no Arthur. He didn't fit in with her idea of The Husband at all. He wasn't domineering, he didn't expect to be waited upon, nor for his wish to be law within his house. He never pulled any kind of rank and sometimes she thought he should. She remonstrated with me and with the children – 'That is your *husband* you're speaking to' and 'That is your *father* talking to you', she'd say. But since Hunter didn't seem to care about imposing what she saw as his rightful authority, there wasn't much to be done about it. 'You'd never know who was boss in this house,' she'd occasionally say, and I'd be quick to laugh and announce there was no boss, that the idea of the husband as boss came from him being the wage-earner and now women, the wives, were wage-earners too, both had power.

She didn't want to leave our unruly household and go

home, though. When, on the morning of departure, it looked as though the ferry might not run and my parents would miss their plane, she said she was glad. My father wasn't, though he was the one who'd had the best holiday. But the ferry did run and they began the long journey home. 'Grand', was my father's verdict on abroad before he left, 'champion'. My mother was annoyed that she couldn't improve on his two-word summary even though she'd kept a diary. Every detail of what she had done, where she had been, whom she had met, was written down together with names and prices and weather reports, and yet none of it conveyed the excitement she had felt, nor was there a hint of disillusionment. 'That's it,' she said as they left, 'we'll never go abroad again, never.' She wanted the Gozo trip to have been the start of adventures not the beginning and end. To travel, whether she liked it or not, was to see and she'd only just begun to open her eyes. The gates, she felt, were clanging shut just after they had so miraculously swung open and all she'd managed was a glimpse of a different life. The fact that she wasn't sure she had liked it was irrelevant.

After five months on Gozo we packed up and moved to the Algarve, no longer interested in sticking to an English-speaking country and realizing how silly we were being not to live somewhere more interesting. The Algarve was definitely more interesting but my parents could not be persuaded to come to sample its winter sunshine. My sister and her husband and their two small sons came and stayed, which pleased my mother. Pauline had been very ill and needed to recuperate and it not only relieved my mother to think of her enjoying some winter sunshine but it was evidence, too, of the sort of sisterly solidarity she wanted to have proved still existed, as it had done in hard times between herself and Jean and Nan. It was almost a year until I saw my mother again and during that time she'd had some serious eye disease which had meant having her eyelid stitched up for weeks. The accompanying pain was borne with great fortitude but when I next saw her she seemed suddenly much older, and quite frail, and my father was already turning into the carer, which she appreciated but didn't like at all.

The eye healed and she came to stay in the summer of 1969, looking more like her old self. I was by then a housewife and mother of some experience and I saw her judging me. She wasn't in the least censorious but she noticed things and I noticed her noticing. My standards were not hers. Hers were her mother's (and whose those were nobody can tell). I didn't dust much for a start. My mother was a great duster, but then in her house there was plenty to dust (and she'd never got used to there being only half the dust there had once been now that she had no dirty coal fire). She'd ask me where my duster bag was and I'd say I didn't have one. Her dusters were the standard yellow fleecy sort, washed after each ferocious bout of dusting, then pegged on the clothes-line and finally folded and put in a bag hanging behind a cupboard door. I'd offer her a damp cloth, pointing out that the shelves and other surfaces we had were pinewood and better wiped than dusted. I didn't have any ornaments or photo frames or knick-knacks either. But, as my mother said, there were hundreds of books, all crying out for a good dusting. It was true. Books are filthy things. I said I'd dust those I took from the shelves, as they were used, but that wasn't good enough for my mother, who laboriously dusted every one for me. There was dust under the beds too, but I was happy only to vacuum it up at irregular intervals – I wasn't going to go in for a weekly moving-of-the-beds and meticulous cleaning. Doors were another black mark – literally. I didn't very often clean grubby fingerprints off them – and as for skirting-boards I didn't notice they needed attention. My house still looked perfectly clean to me however low my standards. I was never going to become a slave to it – if the housework could be done and enjoyed, with the help of every machine available, in a quarter of the time it had taken my mother, then I wasn't going to look for extra jobs and wipe out the advantage I'd gained.

What my mother was always trying to work out was why, when we were clearly a prospering young couple, we chose to live as we did. Why did we eat in the kitchen? Why didn't we have a dining-room and an oak or a walnut table, something upon which a shine could be put? Why did we have those flimsy Habitat chairs with metal frames and bright yellow soft cushions that gave no support and that thing called a day-bed which was just a wooden frame and mattress? Why did we have sanded floorboards, so cold, when we could have had a good Wilton or Axminster? Her point was, we were doing well for ourselves but nobody would ever know it. She saw these choices, which were no more significant than a matter of taste and fashion, as perverse. She wanted me to have the ideal house she'd never had and always craved. Our old battered house in a typical London street didn't appeal to her. She wanted to see me in leafy Surrey in a detached double-fronted modern house with a drive and a rose garden.

The life I led inside my house also puzzled her. Much of my time was spent cooking and she observed this with something close to astonishment. Cooking for her had always been a burden, a necessary daily ritual with little pleasure in it. The family had to eat, the meals had to be cooked and it was such a nuisance thinking what to have (though what we had was dictated by what day of the week it was, so rigid were the culinary rules). But I had cookery books, mostly Elizabeth David's, and I'd pore over them and experiment. I had a sunny, pretty kitchen too, a place it was pleasant to be in and not the ugly, cold, ill-equipped slot she'd wedged herself into most of her cooking life. She watched as I chopped vegetables she'd never heard of, still not obtainable in Carlisle then, and flung the wine and herbs around – she saw me enjoying myself, whereas to her all food preparation had been not just a chore but a constant anxiety. I'd cheerfully break six eggs into a bowl and watch her gasp, memories of dried egg filling her head. 'This must cost a fortune,' she'd say, slightly accusingly, slightly disapproving of money being spent on food in this way. There was no adequate answer to that. Compared with what she'd had to spend on food then, I did spend a fortune.

We began to drink wine with our meals after we came back from the Algarve and my mother was not pleased. The too-often-heard words 'God, I could do with a drink', alarmed her even though she saw we bore no ill-effects. We didn't stagger about as though we'd just come out of the Horse and Farrier in Raffles. Knowing her horror of drink, all drink, and pubs, it was wicked of us to trick her into going into one without her being aware of it. No pubs in Carlisle had gardens then and certainly no outrageous objects such as attractive benches and tables and umbrellas, so when we walked across the Heath and went into the garden of the Spaniards by the back way she was charmed. She was quite happy to sit with her glass of tonic water and watch the children have their orange juice and us our white wine.

There were no drunken louts to spoil her enjoyment (not when we were there anyway) and a whole new complexion was put on going to a pub. If pubs had gardens like this, if she could sit under a rose trellis, if everything was civilized and orderly, then she was prepared to relax. My father, who had long since 'come round', and also came to stay, hated the Spaniards and other pubs like it. Women and children shouldn't be in pubs. Pubs shouldn't be made into play-pens, it ruined them. They were places for men only, for serious drinking.

The part of my life my mother liked best was the part similar to her own as a young wife. I met my children out of school, always. I took them there, or Hunter did, and I met them and it was such a relief to her to light on this similarity when everything else about how I lived seemed so different. She'd always taken and met me until she was rejected – every day I'd come out of school, up to the age of eight, absolutely secure in the knowledge my mother would be there, holding out a raincoat if it was wet, standing patiently however cold it was. I loved the sight of her. I'd fly into her arms and hug her. And now I did the same as she had done and she came with me and watched my own children recognize and rush to me. It was what mothers were for and in spite of my fancy ways in other respects I was bowing to breeding and convention. It was the same when I spent the afternoon on the Heath before the children were at school. She liked me to take them to feed the ducks or play in the sandpit. She approved of these routines and yet the evidence that I was being at these times the kind of mother she had been didn't create any real harmony between us.

Often, she was bored, if approving, the boredom that came from being bored with herself. Once, as we were sitting on a bench at the swings watching the children play, I said I'd just go over to the slide and say hello to a friend I'd seen putting her child on it. 'What?' my mother said, quite sharply for her, 'and leave me sitting here like a pot slop?' I laughed – it was such an odd expression, I didn't even know what a pot slop was – and sat down again saying fine, it didn't matter, I'd talk to my friend later. After a while my mother said she was sorry, she didn't know what had got into her and that of course I should speak to my friend. So I did, and brought her over, and introduced her to my mother, who was charming and smiled and chatted and gave every appearance of being totally happy and comfortable. But it was a mirage, the apparent ease, the mother-and-daughter closeness, the united front. We weren't united. We were miles and miles apart in thought and feeling while caring deeply for each other. We needed the children to bind us together. As long as they were demanding our attention real communication was avoided. Once they were in bed my mother didn't know what to do. We ate, we chatted, but she remained expectant somehow and as usual I didn't know either precisely what her expectations were, or how to satisfy them. I wanted to read and knew she would resent this. The best solution, though obviously it wasn't one that could happen every night, was to take her to the theatre or to see a film. She adored the musical *Oliver!* and came home transformed by the excitement of her pleasure, and when we saw the film *A Man for All Seasons* she was so absorbed she didn't even notice that the man next to us had had a heart attack, in spite of the commotion this caused. But the evenings at home were flat. I wondered what she'd done with her own mother in that tiny house in Raffles. How had they spent their evenings together? She was over the age her mother had been when she died and I was younger than she had been at that period when her mother lived with her, but I wondered if she and Margaret Ann had been happily intimate together and that was what she had expected and not got from her own daughter. Somehow, I doubted it.

But there were no discussions about this, philosophical or otherwise. We talked children, children, children and, if not children, health. I'd never thought of my mother as unhealthy, except for her eye trouble, but suddenly during these weeks when she stayed with us I realized she was not fit. She was only five foot four but she weighed eleven stone. I was five foot eight but weighed nine stone. She had become plump, more than plump, fat, and it made her breathless carrying that weight. She'd never taken any real exercise in her life but was under the impression that the housework she did plus going to and from the shops and church amounted to all the exercise she needed. Good heavens, who had spare energy for *exercise*, it was ridiculous. She'd never played any kind of game, not even as a young unmarried woman, though in the twenties there was such a vogue for tennis and cycling and exercise classes with music. Games were a luxury and not one she envied. I hate games myself, all games, just a waste of good reading time, but on the other hand I'd always gone fell-walking and swimming and at one time was a cycling fanatic. I saw that compared with my mother I was extremely fit and always had been. Now she was aggrieved and bewildered by her own weight gain and kept saying she didn't understand it, that she didn't eat much. But it was easy to understand. She wasn't expending anything like the energy she had once done now she was in her easy-to-look-after bungalow and yet she was eating the same amount of food and the same kind – cakes, scones, biscuits, puddings and still potatoes with main meals. She had the money now to indulge her taste for pastries and cream and Cumberland rum butter and all the fattening things. She didn't like fruit, except for grapes, and wasn't keen on salads or any vegetable except cauliflower. Her tea was always sugared and so was her cocoa, heavily. Any suggestion she should diet made her miserable. The only gesture towards dieting she made was to give up the boxes of Terry's All Gold chocolates she loved. The weight built up and so did her blood pressure and that finally forced her to go to see her GP.

Her doctor was fat himself and quite jovial about her weight. He told her to cut down on sweet things but didn't give her any specific advice about diet in general. She came away with the feeling nothing could be done about her weight and angry at the doctor's joke about joining a keep fit class. She was mortified at the very thought – at her age, the very idea.

Her first stroke was no real surprise.

XVIII

The bad years began in the early seventies and lasted a decade. First there were more eye operations, this time for cataracts, then the strokes, each more serious than the last, leaving my mother with her left arm useless and her left leg weak, then a bowel obstruction followed by shingles and finally heart failure. Ten years of acute illness, of having all real independence taken away, of deep depression, of a wish to have done with it and die.

My father was brilliant. He looked after my mother with total devotion, watching over her in every way. He learned at the age of seventy-two to shop and cook and clean. But though she was grateful my mother still wanted her daughters; there was no substitute for us. She had looked after her mother and her mother-in-law, she'd given them a daughter's tender care, the kind no man could give however devoted. But everything had changed. Families were no longer near to each other. Her daughters lived too far away to pop in daily with tasty things to eat, with clean washing, with little feminine services to perform. In a crisis, of course, and there were plenty of those, we always went, my sister or I, often both of us. We would relieve each other, never even suggesting our brother should take his turn – this was women's work, he was not expected to respond in the same way. He was a man and had a man's work to do. Pauline was a teacher and a wife and a mother of two boys. But that was different, oh heavens yes, and I was only a writer and that couldn't be called work, could it? There was no need to ask if I could have time off. I could just take it.

It was true. I could, and did: family first. But I had just had another baby, Flora, when my mother's illnesses began in 1972, and though I put her in a carry-cot, only a few weeks old, and leapt on a train when the need arose, it added to the strain. How many times was I going to have to do this? Very many. Nine more years to go. In the middle of them, Jean died, just like that, a heart attack, her mother's sort of heart attack at her mother's sort of age. My own mother was distraught, not just with grief but envy – *she* was the eldest, she should have gone first. And Nan was in an appalling state of distress too, but that was more because of the shock of realizing her own generation was mortal – if Jean could die so could she and it terrified her. My mother couldn't go to her sister's funeral, she was too ill, so I went *in loco parentis* rather than as the devoted niece. At the funeral I speculated about Jean's life. How much more fulfilled had she been than her mother Margaret Ann? Her only work had been in Carr's offices and, once married, she had been a full-time wife and mother. But what I didn't know, because I'd never been close to Jean, was whether those roles had left her as unsatisfied as my mother. Well, she'd missed the bad years, that was one thing. No long, slow decline for Jean, a fact much commented on at the funeral.

Nan found it too terrible to think about and yet she could think about nothing else. And her own life was now so sad. True, she had a splendid mansion in its own grounds, the sort she had always wanted, and there was a Silver Cloud Rolls-Royce in the garage, even if she couldn't drive, and she had a mink coat and beautiful jewels and all the new clothes she wanted. She had all the champagne and smoked salmon she'd craved, all the worldly goods she'd vowed to acquire – her mother would never have believed it – the fine china, the antique furniture, the lush carpets. She lived with Jack in style. But style meant nothing because of what had happened to her only son Michael. Michael had multiple sclerosis. He was entirely bedridden, able to move only his arms and speaking with difficulty. He'd been taken to every specialist available and it was no good, he was incurable, and poor Nan grieved inconsolably. Jean's sudden and untimely death made her see her own as imminent, and then what would happen to Michael?

Sitting with her the day after Jean's funeral, I was more affected by Nan than I had expected. She was still, in her mid sixties, a beautiful woman, looking at least ten years younger, what with her good and carefully looked after skin and her strong bone structure and the clever make-up and elegant clothes and discreetly tinted hair. A woman of a certain era, true, but highly attractive all the same, the dated style having its own appeal. Only the lovely mouth told of her tears and unhappiness and disappointment. It was twisted into a bitter pout; it pulled the shape of her whole face down and gave it a wretched look. The large blue eyes still sparkled but with tears of rage at the way life had turned out. And she was angry that day, angry with me. She wanted to know why I hadn't been to see her for a whole year. 'After all I did for you,' she said. I tried to explain – a new baby . . . my mother's illness . . . my work . . . three children to look after . . . the house. Excuses, she saw them as excuses, and trumped up at that. She was contemptuous, told me I could have come if I'd wanted to, said I'd let her down badly, I hadn't behaved like a niece upon whom so much time and money had been lavished in her youth. 'What happened?' she asked as I left, shaking her head, refusing to accept my awkwardly offered embrace. I was speechless.

It was only later, on the way home, that I thought of asking Nan about herself at my age. Whom had she visited? Whose generosity had she repaid? Which beds-of-illness had she attended? And her load had been light, with one child at boarding-school, no work, a woman to clean for her. She was no more the caring, compassionate daughter or niece than I was. Nor did she have the slightest appreciation of how hectic my life was, not an inkling. But most of all I resented this assumption of hers that in families everything must be paid for. Hadn't she enjoyed having me to stay, hadn't I been useful as a companion for Michael? Of course she had, of course I had been. But she had imagined this would bind me to her in a way it never should have been expected to, not once it was revealed how different we were in spite of first appearances, how we had nothing in common, neither standards nor tastes, once I was a person in my own right.

But I knew that kind of reaction of mine was foolish. Nan's resentment was more against fate than against me. Her life had only on the surface turned out how she wanted it to. A life of ease, a life with none of the hardship her mother had known, and from which she had wanted to escape, but a life with far less contentment in it and no acceptance at all of its random cruelties. She had only Michael and he was a tragedy. He had had no time to marry and have children before MS struck and she had been denied the grandchildren she wanted. She saw my mother at the apex of an ever-growing family – and family, it had been impressed upon her from the earliest age, was what a woman's life was about. For Nan, nieces were the only hope, nieces, and, if they failed (as we did), nephews: Jean's two unmarried sons who both lived near her and were her only family. She was in a panic of reproach that day and I was there to be accused. It would have been useless to tell Nan to blame herself for the emptiness of her days. It was no good pointing out to her that she could find interest and pleasure in educating herself as plenty of her generation were doing (her old friend Peggy Farish, for example, who went on all kinds of courses, who travelled on her own and in general made up for the deficiencies of the Board Schools). She didn't want to be educated, she didn't want to develop interests. She wanted people, she wanted *family* around her.

My mother had been no more willing to broaden her cultural horizons. Once, before the eye trouble and strokes, at that time when she was so restless and aware that her days were becoming empty, I suggested she should attend some Adult Education class – she was clever, after all; she'd have no problems whatever she chose to study. But she chose nothing. I showed her a leaflet, listing what was available in Carlisle, and she ran her eye over it and shook her head. Why not French classes? No, it was too late to learn. There was no point in learning French. Music appreciation, then? No. She had a wireless if she wanted to listen to music and she really only liked hymns and needed no help appreciating those. What about history, local history? Surely she'd admit she had always been interested in history. Yes, she was, but she couldn't be bothered. What she wanted was to return to the doing of those good works which had made her feel so useful and needed. If she couldn't help people but had to be helped instead, what was the point in being alive? Her life had been about giving, mainly to her family, and without this giving she was bereft.

My mother thought any kind of voluntary work was not something I'd deign to do. In her opinion I was above it, whereas women like her were made for it. This annoyed me. I hated the demarcation line she drew in her mind – she on one side, I on the other. After her first stroke she was in bed a couple of weeks and couldn't do her turn at the Infirmary, taking round the tea trolley for Out-patients. She was agitated and the agitation was all because she didn't like to ask me to do it for her and so avoid letting down her partner on the rota. I said *of course* I'd go in her place and why ever had she imagined I wouldn't? 'Well,' she said, 'you don't do that sort of thing. I thought . . .' But what she thought could not then be dragged out of her.

Off I went to the Infirmary, desperate to prove I could be an adequate tea-trolley lady and so be worthy of my mother. I walked there, trying to think myself into my mother's shoes. Shoes, yes. She'd wear her plain black court shoes, the ones with the lower heel, good for walking in her opinion, useless in mine. I couldn't do anything about my plimsolls but at least they were pristine white. She would dress with care, as usual. She'd wear something she considered suitable for a hospital, probably her blue flowered dress with the white collar. I didn't have such a dress but I was soberly attired in a plain grey cotton skirt and a white shirt. She'd leave plenty of time to walk there – rushing made her red and dizzy – and she'd take the shortest route down Stanhope Road and into Granville Road, and there she'd be, opposite the Infirmary. Couldn't be simpler. It would take her about half an hour and she'd be pleased at the exercise and fresh air. It took me ten minutes. I reported to the desk and met my partner who looked rather like my mother and was very pleased to see me because she was worried about being able to manage on her own.

We didn't push the trolley very far, just did a circuit of the Out-patients department. I poured the tea and added milk and sugar if required and handed the cups out while my companion took the money and offered biscuits. We were a popular service. People were desperate for tea and weren't always able to go to the actual cafeteria (which wasn't always open anyway). Such gratitude there was, such pleasure and comfort the tea brought. It was easy to understand why doing this made my mother happy, why she found it rewarding. She'd be so compassionate too. I could imagine her helping those with slings or plasters to manage the tea, I could see her eager to hold howling babies for distracted mothers while they gulped their tea. The time flew. Round and round we went, making sure no one had been missed, constantly searching for the perpetual influx of new patients. At the end of our stint we went into a little sluice room and washed the cups – ours were real cups, no plastic or polystyrene – and dried them and stacked them and cleaned the trolley. We'd brought our own tea-towels, two each (my mother equipped me before I set off), and they were sopping wet when we finished. What a good job we'd done.

My mother was avid for every detail. Had there been a float to start with? Yes, there had been five pounds' worth of small change. Good. She smiled with satisfaction. When she began doing the job there was never any change and she'd insisted there should be and had often provided it herself. Had there been a variety of biscuits on offer? No, only digestives. She was exasperated. How many times had she pointed out a choice made patients so much happier and heaven knew it was easy enough to provide with Carr's Biscuits almost next door. But at least the only choice hadn't been chocolate biscuits, Carr's Sports, beloved by children but expensive and messy for them to eat when mothers were trying to keep them clean for the doctor. Was it busy? Yes, very. Hordes of people the whole three hours. My mother sighed with longing and regret. She loved it to be busy. Had I managed all right? Perfectly. I wasn't bored? No, I wasn't bored. I'd do it again, any time. But I never did. My mother's name had to be taken off the rota because she was clearly never going to be able to do the tea-trolley rounds again. I never volunteered to do similar work at my own local hospital. Thought about it, but never volunteered. I suspected my own motives, that was the trouble. My mother's had been pure – she wanted to give help because giving it made her feel useful and being useful made her happy. I'd have been volunteering out of a feeling of cold duty, thinking I *ought* to offer my services but not really wanting to.

My mother didn't like to go out of the house after her second, much more serious, stroke. She didn't want people staring. Nobody did stare; there was nothing to stare at. The useless left arm was not disfiguring and, though her left foot dragged just a little bit, her walking was not particularly ungainly for a woman in her late seventies. But she felt an object of pity. She felt she didn't 'look nice', so she wouldn't go anywhere except to church. My father thought going to church was bad for her. He was quite definite about it, all that standing and kneeling, all that up and down. It was just what she shouldn't do. And she couldn't go on her own, that was out of the question. So for a while he took and collected her, like taking a child to and from school, until a fellow parishioner began picking her up in her car. Eventually even that proved too difficult, then the vicar came and gave her Holy Communion at home. Much better, my father thought, but my mother missed church. Without being in the actual church she didn't feel the holiness she'd always loved.

She missed the shops more than the church, though. Just being able to go 'up street' on the bus and potter about on her own, looking not buying most of the time, and meeting Ruby Gillespie in Binn's. Shopping was a ceremony to her. She loved getting ready for it and then following her own invented rituals. But she loved the shops themselves, the atmosphere of them, the new goods, the very bustle of that kind of commerce. She had always regretted my lack of interest in shopping. Whenever I went with her as an adult it was obvious I had no idea how to enjoy shopping – with me, it was all speed, in, out. I never *savoured* shops, never lingered lovingly over the displays. But now that my mother couldn't go shopping any more and missed it so desperately, it was up to me to take her. I took her at least once every school holiday we were up there (staying now in a cottage we'd bought at Caldbeck, up on the fells but only half an hour from Carlisle). Hunter would take my father and our three children off to Silloth and I would guide my mother round the shops. A delicate task. She still liked Binn's best but regretted all the changes – Binn's wasn't so smart any more; the clothes were too crowded together. She now couldn't handle the racks, so I had to pull the hanger slowly along while endless garments were scrutinized. Inevitably, she would decide none appealed to her and that what she had would 'see me out'.

Once, I went to Carlisle specially to take my mother Christmas shopping. Her excitement was terrible. Her face was flushed even before we began and my father admonished her sternly – 'Settle yourself or you'll have another stroke.' We took a taxi to town, a five-minute ride but itself an adventure, and started in Binn's, where else. Cards first, then slippers for my father. Slippers were looked at in comfort, sitting down, and it brought her great pleasure. She was quite relaxed looking at twelve pairs of men's slippers, comparing colours and linings and the relative values of different kinds of soles. Finally a pair was purchased and then we went for lunch but not to Binn's café, now *déclassé* for lunch in my mother's opinion, but to Bullough's. We had a table overlooking the cathedral, in full view of Paternoster Row where Margaret Ann had served the Stephensons, and a mere five hundred yards from where Annie Jordan had lived. We ate plaice, grilled. I had a glass of white wine with mine. I was in need of it. I'd have happily drunk a whole bottle, but it would have upset my mother. I sipped my miserable one small glass carefully, trying to make not just it but the whole lunch last as long as possible. 'I've been looking forward to this so much,' my mother suddenly blurted out, 'you've no idea how much.' This was said so emotionally I was startled. 'I could stay here for ever,' she went on. 'Nice view, nice table, nice food. It's all so nice.' I couldn't help smiling but that was a mistake. 'Of course,' she said quickly, quite fiercely, 'it's nothing to you. You have lunches out all the time in London.' 'I don't,' I said. 'You could if you wanted to,' my mother said. 'Yes,' I admitted, 'I could. But I don't want to, so I don't.' 'It's wasted on you,' my mother sighed. 'All the opportunities you have that I never had and you don't take them. I wish I'd had your life.'

It was painful, somehow, hearing her say that. I didn't want her to want my life. I wanted her to have enjoyed her own. And what she was concentrating on, in her desire, were only the superficial things in my life. Given my income, my mother would have been a spender. Given the chance, it would have been on with the designer clothes, out Nan-ing Nan. She would have been a lady who lunched, at the Savoy Grill, at the Ritz. She didn't know anything about my real life, the part that *was* enviable, the hours spent writing and reading which put being a wife and mother into a different context. She was right, life *had* changed for women and I'd benefited from the changes, but the greatest change of all was not one she either saw or appreciated. I was having a career as well as everything else and that was what, if anything, she should have yearned for.

Over the pudding – my mother loved puddings, so she was at her most content, it was a good time to choose – I thought I should try to enlighten her a little, straighten out a few of her fantasies. 'A lot of my life,' I said, 'is the same as yours was at my age.' She gave a little snort of disbelief but her mouth was full of apple pie and cream. 'No, really,' I said, 'my day-to-day life is looking after the children, just as you did, and being a housewife, cleaning and tidying and cooking and shopping. It's all easy for me. It isn't the hard slog it was for you, and money makes it all even easier. But the feeling is the same, I get just as tired as you did.' 'You should get help,' my mother said, 'you're silly. You should have someone to clean, and a nanny. You're wearing yourself out in that big house of yours and you've got the money to afford servants.' 'Servants?' I echoed. 'You think I should have *servants*?' 'Certainly,' my mother said. 'I'd have had servants, if you can call them that these days. Nothing wrong with servants. You can't do everything, you know. You can't do this writing business and everything else, it's daft. Women weren't meant to do everything, I'm sure they weren't.'

I didn't even attempt to answer her. It was the most serious conversation we had ever had, but I couldn't bear to spoil the lunch by arguing. Anyway, the meal was over. We couldn't go on sitting in Bullough's window for ever. The restaurant had emptied and there were other presents to buy. 'That was lovely,' my mother repeated as I paid the bill. Then, 'I don't know when I'll get out to have lunch again. Never, probably.' She looked out of the window, her eyes unable to avoid Paternoster Row. 'But I shouldn't complain,' she went on, 'my poor mother never had lunch in a shop in her life. Nobody did, though, not ordinary women, not then.' We made our slow way through Bullough's, my mother often stopping to finger things she liked the look of. 'Lovely things,' she murmured, 'they have some lovely things here. I wish I'd had lovely things.' It really was unbearable, the tone of her voice. 'What would you have liked exactly?' I asked, quite sharply. 'Come on, what lovely things in particular?' She gazed about vaguely. We were passing through the linen department at that point. 'Towels,' she said, 'you see them in films, great big fluffy towels in beautiful colours.' 'Mum,' I said, almost shouted, 'for God's sake, you can have any towel you want.' 'Not *now*,' she protested, 'I didn't mean *now*. It's too late now.' But it wasn't too late. I'd already stopped and told an assistant to give me the biggest, the fluffiest, the most beautiful blue towel in the shop and to wrap it up for my mother. 'There,' I said, distressed but somehow also furious, 'at least you've got a towel.'

XIX

Right up to the end of her life my mother cared about her appearance – she never, ever, became an untidy, dishevelled old woman long past caring about looks. In particular, she cared about her hair, such beautiful hair, still thick and healthy while the rest of her was sick. She liked it 'kept nice' and the only way it could, for her, reach the right level of niceness was to have a perm regularly. Nothing else was acceptable. For this she was prepared to go to a hairdresser (though if she was very weak the hairdresser came to her) and risk being, as she imagined, stared at and pitied. My father marched her there, stood sentry outside, and marched her back. Once permed, her lovely white hair would look tortured, rigidly tight, but then within a week or so it would begin to soften and after a month the loose, gentle waves were just what she liked.

She went to the hairdresser a month before she died as though in preparation for the greater appointment with death that she didn't know about. Shortly afterwards, just as we arrived in Caldbeck for the summer holidays, she contracted shingles. I came in to find her face covered in scabs and the greatest concentration of them near her eyes. I called the doctor who said she needed hospital treatment, and I took her to the Infirmary at once. She was so glad I was the one taking her, having this firm belief that I knew how to talk to doctors, or anyone in authority, and it would make a difference, she would be respected. 'How long has she had this?' the hospital doctor asked when finally our turn came. 'Why don't you ask my mother herself?' I said. 'Her name is Mrs Forster. She may have shingles but this doesn't mean she is deaf or stupid.' I hope I said this quietly, without anger, but maybe I didn't. The doctor blushed. My mother squeezed my hand. He asked her the same question and she replied, clearly and with great dignity, and visibly chastened he mumbled, 'Sorry about that.' He told my mother he thought she should be admitted just for a couple of days because when shingles spread to the eyes, and hers already had, it could be very serious and was best dealt with in hospital conditions. My mother didn't seem to mind having to stay as long as she wasn't going to be in the geriatric ward. I took her up to the wards and when she found she was in the women's surgical in the new wing she was relieved. Then I went back to fetch her things.

At first she was a model patient. She looked so sweet in the hospital bed, lovely hair and all, blue nightgown, blue lacy bed-jacket, lying so still and obedient, propped up on her pillows. The shingles began to clear quite rapidly but then, just as we were told she could go home the next day, she had another stroke. From then on she deteriorated every day, though, after another two weeks, she was said to be 'on the mend'. The days of 'on the mend' were tense. The prospect of my mother going home to be looked after by my eighty-year-old father was appalling – the ever-loving, ever-willing, ever-conscientious Arthur wouldn't be able to manage, not now her left leg was completely useless and she couldn't walk. He was still strong but not strong enough to lift her. She would have to go into a Home but he would never accept that until it was forced upon him by his own realization that he couldn't manage. We were in for an agonizing period while he came to this pitiful decision. And there was my own promise to remember and rescind. All her life my mother's greatest fear had been that she would end up in a Home. 'Look,' she used to say to me as we walked down Norfolk Road, passing an old people's Home where the inmates sat, mostly in wheelchairs, in the window, 'look. That will be me one day.' And I'd become quite hysterical in my vehemence, vowing that never, *never* would it be her. She was my mother, she would be with me. Having a family was what kept you out of Homes – the family put you first as once you had put them. I should gather my poor mother up and take her to my home and lavish upon her the love and care she had lavished upon me.

On 11 August 1981, a hot sunny day, I went in to see my mother as usual. Hunter and the children had taken my father to Port Carlisle, to the sea. There were rails up round my mother's bed now. She was no longer a model patient. In the week since the stroke she'd turned violent. She'd taken to getting out of her bed and wandering around shouting and yelling. I found this hard to credit when the nurses told me that was why they had had to box her in – Lilian, the quiet, well-behaved Lily, *shouting*? In public, as it were? But the other women in the ward assured me it was true. My mother had shouted and what she had shouted was mostly abuse, about me – Where is Margaret, damn her? Why isn't she here, the bitch? Where is she? Why doesn't she take me home . . .? It was distressing even hearing this. Drugs, it must be the effect of the drugs they were giving her. My mother had never sworn in any way whatsoever. The language of swearing, the vocabulary, was alien to her. So it was not really my mother shouting. But on the other hand the resentment expressed rang true. She'd never voiced it but I could believe she felt it. Her expression, her tone of voice, her whole demeanour had for many years now told me what she had finally shouted in her drugged state. 'She doesn't mean it, pet,' one of the women kindly said. 'She doesn't know what she's saying.' I knew she did.

But she wasn't moving now or shouting. She lay still and whispered. I did the talking, trying to entertain with anecdotes about the children. It was hard to keep going when there was little response beyond 'really' and 'oh, yes'. There was the sense, too, that it was wicked to be indulging in this kind of trite chat when there was so much that was important which should be said if only I could divine what. Then, in the middle of one of my rambling sentences, my mother said, 'I feel as if I'm in a waiting-room. It's so tiring, waiting, waiting. I wish my turn would come. I wish I didn't have to wait. I want to leave. I want to go somewhere nice.'

'Where? Where would be nice?'

'Oh, Silloth, of course. I'd like to be on the Green at Silloth. Lovely.'

'Who with?'

'Jean and Nan and Peggy Farish.'

'What would you do? Have a picnic?'

'No, no, the grass is too damp.'

'So what will you do?'

'Oh, sit on a bench for a while, then have a walk along the sea wall, watch the tide come in, have an ice-cream, watch the men fish. Plenty to do.'

'What will you wear?'

'My blue dress, the one with the sailor collar.'

'And what . . .'

'Oh STOP IT!' she suddenly snapped. 'This is *silly*.' It was

301

said so viciously, with a strength I didn't know she still had, and yet I'd thought she was enjoying what seemed a harmless game, a soothing fantasy. I could have played it for hours. I *wanted* to play it for hours. She tossed and turned on her pillow and sighed. 'Anyway,' she said, 'I've had enough.'

'What of?' I asked, nervously, knowing I mustn't anger her by starting another evasive dialogue.

'This. I've had enough. I want done with it. It hasn't amounted to much, my life.'

'Mum, *please* . . .'

'No, it hasn't. It's been all work and worry. I've done nothing with myself.'

It was the old cry, the more painful for being said, as it was said now, without any desire to arouse sympathy, without the slightest hint of wishing to be contradicted and persuaded otherwise.

'Mum, please, listen. You've led a good life, you have . . . You've done so much good in it. You've been a wonderful daughter and wife and mother. Nobody could have been better . . . You've had and brought up three children. You've always put your family first . . . Isn't that making something of your life? Isn't it?'

'No. It isn't what I mean. Look at you . . .'

'Mum! I can't bear it. You go on as though I'd climbed Everest or discovered penicillin. I haven't done any more than you have. My life is no more commendable than yours. There's no real difference in what we've achieved. A few skittery books doesn't amount to much . . .'

'It's how I feel. And I've had enough anyway.'

The nurse came and took her pulse. 'Is your father coming?' she asked. I said he was. He'd take over from me and spend the evening here as usual. She nodded, said my mother's pulse was very weak, though this wasn't necessarily significant. It could mean a sudden collapse was imminent but on the other hand it might not happen tonight or tomorrow, or the next day, there was no real knowing. So I left and my father came. He stayed an hour and then made his sad way home, no words having been spoken by my mother. She died at four o'clock the next morning, 12 August. We rushed in from Caldbeck and went with my father to see my mother's body – he was insistent we should see it. 'That's not her,' he said, at the sight of her corpse. 'That's one thing I know, it's not her. She's gone.' He was right. The dead body was nothing, aroused no emotion except relief. 'Take her ring off,' my father instructed, 'we don't want them lot having it.' With difficulty I worked my mother's wedding ring off her stiff, cold finger, loathing the touching of her. I would give it to my sister (on holiday in France, not even knowing before she went that my mother was so ill).

Another glorious day for this funeral too. Nan came, not as distressed as she had been at Jean's, but then this time she had been prepared. There wasn't the same sense of shock. 'Oh, it's awful being old,' she sighed, 'awful.' She said Jack wasn't well enough to come ('a likely story' my father muttered, audibly, but nobody felt like challenging him). Michael was now so paralysed with MS he couldn't talk, but Nan said tears had rolled down his cheeks when she told him Aunt Lily was dead and she was leaving him for two days to go to her funeral. Standing watching the coffin slide off to be cremated, I could only think of my mother's last words to me: 'I've had enough . . . It hasn't amounted to much, my life.'

It had amounted to us, standing there, it had amounted to her family. Yet she was a woman who had felt cheated, but of what exactly? Had we failed her as a family? Had the concept of family itself failed her? I knew that whenever I lay dying I would not be feeling the dreadful sense of waste she felt.

After the funeral I began the attempt to inquire into my grandmother's past which began this book, wanting not just to satisfy my own curiosity but believing that what I said was true – I can't understand my own history unless I understand my grandmother's, my mother's and that of the women like them, the ordinary working-class women from whom I come. The mission is only half accomplished.

My curiosity certainly isn't satisfied. I haven't found out nearly enough about my grandmother or about her first illegitimate daughter Alice. I hate having to accept that I will never know what happened to Margaret Ann between the ages of two and twenty-three. I will never know the circumstances of Alice's conception nor what happened to her as a child. It is how my grandmother wanted it. She successfully concealed from her legitimate daughters every scrap of her past before 1893, the perfect crime except there was no crime involved. She was a woman determined to have no past, or at least to decree it should start when she was twenty-three.

Twenty-three years old . . . If I suppressed the first twenty-three years of my own life it could never properly be understood by me or anyone else. If I knew nothing of the first twenty-three years of my mother's life I could not possibly understand her – those years explain her personality and illuminate her problems to a startling degree. We *are* our past, especially our family past, a truism if ever there was one. But my grandmother could not bear to acknowledge this. Locked up inside her was an unfathomable amount of unhappiness, perhaps even horror, if of a sadly conventional kind, and the only way she could deal with it was by pretending it never existed – so much pretending women like my grandmother had to do. The urge in her to be respectable and above reproach was so strong, and the rules of that respectability so rigid, that it overrode all other desires. In our age, my age, when we are encouraged at every level to be open about our upbringing and whatever happened to us in the course of it, women like Margaret Ann Jordan are virtually incomprehensible in their passion for privacy and secrecy.

As for women like Alice . . . Alice died on 2 November 1955, in Garlands, Carlisle's mental hospital, the old Cumberland and Westmorland Lunatic Asylum opened in 1862. Records there are closed for one hundred years so there is no means of telling how long Alice had been there or how many times she had been admitted, or what precisely was the nature of her mental illness. Did my grandmother's rejection of her lead Alice to a complete breakdown? Did her half-sisters' denial that she was who she said she was precipitate nervous collapse eventually?

I visited Alice's grave, with vague hopes of finding on her tombstone something beyond the dates I already knew. William Muir, her husband, bought a plot for Alice to be buried in (and for himself, ten years later) but it is not in Carlisle's main cemetery where her mother and grandmother were buried. It is in Upperby, to the south of Carlisle, the area to which Alice and William moved from Brook Street. I had the number of the grave and a map to locate it. Upperby cemetery lacks both the grandeur and the floral splendour of the main cemetery. It is quite small, with virtually no trees and the only flowers are those laid on the graves. There is a big hedge at the east end of it, hiding a railway line. Alice is buried right up against it. But there is no stone at all to mark the spot. The other graves have headstones but not 12-D3, Alice's plot. There is nothing to mark that she is there. A blank. A path of smooth grass. It looks odd, as though a mistake has been made ... How can I forgive my grandmother for her treatment of Alice?

To answer that is the stuff of fiction – so tempting to invent a history for Alice, to imagine a plausible explanation for my grandmother's apparently callous treatment of her and be then able, graciously, to forgive her, but it would not be a satisfactory solution in this case. But it is not my grandmother who needs to be forgiven. It is the times she lived in, those harsh times for women, the times that led to waste of a far more savage kind than my mother ever experienced. It gives me such satisfaction to prove, to myself at least, that what I hoped was true *is* true – my chances, my lot, my expectations, born as I was into a working-class family in which women had always served rather than led, were always hundreds of times better than my grandmother's or mother's. All of us, all three representatives of different generations, always have put family first but in my case, in the case of my generation, it has not been at ruinous cost. I'm not, and haven't been, crippled by the family. I don't pay an enormous emotional price for the having of one. I have been able to be myself within its confines.

Margaret Ann Jordan, Lilian Hind, Jean Wallace, Nan Marshallsay, even poor Alice, all the women whose lives and times I have touched upon, would have been able to fulfil themselves in an entirely different and much more gratifying way if they could have benefited from the radical changes in the last half century from which I have benefited. Let no one say nothing has changed, that women have it as bad as ever.

They do not. My personal curiosity may not have been satisfied but my larger curiosity, as to whether life has indeed improved for women like my immediate ancestors, is. And I am glad, glad not to have been born a working-class girl in 1869 or 1901. Everything, for a woman, is better now, even if it is still not as good as it could be. To forget or deny that is an insult to the women who have gone before, women like my grandmother and mother.

Author's Note

In one sense there was no real research, or what I would term research, needed for this book, since it relies so heavily on personal memory of one kind or another, but attempting to place these memories, many of them not mine, in some historical context did lead to a great deal of delving into the Cumbria County Council Archives, housed in Carlisle Castle. I am grateful for the help of the efficient and enthusiastic staff there and also for the help of Denis Perriam, Haydn Charlesworth and Rosemary Southey who looked up information when I had returned to London (where I live half the year). Harry Arkle undertook further searches for me at the Newcastle end.

It was a strange feeling, every time I made my way to the castle, to be walking past the house where my grandmother worked as a servant. I'd day-dream along Paternoster Row and into Castle Street and reach the Records Office convinced there was something in the power of place. A memoir, of whatever kind, is such a living thing, its subject matter so hypnotic, especially when it is rooted in local history, as this one is. The past – my grandmother's, my mother's, my aunts' – did not seem a foreign country to me as I daily walked its streets. I passed over and over again the places where they had lived and worked and shopped until the empathy with them was so strong, and the recollection of my childhood self so sharp, that we all walked together. But that perhaps is the point of any memoir – to walk with the dead and yet see them with our eyes, from our vantage point.

READ MORE IN PENGUIN

In every corner of the world, on every subject under the sun, Penguin represents quality and variety – the very best in publishing today.

For complete information about books available from Penguin – including Puffins, Penguin Classics and Arkana – and how to order them, write to us at the appropriate address below. Please note that for copyright reasons the selection of books varies from country to country.

In the United Kingdom: Please write to *Dept. EP, Penguin Books Ltd, Bath Road, Harmondsworth, West Drayton, Middlesex UB7 ODA*

In the United States: Please write to *Consumer Sales, Penguin USA, P.O. Box 999, Dept. 17109, Bergenfield, New Jersey 07621-0120*. VISA and MasterCard holders call 1-800-253-6476 to order Penguin titles

In Canada: Please write to *Penguin Books Canada Ltd, 10 Alcorn Avenue, Suite 300, Toronto, Ontario M4V 3B2*

In Australia: Please write to *Penguin Books Australia Ltd, P.O. Box 257, Ringwood, Victoria 3134*

In New Zealand: Please write to *Penguin Books (NZ) Ltd, Private Bag 102902, North Shore Mail Centre, Auckland 10*

In India: Please write to *Penguin Books India Pvt Ltd, 706 Eros Apartments, 56 Nehru Place, New Delhi 110 019*

In the Netherlands: Please write to *Penguin Books Netherlands bv, Postbus 3507, NL-1001 AH Amsterdam*

In Germany: Please write to *Penguin Books Deutschland GmbH, Metzlerstrasse 26, 60594 Frankfurt am Main*

In Spain: Please write to *Penguin Books S. A., Bravo Murillo 19, 1° B, 28015 Madrid*

In Italy: Please write to *Penguin Italia s.r.l., Via Felice Casati 20, I–20124 Milano*

In France: Please write to *Penguin France S. A., 17 rue Lejeune, F–31000 Toulouse*

In Japan: Please write to *Penguin Books Japan, Ishikiribashi Building, 2–5–4, Suido, Bunkyo-ku, Tokyo 112*

In South Africa: Please write to *Longman Penguin Southern Africa (Pty) Ltd, Private Bag X08, Bertsham 2013*

BY THE SAME AUTHOR

The Seduction of Mrs Pendlebury

Rose and Stanley Pendlebury, aging and alone in their antiquated Islington house, have a relationship based on mutual tolerance. Rose, 'brittle as thin toffee', finds the whole world an offence. Until gradually, reluctantly, she allows her neighbours – especially their delightful toddler Amy – to prove that she is not too old for friendship and hope.

'Beautifully written and a joy to read' – Auberon Waugh in the *Evening Standard*

Private Papers

'A brilliant, sometimes terrible novel about the generation war within a family, as witty and cool as it is heart-rending' – Auberon Waugh the *Daily Mail*

'Painful ... gripping ... her 'private' story reaches far beyond the merely personal' – *Observer*

and

Significant Sisters
The Grassroots of Active Feminism 1839–1939

Significant Sisters traces the lives and careers of eight women, each of whom pioneered vital changes in the spheres of law, education, the professions, morals or politics. Each forged her own particular brand of feminism, yet all engaged with courage and determination in the battle against the injustices and limitations imposed upon women's freedom.

'A serious book but immensely readable because it is so well-written' – Susan Hill

BY THE SAME AUTHOR

Georgy Girl

Made into a successful film that starred Lynn Redgrave and Charlotte Rampling, *Georgy Girl* is a sharp, affectionate and very funny
portrait of a large, lachrymose and self-confessed ugly duckling, who
pursues the chimera of true love, only to find that there are other
alternatives in life.

'Almost uncannily readable' – *Sunday Times*

Mother Can You Hear Me?

Angela Bradbury's mother certainly makes the most of life's dis-
appointments – in those endless insidious sacrifices bravely borne, for
which her children can never be quite grateful enough.

Even now just one phone-call from Mother can send Angela into a
maelstrom of complicity, guilt and regret. And her own daughter,
Sadie, has developed into a scornful, slovenly, selfish adolescent. It
seems that motherhood is a heritage of broken promises. But Angela
is determined that, somehow, her relationship with Sadie will be
different.

Lady's Maid

'Compulsively readable ... at each climax of the story, from the
Brownings' runaway romance to her own equally compromised and
complicated marriage, the lady's maid speaks directly and at the last
most movingly' – *Guardian*

'Fact and fiction are skilfully interwoven ... beautifully done' –
Evening Standard

BY THE SAME AUTHOR

Mothers' Boys

The attack on fifteen-year-old Joe Kennedy was particularly squalid and vicious. Sheila Armstrong's grandson Leo was found holding the knife. Harriet Kennedy cannot cope with her son's continuing pain; Sheila, who reared Leo, cannot bear the lasting guilt. In a moving tale of suffering and forgiveness, the two women confront the complex range of emotions that motherhood entails.

'Margaret Forster has the gift of making you care deeply about what happens to her characters . . . I doubt if I shall read a better novel this year. It is time Forster's reputation matched her achievement' – Allan Massie in the *Scotsman*

The Battle for Christabel

Rowena wants a baby. What she doesn't want is the baby's father. Yet five years after the birth of Christabel, Rowena is dead, tragically killed in a climbing accident. The battle for Christabel has begun . . .

'Forster has the essential capacity to see everyone's point of view, whether it is the social workers who resent the upper-middle class assumptions of Christabel's grandmother, Isobel's lover who believes she should adopt the child, or Christabel's foster mother Betty . . . in that territory of dread and reconciliation which is the family, Forster reigns supreme' – *Guardian*

Have the Men Had Enough?

'Mercilessly exact and unsentimental about the desolation of old age and the barnacles of family life . . . It is a moving love story, a condemnation of the way we treat our old friends and loves, a rage against the dying of the light' – Philip Howard in *The Times*

'It is close to real life in a way we hardly expect a novel to be, and finally very moving' – Hilary Mantel in the *Daily Telegraph*